On the Art of the
Nō Drama

The Major Treatises of Zeami

translated by J. Thomas Rimer
Yamazaki Masakazu

Princeton University Press | Princeton, N.J.

Copyright © 1984 by Princeton University Press
Published by Princeton University Press,
41 William Street, Princeton, New Jersey 08540
in the United Kingdom: Princeton University Press,
Chichester, West Sussex

Library of Congress Cataloging in Publication Data
Zeami, 1363-1443.
On the art of the nō drama.
(Princeton library of Asian translations)
Bibliography: p.   Includes index.
1. Nō. I. Rimer, J. Thomas. II. Yamazaki, Masakazu, 1934-   .
III. Title. IV. Series.
PN2924.5.N6Z4213 1984   895.6'2'009   83–42573
ISBN 0-691-06582-9   ISBN 0-691-10154-X (pbk.)
(Rev.)

The text of this book has been composed in
Linotron Sabon with Optima display.
The glossaries have been composed in
Monophoto Bembo with Optima display
by Asco Trade Typesetting.

Princeton University Press books are printed on acid-free paper
and meet the guidelines for permanence and durability of the
Committee on Production Guidelines for Book Longevity
of the Council on Library Resources

Printed in the United States of America by Princeton Academic Press

The preparation of this volume was made possible in part
by a grant from the Translation Program
of the National Endowment for the Humanities,
an independent federal agency

Funding for the reproduction of the color plates in the third printing was
generously supplied by the Toshiba International Foundation

4   5   6   7   8   9   10

Contents

Glossaries

A modern performance of the ceremonial play *Okina*.

Foreword

When you read these miscellaneous notes,
you will find dew-like gems,
polish them and flowers will
bloom in endless profusion.

When I was a young man,
I received this collection of
teachings from my teacher Zeami.
Zenchiku, 1453

Indeed, this book is full of "dew-like gems" valuable to a wide range of readers—from the serious student of Japanese culture to the professional theater practitioner in search of enlarging his understanding of his craft. Zeami was a genius at his art, as actor, dancer, playwright, and producer, and has much to teach us six hundred years later.

With his father, Kan'ami, Zeami is considered to be the founder of *nō* drama, the classical dance-drama of Japan. They were both Buddhists and, like many seminal theater artists, were deeply religious men. Zeami wrote that the *nō* is a "means to pacify people's hearts, to bring about a sense of contentment and to promote a long life." He was strongly motivated by a desire to enlighten his audience through theatrical production.

This enlightenment can only be brought about by those actors who are masters of their craft: the ritual/play must be performed brilliantly, it must be done right, or it will not "pacify the devils." Are the devils referred to the evil spirits of the underworld, or are they the critics? At any rate, the gods must be appeased, and will be if the acting is good.

Like many artisans of all ages, Zeami was very concerned about preserving the mystique of the artist. These essays were all considered by him to be secret treatises, to be seen only by members of his immediate family, the Kanze *nō* School. This not-for-publication approach seems in part to be a desire to keep covert his tricks of the trade, and in part a desire to maintain an aura of religious ceremony—wherein the actor is not just a performer, but a priest who transmits enlightenment to his devotees. This attitude of secrecy is not exclusive to Zeami; many modern performers don't like to talk about their craft, or if they do, don't speak about it with any particular coherence.

This attitude is all well and good, but it reinforces the notion that fine acting just "happens," rather than as a result of a hard-won, lifelong devotion to craft. "How did you learn all those lines?" seems to be the most common question of the performer. It is useful, on this level alone, to read these essays in search of what it is that an actor does.

Zeami does state that the excellent actor must appear to work effortlessly, and perform with ease: "the harder the actor tries to perform, the less interesting he is to become." And that "reserves of skill (must) seem to lie behind his accomplishments." This is similar to modern Western theater parlance, where the actor is trained to underplay, to "save it," to not "give it all away."

The most extraordinary aspect of Zeami's discussions of the art of the actor center around the concept of *hana* ("flowers will bloom in endless profusion"). The literal translation of the word is "flower," and it may be taken to be a comparison of the aroma of a flower with the aura of an actor. Perhaps what Zeami is talking about is what we speak of today as stage presence. An actor's livelihood is dependent on his ability to sustain his influence over an audience, his "way" over a group of people.

Hana, for Zeami, also is a term of approbation, of an achievement of the highest critical standard, representing the ultimate in physical, vocal, and spiritual technique. The *nō* actor has been rightly termed the most disciplined in the world, as Peter Arnott reminds us in his fine book *The Theatres of*

Japan. He undergoes rigorous training, which does not stop at graduation. There is only gradual growth as the actor reaches out for his fullest artistic expression, when his *hana* is at its fullest.

The image of a flower is particularly apt because of the idea of an artist "flowering" at the height of his powers: the growth of a flower from bud, to opening, to maturity, is a marvelous concept for the development of an artist.

And Zeami is quite specific. The potential actor must begin his training at the age of seven, and he must continue training until he is too old to perform. The path of the *nō* actor must be one of monastic dedication: sex, gambling, heavy drinking are distractions to be avoided. At seventeen, the actor must decide to give his life completely to the pursuit of *hana* and must continue to perfect his craft until he reaches the heights, which he suggests occurs in the forties.

He warns the young actor, attractive and flashy, against appealing to the audience with a *hana* that is merely temporary, superficial, inconsequential; not to "lose oneself in the foolish praise of a night." These traps can prevent full maturity in the art if the young actor stops growing as a result of early success.

Zeami also speaks of *hana* as a "means to give rise to the unexpected in the hearts of the audience." Great acting, indeed, is always novel, offering striking insights into human behavior. The brilliant moment of an Olivier or a Gielgud is always unexpected, always fresh and insightful—jolting the audience into a fuller understanding of character, play, or "the heart of the matter."

Zeami also speaks of *hana* as "essence"—an essence that is a distillation, a crystallizing of experience, the flowering of one's talent that leads to an understanding of a Zenlike essence of the human condition in a single gesture or a turn of the head.

Hana is, finally, the pursuit of excellence, a quest for the highest levels of artistry. Late in one's career, one may achieve "the flower of proud benevolence," and beyond that become an initiate into the "art of the mysterious flower" in which the spirit of the actor and his manifestation of that power are indivisible. Great performers seem to not be working, but just "being." The blending of form and content is particularly difficult when it comes to the human body performing a play; Zeami is quite sure it can be achieved.

Zeami sounds very much like the modern director when he speaks of "the sensation of mutuality" as essential to an acting company; the highest level of achievement cannot be reached without a strong ensemble, a strong sharing of all those on stage.

Finally, one admires Zeami because of his comments about such matters as performing a bad play: "A bad play that one can yet make something of by taking advantage of its very defects and 'breaking one's bones' in the acting of it." Is this not the medieval Japanese equivalent of "chewing up the scenery"?

And Zeami is again endearing when he speaks of playing "a bit more forcefully" when the audience is inattentive. He is not opposed to trying out new things in the provinces, perfecting the work before bringing it to the cultural capital: he has had his Boston-New Haven-New York City circuit. But he does not believe in condescending to the less sophisticated audience—one must be able to achieve *hana* with the audience, no matter what the social setting.

This is a valuable, intriguing book. It is a delight to discover that there is nothing new under the theatrical sun, and that so much can be learned from someone who trod the boards six hundred years ago!

Wallace Chappell
Artistic Director
The Repertory Theatre
of St. Louis

Acknowledgments

The preparation of this translation, whatever its present virtues and faults, has been a labor of love on the part of both of us. Without the help and enthusiasm of many, however, what follows could not have appeared here in as complete and accurate a form as it has.

Our first thanks go to Dr. Susan Mango of the Translations Program of the National Endowment for the Humanities, whose enthusiasm for the project provided the first and most important stimulus for the undertaking. NEH provided funding for two summers of work, which helped us on our way, but without Dr. Mango's constant support and encouragement, we might not have had the courage to attempt what turned out to be a more difficult, and indeed, a more exciting project than any of us first imagined.

Zeami's treatises range over a wide variety of subjects, and specialized knowledge was sought from a number of specialists. Professor Kenneth DeWoskin provided invaluable information on the traditions of Chinese music. Peter Holman, the British musicologist, and his assistant Bruce Carvell, were particularly helpful in consolidating our usage of various Western musical analogies. Dr. Robert Morrell supplied a great deal of information on Buddhist terminology and bibliography, and Professor Robert Hegel contributed important information on traditional Chinese literary references. Professor Mae Smethurst read much of the manuscript and provided a number of important insights based on her comparative research into Greek and Japanese theater. Professor Joseph Roach gave careful guidance in Western theater history and terminology. Professor Thomas Hare was of the greatest assistance, both because of his knowledge of Zeami and the nō theater, and because of his enthusiasm for our project. Mrs. Mie Kakigahara provided useful assistance in the preparation of the translation of the essay "The Aesthetics of Ambiguity." Mrs. Robert Morrell provided an important service in rendering the Japanese characters used in the text and glossaries.

We would also like to thank the Research Institute for the Nō Theatre of Hosei University, Tokyo, for providing us with the photographs of the original illustrations for the Two Basic Arts and the Three Role Types (*Nikyoku santai*) and for the calligraphy attributed to Zeami. We would also like to thank the *nō* master Sano Yoshiyuki and the photographer Imakoma Kiyonari for making various arrangements for us to use the other photographs included in the book.

We would also like to offer special thanks to Mr. Wallace Chappell, Artistic Director of the Repertory Theatre of St. Louis, whose abiding interest in Zeami as a professional theater director provided particularly useful insights. We have asked him to share some of those insights with the readers of this book, which he has kindly done in his Foreword.

Finally, we would like to thank Debra Jones, of the Department of Chinese and Japanese at Washington University in St. Louis, for her careful preparation of the manuscript.

In addition, we would like to express our appreciation to the readers of the manuscript chosen by Princeton University Press, who provided us with a number of cogent suggestions for changes and amendments to our original versions. Finally, our warm regards go to Miriam Brokaw and Margaret Case, who did so much to make the final book so useful, and so attractive.

J. Thomas Rimer
St. Louis, Mo.
December 1982

A Note to the Reader

In order to reduce the number of footnotes and to facilitate the reader's progress through the treatises, we have prepared a series of glossaries that can be found at the back of the book.

Glossary 1 is an English-Japanese compilation of our translations of aesthetic and other terms used throughout the treatises. We felt that it was better to have attempted working translations of these terms, however inadequate such renderings might be, rather than to overload the actual text with too much romanized Japanese. These terms can be quickly identified, as they are capitalized throughout. We have put brief definitions in the glossary, as well. In the course of the treatises, Zeami uses these terms in different ways, but we have left our translated terms the same, so that each word might pick up increased nuance in a variety of settings, just as do the originals.

Glossary 2 is a compilation of Japanese words, mostly terms for musical performance and articles of clothing, for which no suitable English equivalents could be found.

Glossary 3 is a list of important persons—historical, theatrical, and literary—mentioned in the text.

Glossary 4 provides a list of *nō* plays mentioned in the text, as well as some information about their contents.

In the translation itself, parentheses ( ) are used when Zeami himself has presented information in the form of an aside. Brackets [ ] are used when the elliptical nature of the text has required specific additions by Mr. Yamazaki and myself. When the meaning of the original seems basically clear, however, we have not used the brackets but simply accepted the general sense of the passage as established by the various scholarly editions of the treatises.

As is customary, all Japanese names are given with the surname first.

The Background of Zeami's Treatises

by J. Thomas Rimer

The *nō* theater of Japan, one of the most remarkable performing traditions in world theater, was brought to its first and highest flowering by Zeami Motokiyo (1363-1443). Zeami, building on the insights and experiences of his father Kan'ami, was able through his own skills and abilities to transform what had been essentially a country entertainment with strong ritual overtones into a superb total theatrical experience in which mime, dance, poetry, and song were combined so that each art could be transcended in order to produce for his audiences an experience of profundity and almost religious exhilaration.

Zeami's treatises, in which he discusses the principles of his art, remain unique documents in the history of the *nō*. They stand as crucial statements that can inform a modern reader, just as they were meant to inform Zeami's professional colleagues, of the essential elements in the theatrical process as Zeami understood them. From our twentieth-century point of view, the treatises seem to serve two widely differing functions. On the one hand, Zeami's notions of the interlocking functions of acting, music, and movement in the *nō* reveal a remarkably contemporary consciousness. Despite the poetic and often arcane language Zeami uses, a performer can still find much here that seems altogether appropriate to the craft of acting. My colleague, Mr. Yamazaki concentrates on this aspect of the treatises in his essay. On the other hand, the treatises tell us an enormous amount about the early development of the *nō*, a form of theater profoundly grounded in the specifics of medieval Japanese culture. My purpose here is to suggest enough of the historical background to provide a useful context for an understanding of Zeami's concerns.

Considering the stature of Zeami, a celebrity during his own lifetime, it seems remarkable that we know so little about him.[1] He was a child performer in the troupe of his father Kan'ami (1333-1384). When he was a boy of twelve, his remarkable talents were first noticed by the Shōgun Ashikaga Yoshimitsu (1358-1408), as powerful a patron of the arts as he was a political figure. Zeami's beauty both as a boy and as a performer attracted Yoshimitsu's patronage, as well as the encouragement and support of Nijō Yoshimoto (1320-1388), a leading *renga* poet of the time. Zeami's intellectual and artistic training was surely encouraged by such men in the court as these, for it is clear from the treatises that Zeami was a man well-versed in the details of literature, poetry, and philosophy. Normally, such matters would have been little known to an actor, since the social status of performers at this period was low indeed.

Zeami's father died when the young actor was only twenty-two, leaving him with the considerable responsibility of carrying on the tradition of his family troupe. Indeed, Zeami's stated purpose in writing his first treatise, *Teachings on Style and the Flower*, was to record the experiences of his gifted father and to comment on his own observations as a performer who attempted to follow in that tradition.

Zeami and his troupe evidently enjoyed the continuing patronage of Yoshimitsu until his death in 1408, but the Ashikaga successor, Yoshimitsu's eldest son Yoshimochi (1386-1428) seems to have favored another actor Zōami, a gifted performer in a rival *dengaku* troupe. Zeami admired Zōami and others of his contemporaries as well, and he learned from them, as the treatises make clear.

---

[1] For a judicious and detailed treatment of Zeami's life, see Thomas Hare's introduction in his dissertation (not yet published), "Zeami's Style: A Study of the 'mugen' Noh Plays of Zeami Motokiyo," University of Michigan, 1981. Yamazaki Masakazu's 1963 play *Zeami* is an attempt to dramatize many of those same facts. A translation is available in the volume *Mask and Sword: Two Plays for the Contemporary Japanese Theatre by Yamazaki Masakazu* (New York: Columbia University Press, 1980).

Yoshimochi may have been indifferent to Zeami, but after the Shōgun's death in 1428, when Zeami was sixty-six, Yoshimochi's younger brother Yoshinori (1394-1441) took over the reigns of government. From this time on, Zeami and his family suffered real personal difficulties. In 1434, when Zeami was seventy-two, he was banished to the island of Sado, a remote area near Niigata, in the Japan Sea. Four years before, Zeami's second son Motoyoshi (who wrote down the text of *Zeami's Reflections on Art*) abandoned the acting profession and became a Buddhist priest. In 1432, Zeami's older son Motomasa died, and there is some suggestion that he was murdered. On'ami (1398-1467), a nephew of Zeami, was officially appointed head of Zeami's family troupe by the Shōgunate when Motomasa died. The reasons for these terrible events have never been made clear, but it may have been Zeami's opposition to On'ami, whom he considered an inferior artist, that caused his exile, and indeed Zeami did insist on passing his treatises on to his gifted son-in-law Komparu Zenchiku (1405-1468), refusing to give them to On'ami. Zenchiku himself became a playwright and a theoretician of the *nō* second in importance only to Zeami himself.

Yoshinori was assassinated in 1441. Tradition has it that Zeami was pardoned and allowed to return to the mainland before his death in 1443. Few details concerning the end of his life are known, however, and inference and speculation often account for many important details of his career. In terms of Zeami's artistic and intellectual attitudes, however, the treatises do tell us much about his convictions and enthusiasms. In that way, at least, the spirit of this remarkable artist can be known to us.

Zeami, of course, never imagined that the works translated in this volume would ever be widely read. They were originally intended for a small circle of intimates and were written for the purpose of passing on matters of professional concern from one generation to the next. Zeami's troupe, like the others performing at his time, was organized on an hereditary basis, and these treatises were written for those already initiated into the art.

The idea of writing such secret treatises did not originate with Zeami. Such documents have always been important in Japanese culture, first perhaps in the esoteric sects of Buddhism, then in the realm of court poetry composition, where secret traditions for the writing of *waka* and *renga* were passed on through successive generations of the great court families, who jealously guarded their private treatises on the secrets of excellence in poetic composition.[2] As far as modern scholarship has been able to ascertain, however, no such elaborate treatises on the art of the *nō* were written before Zeami's time. Perhaps Zeami's early training in poetry through his contacts with Yoshimoto and Yoshimitsu helped suggest to him the idea of composing such documents, and indeed the very existence of such treatises would doubtless help to dignify a profession that had heretofore seemed of little social account. In order to insure continued patronage, Zeami must surely have felt it necessary to consolidate what he learned from his father and to do all that he could to insure that his descendants might be as successful as possible, financially and artistically, in their endeavors. It is clear, however, from various remarks in the treatises, that these documents contained information that was not to be shared with other actors outside the family, or with the public, in any form. The secrets of the art were to be passed on privately, and the treatises shown only to those who were properly initiated.

For that reason, the texts of these works were not available to the Japanese public until the twentieth century. After Zeami's time, the *nō* continued as a theatrical form of great popularity, and by the seventeenth century, in the early Tokugawa period, the development of printing and the interest shown by a growing number of amateurs in the *nō* gave rise

[2] See various entries in Brower and Miner, *Japanese Court Poetry*, for the development and transmission of poetic treatises. There is also a useful article on the subject of Komiya Toyotaka, "Nō to hiden," in Nogami Toyoichirō, ed., *Nōgaku zensho* (Tokyo: Sōgensha, 1942-1944), I, 275-315.

to the publication of certain play texts and a much bowdlerized version of portions of *Teachings on Style and the Flower*. The authentic texts by Zeami, however, remained in private hands until 1908, when a collection of the genuine treatises was discovered in a Tokyo secondhand bookstore. Purchased by a wealthy collector, they were edited by the writer Yoshida Tōgo and published in 1909 under the auspices of the Society for the Study of Nō Literature. These texts were collated with other versions that came to light, and the first set of definitive texts were published in the 1940s by a leading scholar of the *nō* , Nose Asaji, in his two-volume *Zeami jūroku bushū* (The Sixteen Treatises of Zeami). Since the war, another generation of meticulous Japanese scholarship has produced the now standard editions used in the preparation of these present translations. Certain pieces of information are missing, and some passages remain obscure, but we now have a fuller view of the critical writing of Zeami than would ever have been thought possible a few generations ago.

The range of the nine treatises included in the present volume is sufficiently wide that the reader can observe the changes in Zeami's own experience, from the early *Teachings on Style and the Flower*, in which he chronicles what he has learned from his father, to *An Account of Zeami's Reflections on Art*, taken down by his son Motoyoshi in 1430. A close study of the texts can show how Zeami's concepts developed as he gained experience. In the later treatises there seems an increasing predilection for searching out metaphysical explanations, often Buddhist in tone, for the kinds of practical insights that Zeami had learned both as a writer and as a performer. And, indeed, the treatises read more clearly and are more comprehensible as a whole than when read singly. Much that is unstated in one context is explained in another. Zeami conceived of the Way of the *nō*, as he sometimes put it, in a manner similar to that of the Way of the *waka* poet or the Buddhist adept. The Way (*michi* in Japanese) suggests commitment, constant practice, and a genuine humility on the part of the one who is sincere in seeking a true path toward enlightenment or excellence.[3] It is not by accident that the word Path or Way occurs in the titles of several of Zeami's treatises, and it is the concept that ties all of them together.

For all the importance that Zeami places on the need for an inner concentration leading to a fixed goal, a modern reader will be struck again and again by Zeami's fascination with the freedom of the process involved. Nō may have grown out of ritual and folk art, but Zeami brought to such traditional assumptions an opportunity for a new and profound originality through his commitment to pleasing his audience, a process that required a judicious use of the traditional and the unexpected. In this sense, the treatises show an almost revolutionary spirit at work. Zeami was willing to set aside canons of traditional taste when the occasion demanded it. In this regard, he goes beyond his mentors in the field of *waka* and *renga*.

The important aesthetic concepts developed by Zeami in the course of these treatises could well form the basis for an extended study. In any case, he explains his ideas in such striking and poetic language that no lengthy preface is required here. At the least, however, it might be well to mention here several key terms as a signal to the reader that these concepts— which usually become more clear when all the treatises are read—are crucial to Zeami's central patterns of thought.

One is that of the Flower (*hana*), a symbol used by Zeami for the true beauty created by the actor's performances in different ways throughout his career. By the use of this natural symbol, Zeami maintains a deep connection between the forces and movements of nature and the work of the committed actor, who in his art must attempt to recreate and symbolize those patterns and relationships. Then too, as Arthur Waley first suggested in his 1921 volume *The Nō Plays of Japan*, the idea of mystic transmission is involved in the concept of the Flower. The alternate title of the *Fūshikaden* (which we have

[3] See Brower and Miner, *Japanese Court Poetry*, p. 257. For a full discussion of the concept of *michi* in medieval Japanese aesthetics, see Konishi Jin'ichi, *Michi—chūsei no rinen* (Tokyo: Kōdansha, 1975).

rendered as *Teachings on Style and the Flower*) is the *Kaden-sho*, which might be literally translated as "The Book for the Transmission of the Flower," perhaps a reference to the mysterious transfer of thought from the Buddha to his disciple Kāśyapa, an incident mentioned in the treatises by Zeami himself. It is doubtless for this reason that Zeami often observes in the course of the treatises that some particular point cannot be explained in words alone but requires an intuitive understanding on the part of the actor.

Another concept crucial to Zeami's thought is that of a fundamental rhythm basic to the *nō*, and, as he points out on several occasions, to all of nature itself. Zeami categorizes this basic rhythmical movement as *jo* (introduction), *ha* (breaking), and *kyū* (rapid), a gradual increase of pace from slow to fast. Scholars have identified various sources for this concept that go back as far as the patternings for the *bugaku* dances imported into Japan from China in the Heian period (794-1185). Zeami, however, seems to have been the first to use such a rhythmic pattern as a metaphor for the deepest psychological movement inherent in a successful theatrical experience.

Another powerful idea in Zeami's treatises concerns the relationship of *yūgen*, which we have translated as Grace, with the concept of *monomane*, sometimes translated as imitation but rendered in our translation by the term Role Playing so as to avoid too strict a suggestion of Western *mimesis*. A number of the most striking passages in the treatises deal with a need to create in the spectators a sense of the beauty that lies behind and beyond the kind of surface portrayal possible through the creation by the actor of any mere outward verisimilitude of the character being portrayed.

In addition to Zeami's own concepts, these treatises also provide for the student of comparative theater history or of Japanese medieval culture an enormous amount of fascinating specific information, often presented in a vivid fashion, of artistic life during Zeami's lifetime. Although it is true that methods of performing the *nō* established at that period still continue, the kind of stately experience usually offered today seems at some variance with the rough-and-tumble world described in the treatises. Zeami's milieu involved constant competition, and he always remained anxious to make his troupe successful and to keep it so. He has praise for others, but he shows himself as well an astute critic of performers from rival groups; and, indeed, his comments are so shrewd that, although the particulars of the acting styles are no longer always clear to us, the general import of his remarks always remains precise and vivid.

Four of the major troupes that perform today can trace their lineage back to the time of Zeami (see chart 1). The fifth troupe now performing, usually referred to as the Kita school, was formed in 1618 by a gifted amateur actor, Shichidayū (1586-1653), who received special patronage from the all-powerful Tokugawa family. From this time on, official support for the nō from the Tokugawa Shōguns helped remove this form of drama from the public scene and brought about as well a standardization, an increased emphasis on elegance, and a slower pace to performances. The nō that we witness today has been filtered through the Tokugawa process of gentrification, with both gains and losses.

One important change during the early Tokugawa period involved the establishment of fixed dimensions for the nō stage. The treatises make clear, however, that actors during Zeami's lifetime were quite prepared to perform in a variety of playing spaces; indeed, one test of their skill as performers concerned their abilities to adjust their movements and vocal production to a variety of environments. Evidently there was no regularized playing space during Zeami's lifetime, or at least there is no information remaining that allows us to describe such a place with confidence. Figure 1 is a modern rendering of the kind of space used for performances in front of the Shōgun, and so might be considered as somewhat typical.

The treatises also reveal that the method by which the plays were chosen for performance was somewhat at variance with

Chart 1 Various Important Troupes Performing at Zeami's Time

	Dengaku		*Yamato Sarugaku*				*Ōmi Sarugaku*			*Hosshōji Sarugaku*		
Troupes [alternate names]	Honza	Shinza	Yūzaki [Kanze]	Tobi [Hōshō]	Sakado [Kongō]	Emman-i [Takeda]	Yamashina	Shimozaka	Hie	Shinza [Enami]	Honza [Yata]	Shuku
Actors	Itchū ↓	Hanayasha Kiami Zoami ↓	Kan'ami Zeami On'ami			Zenchiku	↓	↓	Dōami Iwatō ↓	Enami ↓	↓	↓
	DIES OUT	DIES OUT					DIES OUT	DIES OUT	DIES OUT	DIES OUT	DIES OUT	DIES OUT
Later Troupe Names			Kanze	Hōshō	Kongō (divides in 17th century into Kongō, Kita)	Komparu						

Figure 1. The Floorplan of a Performing Space Used at the Time of Zeami

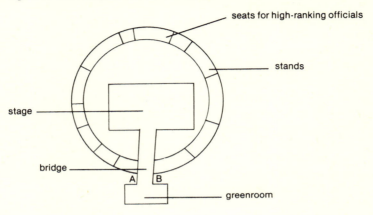

The Floorplan of a Modern *Nō* Stage

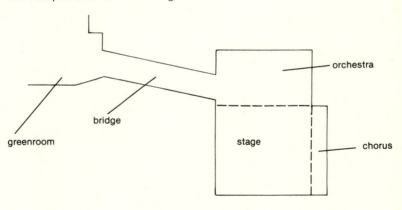

the modern method of selecting a *nō* program. There is no mention in any of the treatises of the so-called Five Groups or Five Categories by which the *nō* are catalogued today, a grouping into plays concerning (1) gods, (2) warriors, (3) women, (4) mad persons, and (5) demons. The pace in this scheme moves from slow to fast, category 1 being the most sedate, and category 5 the most wild and volatile. Such a schematization was evidently imposed later, probably during the Tokugawa period.[4] Zeami's ideas were more flexible and less orthodox, in keeping with the importance he gave to the idea of novelty in his art.

A modern reader will notice at once that the repertory of *nō* pieces performed during Zeami's period was more varied and richer than what can be seen today. The modern repertory is chosen from a body of about two hundred fifty plays, yet a reading of *Zeami's Reflections on Art* shows that a number of important works performed at that time have not been retained in the repertory. Many of these plays still exist in manuscript, and some have been printed in large *nō* collections published in Japan early in this century. If all these texts could be located, a close reading of them and a collation of their themes would doubtless give us a very different, and a much more diverse, picture of the theater and of the mentality of Zeami's time.

Current scholarship indicates that there are in the present canon about fifty works that can fairly be attributed to Zeami. Some of these modern printed versions, however, are often simplified, even bowdlerized. In addition, there are sixteen or seventeen *nō* by Zeami that are not performed and for which texts are difficult to obtain. A few, of course, have been lost. Quite a few of Zeami's plays have been translated into Western languages, but, as *Zeami's Reflections on Art* makes clear, a number of those considered important during his lifetime

---

[4] Scholarly opinion differs as to how and when the various systems of classification for various types of *nō* came into being. For an extended discussion of the problem, see Kanai Kiyomitsu, *Nō no kenkyū* (Tokyo: Ōfusha, 1969), pp. 152-179.

remain quite unknown to modern Japanese or Western readers. Many of these submerged works deal with themes and figures from Shintō myth and legend, pointing to an aspect of ritual and belief that is much less visible in the better-known and often elegant plays based on Buddhist themes. The treatises suggest that the psychological attitudes of Zeami and his contemporaries, for all the affinities we may feel, show strong qualities that are foreign to a modern mentality, Japanese or Western. There remains something rich and strange about Zeami and his world. Working over the treatises, it has seemed to me that, whatever we gained in the centuries since his death, we have lost something as well—a quality perhaps best expressed in that awe Zeami felt before the processes of nature and art, an awe that for him was a necessary prelude to individual creation. If our translations can suggest in some fashion the importance of that awe to Zeami, and perhaps its potential value to us, then Mr. Yamazaki and I will be gratified indeed.

The Aesthetics of Ambiguity:
The Artistic Theories of Zeami

by Yamazaki Masakazu

When compared with the other views of the theater in the world, particularly with various dramatic theories of the West, Zeami's artistic theory clearly demonstrates three major characteristics. First, Zeami attached great importance to the audience that witnessed a performance; second, he laid a particular emphasis on the actor's mental and physical acting among the diverse elements that constitute the theater; third, he gave a high place to stylization in acting.

When speaking of classical dramatic theories of the West, one would cite Aristotle's *Poetics* as the first comprehensive attempt; but in an almost symbolic fashion, this first dramatic theory in the world almost completely lacks reference to the three elements mentioned above. This work by Aristotle is, first of all, a theory of the creation of the drama (as its title in Greek, ΠΕΡΙ ΠΟΙΗΤΙΚΗΣ, shows) and analyzes its structure. Although the author describes precisely and thoroughly how a play should be written, he does not go at all into how the play will be acted or seen by the audience. Aristotle compares literary works, including the drama, with historical narratives, or analyzes art in relation to reality, but he never looks into the relationship between creation and appreciation, or between the work and the audience. One can even say that the very fact the audience does affect the production of art in various subtle ways, and does participate actively in making the theater what it is, was not present in his mind.

Needless to say, according to Aristotle, the essence of the theater is the imitation of action in the form of action, and here the definition "in the form of action," is merely set against the idea of "in the form of narration." In other words, the philosopher is saying that when writing a play the dramatist should not portray his characters from the outside in the fashion of an epic poet, but should enter into them and look at the world from their viewpoints. Within this framework, Aristotle does not completely ignore the importance of acting. In Chapter 17, he even demands of the dramatist a kind of empathic acting.[1] Aristotle insisted that a man who is himself feeling real sorrow and real rage can express such emotions convincingly and make his audience believe in them effectively. However, this view concerned only the internal acting by the dramatist; Aristotle's demand did not extend to the imitation of action by a real actor making use of his voice and body. If the actor's body movements or voice production is considered in Aristotle's theory of the drama at all, it is only in connection with the aural or visual effects of the performance, and even as such, it is subsidiary to references to the plot, characterization, thought, or diction, and is clearly given a peripheral position.[2]

One may say that in the *Poetics* the performance of a play itself is a secondary subject; and if that is so, it is natural that questions of stylization in acting or directing are not seriously considered.

Aristotle was apparently a realist of a sort in his view of internal acting by the dramatist, and seems to have thought

---

[1] "Again, the poet should work out his play, to the best of his power, with appropriate gestures; for those who feel emotion are most convincing through natural sympathy with the characters they represent; and one who is agitated storms, one who is angry rages, with the most life-like reality." S. M. Butcher, trans., *Aristotle's Theory of Poetry and Fine Art* (New York: Dover, 1951), pp. 61-62.

[2] "The spectacle has, indeed, an emotional attraction of its own, but, of all the parts, it is the least artistic, and connected least with the art of poetry. For the power of tragedy, we may be sure, is felt even apart from representation and actors." Butcher, *Aristotle*, p. 29. "Again, tragedy like epic poetry produces its effect even without action; it reveals its power by mere reading." Butcher, *Aristotle*, p. 109.

that the only function of acting is to communicate unadulterated emotions precisely. From their characteristics known today, we may deduce that classical Greek tragedies required highly stylized acting, but the fact that such acting was not of aesthetic interest to Aristotle was decisive for the history of dramatic theories of the West.

Later in the Renaissance period, the West saw signs of Aristotelian poetics reviving along with the resurgence of the theater itself, and on that foundation many literary scholars developed their own dramatic theories. The central argument was again on the writing of the drama—its subject matter, construction, or style. Very little attention was given to the techniques of performance.

The only exception was an Italian humanist, Leone de Somi (1527-1592), who turned his eyes to the art of acting in the latter half of the sixteenth century and wrote a discourse called "A Dialogue on Acting." The eighteenth century finally saw some growth in the interest in the theory of acting: Luigi Riccoboni's *On the Art of Declamation*, his son François Riccoboni's *L'Art du théâtre*, and Pierre Rémond de Sainte-Albine's *Le comédien* were published. This led to the writing of the famous *Paradoxe sur le comédien* by Denis de Diderot.[3]

All these, however, were but fragmentary technical discussions on acting that lacked any firm aesthetic foundation. They were interested in some limited aspect of acting. Their only major argument revolved around opposing ideas as to whether acting should be based on real emotions or on intellectual observation that excluded emotion. In one sense it represented a dispute between the Aristotelian theory of acting and the theory that opposed it.

---

[3] Details concerning these various treatises and translations of important sections from them can be found in various entries in Toby Cole and Helen K. Chinoy, eds., *Actors on Acting* (New York: Crown, 1972). A discussion and evaluation of certain aspects of these treatises from the point of view of a pioneer of the modern theater can be found in chapter 2 of William Archer's *Masks or Faces? A Study in the Psychology of Acting* (London and New York: Longmans, Green & Co., 1888).

This conflict was continued into the nineteenth century, when William Archer discussed the choice between two alternatives, masks or faces. Even then, one may conclude that the mainstream of opinion descended from Aristotle's theory of empathy. For example, Stanislavsky's "method" of realistic acting later came to dominate the modern theater worldwide; it, in short, valued the truth of emotion and denied all stylized acting.

This tradition of the denial of stylization goes back many centuries. In existing records of the Roman era, one can see traces of the fact that actors at that time aimed principally to be realistic. According to Aulus Gellius, the actor named Polus was praised for keeping to himself the sorrow he felt at the death of his son and so making a clever use of it in acting the role of Orestes.[4]

The famous lines in Scene 2 of Act III of *Hamlet* are often cited as an indication of Shakespeare's theory of acting, and the idea that actors should hold a mirror up to nature must also be read as a manifesto on realism in a wider sense of the word. It is widely known that French classicists always asked for the pursuit of "naturalness" at the same time as they demanded a recapitulation of the classics in their concept of the theater. On the Shakespearean stage and in the acting of French classics, various types of stylization were actually required, and lines were written in magnificent verse; yet no theoretical attempt was made to affirm that fact in any positive fashion.

Moreover, even in the modern age, when Stanislavsky and his successors took the center stage, the audience was always treated as a subordinate factor in a performance and was never regarded as an essential part of dramatic creation. Ironically, modern dramatic theories were devised rather as an inquiry into the necessary means to allow the actor to forget the audience and make him independent of it. When the proscenium arch came to be an integral part of theaters and

[4] See *Actors on Acting*, pp. 14-15.

succeeded in physically separating the auditorium from the stage, then and only then did modern realistic acting in the strict sense of the word come into being. Stanislavsky's actors tried to guard the truth of the emotions to be expressed by imagining an invisible "fourth wall" on the auditorium side of the stage and by deliberately disregarding the audience on the other side of that wall.

It is no exaggeration to say that the idea of demanding that the audience participate actively in the performance and the recognition of their worth in dramatic creation as a whole appeared in the West for the first time in the latter half of the twentieth century.

In contrast to these Western views of drama, it is obvious how great an importance Zeami placed on the audience. At the very beginning of his *Teachings on Style and the Flower* (Fūshikaden), he insisted that the ideal of the performing arts is to gain the love and respect of the people. To perform in front of an audience consisting of people of diverse tastes and to capture the heart of all of them was the basic task of an actor. Zeami went so far as to place an extremely difficult responsibility on the actor, which was to perform the *nō* so that it would be enjoyable even to those who have no eye for it. On the one hand, Zeami was an artist who pursued purity in the theater and gave birth to a highly sophisticated theatrical taste, but on the other hand he set for himself the almost contradictory task of pleasing the popular audience at all times.[5] One must not overlook the fact that this emphasis on the

---

[5] Zeami was active at the period when Kyoto, the aristocratic capital, was becoming swollen with new arrivals of different classes—warriors, farmers, merchants—all resulting from the establishment of a new military regime, the Ashikaga bakufu, which took over the middle of the city. Intellectuals of the time, such as Yoshida Kenkō, were keenly aware of the discrepancy in aesthetic tastes between the serene and individualistic "men of breeding," and the crazed "rustic boors who take all their pleasures grossly." See Yoshida Kenkō, *Essays in Idleness*, translated by Donald Keene (New York: Columbia University Press, 1967), p. 118.

audience penetrates deep into his essential idea of the theater and further into his fundamental thoughts on beauty.

Zeami uses the word Flower (*hana*) to describe the beauty of the performing arts or the aesthetic effect of the theater. According to his definition, this Flower is none other than Fascination, and Fascination none other than Novelty. Novelty means something the audience has not seen before, something that always remains fresh in its creative power. In Zeami's mind, Novelty did not mean something odd or something that was singular in kind. It was a quality that emerged out of the technique of making the old look new by various devices used in theatrical presentation. Spectators become bored when shown the same thing repeatedly; on the other hand, it is impossible for an artist to go on producing different qualities infinitely. Zeami managed to repeat the familiar and, by skillfully alternating it with different or unfamiliar elements, to revitalize the image in the spectator's mind. Therein lay the secret of his art.

In that sense, the reason why he compared the beauty of the performing arts to a flower was not simply because a flower is perceived as beautiful in a sensuous fashion. To this great artist, a flower was beautiful because it would shed its petals. In the sense that a flower undergoes constant changes in front of the viewer, it can be compared to an artistic ideal.

His well-known saying, "If hidden, acting shows the Flower; if unhidden, it cannot," for example, comes out of his consideration for his audience and his profound analysis of their psychology. If the audience can see beforehand the performer's calculations in his acting or becomes conscious of his inventions, the dramatic effect that is produced as a result can be neither novel nor fresh. As a consequence, Zeami demands that while showing the results of his acting to the audience, the actor should at all costs hide his self-awareness or the psychological processes that lead to such results from the spectators' eyes. Later this demand was taken even one level higher. The actor was asked to "hide his own mind from himself" or to hide from himself what the awareness of his own efforts does to him. That is the state the actor reaches when he has completely digested his artistic skills through repeated and thorough training and rehearsals, thus integrating his mind and body so that dramatic effects appear almost automatically or spontaneously. In other words, the actor keeps back from the audience the impression that he is controlling their emotions and takes care not to give the impression of the expansion of his self to the audience.

This emphasis on the audience is characteristic not only of Japanese dramatic theories but of its artistic theories in general. Donald Keene in his *Japanese Literature: An Introduction for Western Readers* quotes Ki no Tsurayuki's preface to the early anthology of court poetry, the *Kokinshū*, and points out that an idea completely opposed to Western aesthetics is recognizable in Tsurayuki's thought. The Japanese poet held that poetry grows out of the human heart, touches it and goes beyond human beings to move even nature and supernatural beings. According to Mr. Keene, Western poetics believe that poetry is born out of the supernatural and moves human beings in the guise of human language.[6] The traditional view of art in the West held that art came into being out of the relations between the artist as an individual and what was called a god or an ideal—in other words, between man and the supernatural. In this context, a work of art was created by a lonely genius outside the common or mundane world; therefore another man's appreciation had only a secondary significance.

From the point of view of this idealistic aestheticism, the value that art must pursue, whether it be beauty or truth, must always be seen as at the end of a one-directional road. Since all realities are but copies of their ideas, the correct appearance of reality is produced by approaching as close as possible to that idea. In classicism, the ideal of beauty was given as an objective canon, whereas romanticism sought to achieve more

---

[6] See Donald Keene, *Japanese Literature, An Introduction for Western Readers* (New York: Grove Press, 1955), p. 22.

direct and subjective unity with ideas. In either case, the artist was required to pursue a pure and one-dimensional objective at all times.

Needless to say, even in the West attempts were made apart from idealism to see man as an ambiguous being, and to understand reality as a paradoxical world. It is widely known that Socrates was a genius of paradoxes. Shakespeare's plays are studded with lines that portray the ambiguity of man's existence, such as "Fair is foul, foul is fair" at the beginning of *Macbeth*. Nevertheless, the fundamental aesthetics of the West ultimately aim to capture an ideal in its purest form, and have tried to eliminate all that is inconclusive or ambiguous; in other words, an attempt has been made to exclude compromises between the artist and the rest of humanity.

Even in the modern age, when people began to believe that art must portray reality, the basic idealism did not change. Realism allowed no compromise on the part of the actor, and demanded that he portray social injustices and human uglinesses relentlessly. In addition, the Western tradition required that the artist be aloof to his secular surroundings. He was expected to make his art outside the framework of actual human relations.

In the Japanese tradition, by contrast, art almost always stemmed from actual human relations. Take lyric poetry, for instance. *Waka* poems were customarily made at various parties and later specifically at poetry parties, which were a unique form of social gathering. At such a party, a poem was considered completed when it was appreciated and evaluated by those present as soon as it was made. Afterwards this custom developed further and produced the form of *renga* in which a number of persons contributed to create one unified work. In the case of the fine arts, as well, a painting was deemed completed only when it was seen by people at a salon and their impression was inscribed on the picture in the form of a poem. Furthermore, Japan produced a unique form of art, the tea ceremony. The fact that social formalities were heightened into art is enough to suggest how the Japanese traditional view of art functioned.

Reflecting such a tradition, Japanese aesthetic thought did not and does not encourage pursuit of any aesthetic ideal in one direction of purification. Rather, to the contrary, all aesthetic effects are believed to become what they are while containing contradictory elements within themselves.

According to Yoshida Kenkō (1283-1350), a noted essayist of the medieval period, a man of good taste should not look directly at anything beautiful, whether it be the moon or a flower. The correct attitude is *yosonagara ni miru*, or to long for it indirectly from some distance.[7] This idea was later succeeded by the aesthetics of *wabi*, according to which anything gorgeous becomes truly beautiful when joined with something subdued, so as to become half concealed by it. One of the originators of the tea ceremony, Murata Shukō (1422-1502), said, "I do not like the moon without clouds." The point of the aesthetics of *wabi* was summed up in the words of Rikyū (1521-1591), the greatest of the tea masters, as "a fine steed tethered in a thatched shack."

In Japanese literature from the Heian to the Edo period, the technique of allusion (*honkadori*) in poetry and of parody (*mojiri*) in fiction were particularly liked, reflecting a taste that valued the duality of imagery—creating, in other words, an aesthetics of paradox.

Whereas a transcendental being essentially represents a single value and never varies its demand, man's existence cannot be separated from his physical senses, and so he cannot endure the pureness of any singular and homogeneous value. However much a man may like brightness, he cannot keep his eyes open in the direct rays of the sun. A man may have a sweet tooth, but if he were forced to keep on taking pure sugar forever, he would find it painful. Man's senses easily become fatigued and bored with any unadulterated object; the only way to keep them satisfied is to change continuously the nature

---

[7] See *Essays in Idleness*, pp. 115-118.

of the stimulation. Moreover, just as sweetness is enhanced by a small amount of salt or bitterness mixed in with it, it is well known that man's sensitivity is heightened by the addition of an opposing element.

Such observations help us to see that since Japanese art is created not before a transcendental being but by one human being for another, it is natural for its aesthetic ideal to show an essentially paradoxical and ambiguous character. It is also easily understandable how in the thinking of Zeami, who worked face to face with his audiences as an artist in the theater, such an aesthetics of paradox came to rule his thought. For example, he set the concept of Grace (*yūgen*) as the supreme goal of his art, but this idea of beauty, of which sophistication and grace constituted the essence, could not be achieved by pursuing it directly.

Zeami's family, who came originally from the farming district in Iga and who represented the artistic taste of the powerful local clan, was particularly good at acting out stories with many dramatic ups and downs and at presenting various characters in a realistic manner. One can imagine that their original style lay in portraying diverse characters with clearly marked personalities. On the technical side they laid emphasis on descriptive gestures and stage speech. Starting from this base of unsophisticated realism, Zeami achieved an urban refinement of expression. In more specific terms, he developed a style that emphasized song and dance. He called this new form of beauty "grace."

In this sense, from the beginning his idea of Grace presupposed its opposite as the condition for its existence, and it came into being through the unification of reality and idealization, of individuality and refinement, of popular traits and aristocratic taste. When an actor is to play the part of a fierce warrior, for instance, Zeami demands that a trace of Grace be added to the realistic representation of the character. According to his own words, the effect must be "like a flower blooming on a rock." In the portrayal of an old man, while demanding an expression of the decline of strength and of the anguish that accompanies human life, Zeami required a shade of splendor and charm; he described the effect as "a flower blooming on a dead tree." Needless to say, what he demanded in these instances was not mere compromise or eclecticism, but a dramatic conflict between two contradictory elements, the rock and the flower, or the dead tree and the flower.

In passing, one should note that Zeami showed a special liking for the figure of a beautiful woman who had lost her sanity. In this case, contrary to the examples above, a realistic element of madness is mixed into the portrayal of elegance, with an aim of unifying the charm of static beauty and that of mobility.

In his *Teachings on Style and the Flower*, Zeami cites the basic components of the *nō*, which he calls the Two Basic Arts of song and dance (*nikyoku*) and the Three Role Types (*santai*). From one point of view, the essential opposition also exists between the Two Basic Arts and the Three Role Types. For a man to sing and dance is to leave the reality of his life, but to play a role is to face reality directly and to reconfirm it. Clearly the former represents the lyrical aspects of acting and the latter the epic. Whereas the former aims for fluidity of movement, the latter attempts at articulation. Zeami regarded the unification of this essential opposition as the central task of acting, and in his mind, acting was itself a paradoxical action. Hegel saw dramatic literature as unifying the lyrical and the epic, and explained it as the dialectic between the subjective spirit and the objective spirit; but Zeami saw the unification occurring in physical acting itself.

Going one step farther and looking into Zeami's analysis of actual acting, one notices that he counterposes two basic methods, imitation and becoming. "Imitation" means to copy gestures and facial expressions realistically. It means to observe a human action, analyze it, and reproduce it consciously in detail. On the other hand, "becoming" means that the actor assimilates himself into the emotions of the character. It means that he sees human action as a stream of consciousness that never slackens, throws himself into the stream, and is carried along by it.

When the actor tries to imitate something, he manipulates his body as an object, or paints, as it were, using his body as the canvas; but he transcends the break between his body and mind when he attempts to "become" the character. When he has completely assimilated himself into the character, he fills his heart and mind with the emotions of that character alone, and tries to allow those emotions to move his body with their own force. At such times, he has become completely united with his own body, and he can forget about each specific gesture and facial expression, while keeping hold on the continuous flow of consciousness.

According to Zeami, ideal acting is founded on the unity of these two methods. He describes it, for instance, as "connecting all the arts through one intensity of mind." All arts here denote the various technical skills of acting that enable the actor to represent the character's actions objectively and analytically. Zeami likens their working to the movements of the limbs of a lifeless puppet. What gives life to this mechanical contraption and incorporates it in flowing movement is Zeam-i's "one mind," the act of keeping a certain level of heightened tension in the mind. In other words, the former is the actor turning the eye of consciousness toward the outside, and the latter toward the inside. It is by no means easy to unite the two in a balanced state. In reality, man tends to control and manipulate his own body as an object, and the actor inclines more toward "imitation" and forgets the maintenance of "one mind."

Well aware of this, Zeami demands that the actor hold the function of "all arts" deliberately in check, and communicate his internal tension directly to the audience. To help achieve that purpose, he quotes a phrase used in criticizing the nō, "the less done the better." Through these words, he is teaching the fact that even when the actor has stopped all exterior movement of his body, the well-disciplined dynamism of the body itself can move the audience.[8]

In regard to the style of dance in the *nō*, Zeami first defines the two opposing basic forms of Self-Conscious Movement (*shuchi*) and Movement beyond Consciousness (*buchi*), and places above them Mutuality in Balance (*sōkyokuchi*), which comes into being as the unification of the two. Self-Conscious Movement is the style based on the articulated movement of various parts of the body, including the limbs, and Movement beyond Consciousness is born out of the actor's committing his body to the continuous flow of movement itself. In explaining the dance in terms of Movement beyond Consciousness, Zeami likens it to a bird spreading its wings and floating in the air. This static state, which is full of tension, must correspond to the ideal of "the less done the better." For Zeami, this internal tension was always the foundation of acting, and any external and articulated movement was to be added on top of it. Needless to say, the ideal was a perfect balance between the two. Indeed, in regard to the dance, he defined that state specifically as the original style called Mutuality in Balance.

What Zeami stresses in his teachings to actors, however, is none other than "becoming" and the possession of "one mind." He calls the actor who has acquired that ability one who can show Internalization (*yūshufū*). Internalization requires that an actor become the complete master of his own movements, and according to Zeami it denotes a state in which the flow of movement has become so well assimilated that the actor loses even the consciousness of controlling it.

---

[8] In performances of *nō* as presently staged, it may seem to some members of the audience that the aspect of "becoming" is overemphasized, and that the technique of "the less done the better" is excessively abused by the actors. It is certainly true that throughout the Tokugawa period (1600-1867), efforts were made, under the strong pressure of the Shōguns, to remove the *nō* from the life of the ordinary people and to reduce realistic and expressive acting in order to make the form as aristocratic as possible. Zeami's assertions must be understood in the context of his own historical period.

In this regard, one can say that this great artist's theory of acting went beyond the argument prevalent in the West since the eighteenth century concerning the opposition between masks and faces. Diderot's stand was that acting which moves the audience rises out of the actor's conscious manipulation of his body. Archer's idea was that, on the contrary, such acting came spontaneously from the actor's own feelings. These two views clearly correspond to the contrast between Zeami's "imitation" and "becoming." However, Zeami did not see the mask and the face as requiring a choice among alternatives; rather he wanted the actor to unify the two while retaining a positive consciousness of their opposition. In connection with the expression of a strong emotion, in particular, Zeami strictly demanded this ambiguous attitude. He carefully warned the actor against indulging in his own emotions as well as using his technique to manipulate them. This concept is clearly shown in his teaching, "What is felt by the heart is ten; what appears in movement is seven," and "Violent body movement, gentle foot movement." He wanted the actor to place his body under a certain amount of control. This idea led Zeami to form a particular attitude about the role of a demon, for example. He insisted that even while playing the part of a ferocious demon, the actor's physical expressions must, to some extent, be elegant and delicate.

What Zeami taught specifically to the actors in order to make them tackle this contradictory task of acting was, first, to understand a role in terms of an attitude and, second, to see action as a rhythmical structure. Either of these can become a direct aim for an actor's efforts, and they may be described as the focus for his consciousness, giving him a target for his attention and saving him from confusion and disruption.

Zeami divides nō characters into three basic types, the old man, the woman, and the warrior, and it is obvious that these three represent the basic attitudes of man toward his world. The old man represents the attitude of retiring from life, and the calm contemplation of it. The warrior shows an aggressive and vigorous attitude. The woman stands between the two, symbolizing an attitude of harmony with the world.

This artist, however, did not see attitudes of man on the spiritual plane alone but also regarded them as very concrete attitudes of the body. For example, the old man's attitude is described in the following single sentence: "Relaxed Heart Looking Afar." In this brief summation, the contradictory characteristics of an old man's behavior are united; that is to say, he has given up on this life but still possesses a final concern over the future, which is physically expressed in his calm look directed afar. Zeami warns the actor who plays the old man's part against merely imitating the decline in physical appearance, and encourages him rather to express the man's desire to remain young. In this feat, also, "imitating" and "becoming" need to be united, and as a specific psychological technique, Zeami teaches his actors to assume one particular mental and bodily attitude.

He also pointed out that there is a modulating structure of jo, ha, and kyū in human actions. He believed that it was a duty of acting to unify actions into one complete image by bringing out this rhythmic structure. All actions form one unit when they begin in an easy manner (jo), develop dramatically (ha), and finish rapidly (kyū); and then they can give the viewer the impression of an organic unity.

In real life, this rhythmical structure meets many obstructions posed by various conditions. Part of the process is broken down or its order disturbed. The structure is manifested in its complete form only when such obstacles are eliminated, and when man can move while consciously giving his attention to it. This kind of special action represents acting, which includes singing and dancing. Or rather, according to Zeami, acting makes a positive use of external conditions in order to give the impression of this rhythm, and the actor can take even the atmosphere of the theater and the general feeling of the audience into the structure of jo, ha, and kyū. By acting well, he gives order to his environment, or, to use a different expression, he reflects the rhythm of reality in his body.

This bodily and mental attitude and the rhythm of action complement each other in acting; the former is the spatial support of acting, and the latter its chronological axis. But, needless to say, each of them takes its reciprocal place in the character of acting in its entirety, which achieves a happy balance between those two aspects. One attitude consists of the internal workings of a man as manifested directly on his outward appearance, and also represents a point of contact between the conscious and the unconscious in movement. When a man takes this attitude, he keeps his consciousness in a completely awakened state, but the details of his action emanate almost automatically from that attitude. Therefore, a man takes an attitude through an active use of his will, but once that attitude is established, he is passively carried along by it. Exactly the same is true of rhythm. A man may consciously create a rhythm, and at the same time be moved by it as if intoxicated. A rhythm is founded on the unity between contradictory elements—drive and restraint, flow and articulation. A man can therefore view it from the outside and also make it three-dimensional by immersing himself in it. As far as his actions are concerned, as long as he makes them sufficiently rhythmical, he is, so to speak, automatically uniting the fact of being outside his actions and inside them.

Attitude and rhythm are found, of course, in all of man's actions. It is obvious that in daily life they are distorted in almost all cases, and often destroyed; man tries to control his actions too consciously or, on the contrary, often leaves them to completely habitual and unconscious progression.

In real life, man tends to be concerned only with the aim and results of his action and, as a consequence, is engrossed only in efficiency and economy of labor for achieving them. When it is difficult to attain his aims, man manipulates his body as a tool and makes haste, leaning forward in the effort. When the goal is easy to attain, man throws away the tension necessary to assume any one attitude and so becomes one with his body, simply carried along by its movement. It goes without saying that in either case his attitude loses its essential balance, and the ambiguous character of the rhythm is destroyed. Acting, as a consequence, will become either imprecise, with the aspect of its fluidity accentuated, or will be reduced to a mechanical and clumsy level, with the aspect of its articulatedness more apparent. In all probability, so long as human civilization swings undecided between utilitarianism and laziness, man's action will always be threatened by both of them, and so will fail to attain a sound and beautiful appearance.

Having discussed this much, it is not necessary any longer to explain why Zeami showed no interest in realism of acting but endeavored to establish a stylized form for it. To this artist, it was song and dance, or the Two Basic Arts, and three basic characters, or Three Role Types, that stylized acting. The reason for this was that they gave action both a stable rhythm and an attitude. To Zeami, a beautiful style meant nothing other than the beautiful attitude for action and the ideal rhythm that all actions should possess. In other words, a style of acting is not a fiction for the stage but a form that all actions should possess in order to attain perfection as action. It is, however, a framework that actions tend to miss in reality. In this sense, if one is to state on Zeami's behalf his tacit and basic understanding, probably one should say that there is no perfect action that one must imitate in this world of reality, and a real action is restored to its ideal state only in stylized acting.

Texts Used for the Translations

The present volume provides a complete translation of the standard text of Zeami's treatises as found in the *Nōgakuronshū*, edited by Nishio Minoru, in Volume 65 of the *Nihon koten bungaku taikei* (Iwanami shoten, 1961).

The text used for the translation of *Learning the Way* (*Shūdōsho*), not available in the Nishio volume, was taken from Volume 2 of the *Zeami jūroku bushū hyōshaku*, edited by Nose Asaji (Iwanami shoten, 1966).

Commentaries and interpretations provided for the various treatises reproduced in Yamazaki Masakazu, ed., *Zeami* (Chūōkōronsha, 1969) have been central in the preparation of the translation.

Other commentaries and notes that have proved particularly helpful in preparing the translation were those found in the two-volume Nose volume cited above, and in the *Zeami geijitsuronshū* edited by Tanaka Yutaka (Shinchō Nihon koten shūsei series, Shinchōsha, 1976). Notes provided for the treatises in Volume 24 of the *Nihon shisō taikei* volume entitled *Zeami, Zenchiku*, edited by Omote Akira and Katō Shūichi (Iwanami shoten, 1974) were also most helpful.

Notes on the Treatises

1. *Teachings on Style and the Flower (Fūshikaden)*, the main text of which is thought to have been completed around 1402, when Zeami was forty, gives a thorough account of Zeami's understanding of the art of his father Kan'ami, and chronicles as well Zeami's own development as a performer and aesthetician up to this stage in his career. The sixth and seventh sections were doubtless written later and added to the original five, as the 1418 date at the end of the seventh section would indicate.

2. *The True Path to the Flower (Shikadō)*, written in 1420, when Zeami was fifty-eight, stresses his views of the fundamentals of the actor's art, and begins to make the kinds of metaphysical and philosophical distinctions concerning various levels of accomplishment in acting that are further developed and elaborated in later treatises.

3. *A Mirror Held to the Flower (Kakyō)* was compiled in 1424, when Zeami was sixty-two. The treatise incorporates the text of an earlier treatise, *Learning the Flower (Kashū)*, finished in 1418. The treatise ranges over a number of significant topics, from instruction in basic performance skills to explanations of psychological sequence, audience response, and the philosophical goals of *nō* performance. Zeami's most extended discussions of his interpretation of Grace (*yūgen*) and Peerless Charm (*myō*) are included here.

4. *Disciplines for the Joy of Art (Yūgaku shūdō fūken)* was composed about 1424, when Zeami was sixty-two, although the exact date is not certain. This short treatise, couched in a metaphysical style, provides examples from Buddhist texts, poetry, and Confucian maxims that relate to the art of the *nō*.

5. *Notes on the Nine Levels* (*Kyūi*) is also thought to have been composed at about the same time as *Disciplines for the Joy of Art*, but the exact date has not been determined. The nine levels of performance are given a definitive and highly poetic explanation. Zeami evokes a terminology allied to Zen Buddhism as a means to explain many of his central insights.

6. *Finding Gems and Gaining the Flower* (*Shūgyoku tokka*) was written in 1428, when Zeami was sixty-six. In this treatise, Zeami answers six questions concerning the art of the *nō*. A number of metaphysical concepts, many of them Buddhist in inspiration, are cited in the text.

7. *The Three Elements in Composing a Play* (*Sandō* or *Nō-sakusho*) was composed in 1423, when Zeami was sixty-one. The text is mainly concerned with practical points related to proper methods of composing a *nō* text, and usually stresses formal requirements.

8. *Learning the Way* (*Shūdōsho*) was composed in 1430, when Zeami was sixty-eight. The treatise provides an excellent introduction to Zeami's views on the nature of ensemble acting.

9. *An Account of Zeami's Reflections on Art* (*Sarugaku dangi*) was written down by Zeami's son Motoyoshi from conversations held with his father. The text is dated 1430, when Zeami was sixty-eight. A wide range of topics is covered, ranging from technical matters related to musical and verbal problems in performance to more general reminiscence and reflection.

In addition to the works translated in the present volume, there are other treatises written by or attributed to Zeami that have not been included. They are as follows:

1. *The specialized treatises on music.* Because of the obscurity of the musical terminology employed, the Japanese scholarly debate over the meaning and significance of the musical systems employed by Zeami, and the difficulty of establishing explanatory terminology comprehensible in English, no translations of these works have been attempted. Fortunately, much of Zeami's nontechnical views on musical performance is re-

peated in other forms in the treatises that have been translated in this volume.

Among the most important of the musical treatises written by, or attributed to, Zeami are the following:

(a) *Ongyoku kowadashi kuden* (*Treatise on Musical and Vocal Production*), a short treatise dealing with the vocalization of *nō* texts.

(b) *Fushizuke shidai* (*Treatise on the Application of Melody*), a short treatise on the creation and performance of melodies to be chanted to a *nō* text.

(c) *Fūkyokushū* (*A Collection Concerning Musical Performance*), a brief discussion of methods of performing the *nō* chant.

(d) *Goongyokujōjō* (*Various Matters Concerning the Five Modes of Musical Expression*), the most complete expression by Zeami of his musical ideas on the *nō*.

(e) *Goon* (*The Five Modes*), another statement of the materials discussed at length in the preceding treatise.

2. *Yūgaku geifū goi* (*Five Levels of Performance for the Joy of Art*). A brief treatise, in classical Chinese, that distinguishes five different styles of excellence in performance.

3. *Rikugi* (*Six Principles*). A brief treatise attributed to Zeami that relates the art of *waka* to the *nō*. Some scholars cite the somewhat arbitrary nature of the text as an indication that Zeami may not have been its author.

4. *Nikkyoku santai zu* (*Illustrations for the Two Basic Arts and Three Role Types*). A brief illustrated treatise. The material presented is basically the same as that in *The True Path of the Flower* and in *Finding Gems and Gaining the Flower*. There is a French translation in Sieffert's *La Tradition secrète du nō*.

5. A group of miscellaneous writings that are not, strictly speaking, treatises on the art of the *nō*. Among them are the following:

(a) *Kyakuraika* (*The Flower of Returning*), a short work that combines reminiscence and general statements of artistic principle. A translation, with copious notes, is available by Mark J. Nearman in *Monumenta Nipponica 35*, Summer 1980.

(b) *Kintōsho* (*The Book of Golden Island*), a literary text based on Zeami's experiences while exiled on the island of Sado. The work is not theoretical in nature, but is usually included among the treatises. A translation with notes is available by Susan Matisoff in *Monumenta Nipponica 32*, Winter 1977.

Drawings by Komparu Zenchiku for the *Nikkyoku santai zu* (Illustrations for the Two Basic Arts and Three Role Types), a brief treatise by Zeami on acting styles. Most of the text is reproduced in *The True Path to the Flower* and *Finding Gems and Gaining the Flower*.

Figure 2. A demon whose movements show Delicacy within Strength, "the Appearance of a Demon, the Heart of a Man"

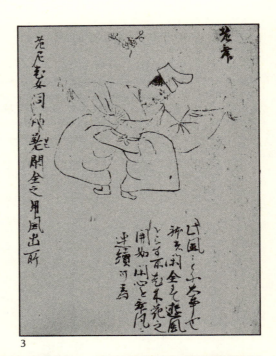

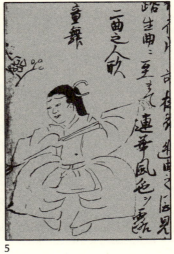

Figure 3. A dance appropriate for the role of an Old Man
Figure 4. A dance appropriate for a Woman's role
Figure 5. A child's dance

6

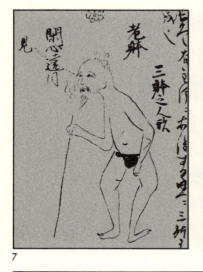

7

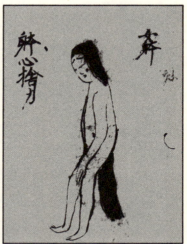

8

Figure 6. A demon whose movements are in the Rough Style, which Zeami did not consider appropriate for his school of performance

Figure 7. The role of an Old Man, "Relaxed Heart, Looking Afar"

Figure 8. The role of a Woman, "Concentration of Mind, Relinquishing Physical Strength"

9

10

Figure 9. The role of a Warrior, ''Physical Strength, Splintered Heart''
Figure 10. The dance of an Angel

The Nine Treatises

Teachings on Style and the Flower
(Fūshikaden)

In searching for the origins of *sarugaku* and *ennen*, some say they came from India, and some say they have been handed down since the age of the gods. Yet as time moves on and those ages grow remote, any proper skill is lacking to learn the ancient ways precisely. The origin of the *nō*, which all enjoy today, goes back to the reign of the Empress Suiko, when Prince Shōtoku commanded Hata no Kōkatsu (some say for the sake of peace in the country, some say to entertain the people) to create sixty-six public entertainments, which were named *sarugaku*. From that time onward, men in every age must have used images of the beauties of nature as a means to render this entertainment more elegant. Later, the descendants of Kōkatsu inherited this art and served at the Kasuga and Hie shrines.[1] This is why, even now, those performers from Yamato and Ōmi perform rites at both temples, which are still flourishing. Therefore, while studying the old and admiring the new, the great traditions of elegance must never be slighted. A truly skillful player is one whose speech lacks no refinement and whose appearance creates a feeling of Grace. One who wishes to follow the path of the *nō* must engage himself in no other art. There is one exception: the art of poetry deserves study, for it is a means to open the actor to the profound beauties of nature and enrich his life. I will note here in general various things I have seen and heard since my youth concerning the practice of the *nō*.

[1] The Yamato *sarugaku* troupe had an official affiliation with the Kasuga Shrine in Nara. A series of *nō* performances was included in the important Wakamiya festival held there. The Ōmi troupe had official ties with the Hie Shrine on Mount Hiei, to the north of Kyoto, the site of the great Buddhist temple complex of Enryakuji.

—Sensual pleasures, gambling, heavy drinking represent the Three Prohibitions. Such was the precept of my late father.

—Rehearse with the greatest effort; do not be overbearing with others.

CHAPTER 1. ITEMS CONCERNING THE PRACTICE OF THE NŌ IN RELATION TO THE AGE OF THE ACTOR

Age Seven

It may be said of our art that one may begin at seven.[2] When a boy practices at this age, he will naturally of his own accord show some elements of beauty in what he does. If, by chance, he should show some special skill in dancing, movement, chanting, or in the kind of powerful gestures required for demon roles, he should be left free to perform them in his own manner, according to his own desires. He should certainly not be instructed as to what he did well and what he did poorly. If rehearsals are too strict, and if the child is admonished too much, he will lose his enthusiasm. If the *nō* becomes unpleasant for him, then his progress will cease. He should only be taught dancing, movement, and the chant. In particular, he should not be instructed in the fine points of Role Playing, even though he may show aptitude for it. He must not be permitted to perform in a *waki sarugaku*, especially on an open stage. Let him perform at a time that seems appropriate, in the third or fourth play in the day's program, when he can be given a part he can perform with skill.

Age of Eleven or Twelve

From this age onward, the voice begins to achieve its proper pitch, and the actor can begin to comprehend the *nō*. There-

[2] Traditionally, ages were calculated so that a person was considered one year old at birth and two at the beginning of the next calendar year. Thus the ages given here are higher than would have been assigned to a Western actor at the same stage of development. Thus Zeami's actor at the age of seventeen or eighteen would probably be, by Western reckoning, between fourteen and sixteen.

fore, various aspects of the art can now be explained. In the first place, a boy's appearance, no matter in what aspect, will produce the sensation of Grace. And his voice at this age will always sound charming as well. Because of those two strong points, any defects can be hidden and the good points will be made all the more evident. On the whole, it is better not to teach any fine points concerning Role Playing for a child's performance, for such knowledge would make his performances at this stage seem inappropriate and, in fact, hinder further progress in his art. Later, as he becomes more skillful, he should be allowed to practice every element of the art. With the appearance and voice of a child, a boy actor, if he shows skill in his performance, can hardly give a bad impression. Still, this Flower is not the true Flower. It is only a temporary bloom. For that reason, practice at this time is easily managed. This does not mean that, because of this one flowering, he will always appear to be so skillful. As rehearsal at this age will always allow the young actor to create the impression of the Flower through his good points, the development of his basic skills is crucial. His movements must be authentic, the words of his chanting distinct, and his positions for dancing must be well fixed. These skills must be carefully and thoroughly rehearsed.

From the Age of Seventeen or Eighteen

This is a particularly crucial period, and not too many kinds of training can be arranged. First of all, since the actor's voice is changing, he loses his first Flower. His physical figure changes as well, and his movements become awkward. Before, his voice was full and beautiful, and it was easy for him to perform; now, realizing that the rules have changed, the actor's will falters. What is more, since the audience may look scornfully at his performance, he now feels embarrassed and discouraged. As concerns training, then, at this age, the actor, even though there are those who may point to him and laugh, must take no note, but retire to his own house, and, in a pitch comfortable to him, practice his chanting, using appropriate techniques for morning and evening.[3] Most important of all, he must vow to himself that, although he is now in a crucial period, he will truly stake his life on the *nō* and never abandon it. Should any actor give up his training at this point, his skill can never increase. In general, although the pitch of the individual voice at this age may vary, it usually lies between the *ōshiki* and the *banshiki*.[4] If the actor tries to regulate the pitch too strictly [by forcing], he risks getting into bad habits with his posture. Then too, this may be the cause of damage to the actor's voice in later life.

From Twenty-four or Twenty-five

It is in this period that the level of artistry of the performer begins to become established. The limits of the actor will be fixed by his training and his self-discipline. His voice will by now have settled, and his body will have matured. These are the strong points required in our art: voice and physical appearance. Both of these become fixed at this period. This is the time in an actor's life when the art is born that will lead to the skills of his later years. In the eyes of others, it may well appear that a new and highly skilled performer has appeared. Therefore, even though he is being judged against a performer who is already highly regarded, it may seem on the occasion of his performance that his Flower is a new and fresh one, and, should he win a competition, others may praise him beyond his due, so that the actor himself comes to believe that he is already highly skilled. I cannot stress often enough that such an attitude serves as an enemy to the actor. For such is not the true Flower. A truly novel Flower comes about because of the actor's age and experience, when his spectators can

[3] Zeami's remark suggests that a certain caution must be used when exercising the voice in the morning, whereas in the evening the voice is freer and can thus be exercised more vigorously.

[4] *Ōshiki* and *banshiki* are two of the twelve pitches in the traditional Japanese musical scales. *Ōshiki* is considered to correspond roughly to the pitch A in the Western musical scale, *banshiki* to B.

truly be surprised. Spectators of real discernment are able to make this distinction. It would indeed be a shame if this early Flower, which actually represents only the actor's first level of accomplishment, should somehow be fixed in the actor's thoughts, so that he sees this phase as the culmination of his art, and therefore indulges himself in what is a deviation from the true path. Actually, even if an actor is praised by his audience and manages to win a competition over a famous performer, he must take cognizance of the fact that his Flower is merely a temporary one; therefore, he will begin at once to study Role Playing with the utmost seriousness and will ask every detail of those who have already achieved a real reputation for their performances, so that he may rehearse all the more diligently. One who believes that this temporary Flower is the real Flower is one who has separated himself from the true way. And indeed, any performer can be taken in by this temporary Flower and so fail to realize that he is losing the real one. Such is the situation of a young actor.

Here is one point that must be considered carefully. If one has a true ability to understand his own level of perfection in his art, then he can never lose that level of the Flower. If an actor thinks he has attained a higher level of skill than he has reached, however, he will lose even the level that he has achieved. This matter must be thought over carefully.

Thirty-four or Thirty-five Years

This age represents the peak of perfection in our art. If an actor grasps the various items set down here, and masters them, he will truly be acknowledged by the public and will achieve a reputation as a great actor. If such public recognition does not come, however, and he does not obtain such a reputation, then no matter how skillful the actor may be, he must recognize the fact that he is not one who has yet found the true Flower. And if he has not obtained such a Flower by this time, his art will begin to decline when he is forty. The proof of this fact will become clear as the actor grows older. An actor is on the rise until he is thirty-four or thirty-five, and he begins to decline after forty. This fact cannot be repeated too often—those who do not achieve a reputation at this stage of their career have not actually mastered the art of the *nō*. Therefore it is in this period that the actor must perfect his self-discipline. At this time in his career, he can recall all that he has learned; it is also the moment when he is able to plan for the means to accomplish what he wishes to in the future. If such things are not mastered at this age, then, let me repeat again, it will be difficult for an actor to find success with audiences later in his career.

Forty-four, Forty-five Years

From this point on, the actor must find new means of showing his skills. Even if he has achieved a fine reputation and has mastered the art of the *nō*, he must be able in turn to have in his troupe young actors who will follow him. Although his real art may not decline, yet, as his years advance, his physical presence and the beauty others find in him will be diminished. Leaving aside the exceptionally handsome performer, even a fairly good-looking actor, as he grows older, should no longer be seen playing roles that do not require a mask. Thus this former aspect of his art will now be lacking. From this point onward, it is best not to perform elaborate parts. On the whole, an actor should choose roles that are congenial to him and that can be played in a relaxed manner without physical strain. He should allow the younger actors to show off their own abilities, and he should play with them in a modest fashion, as an associate. Even if he has no young successor of a suitable caliber, an actor should not himself perform any highly complicated and strenuous roles. In any case, the audience will find no Flower in this sort of performance. If, on the other hand, an actor has not lost his Flower by this age, then it will remain truly his possession. If an actor still possesses his Flower as he approaches fifty, then he must have achieved a real reputation before the age of forty. Even an actor who has gained such a reputation however, if he is truly a master, must most of all know himself, and, therefore, work to give the young actors proper training; he will exert himself to the utmost, without performing roles that may betray his own weaknesses. One who truly knows how to see and reflect upon himself—it is he who has really grasped the nature of our art.

Fifty Years Old and Later

From this point onward, for the most part, there is little more that can be done. There is a saying that "even *ch'i lin*, when old, is worse than a worn out packhorse."[5] Nevertheless, an actor who has truly mastered his art, even though he has lost his ability to perform many of his roles, and although he may manifest less and less of his art in performance, will still have something of his Flower left about him.

My late father died at the age of fifty-two on the nineteenth day of the fifth month [of 1384], and on the fourth day of that same month, he performed the *nō* in connection with religious services at the Sengen shrine in the province of Suruga.[6] The performances that day were particularly colorful, and all the spectators, high-ranking and commoner alike, praised his performances. At that time the various plays were given over to the younger actors, and he performed a few easy roles in a modest way. Yet the beauty of his Flower was all the more striking. For when an artist has achieved a real Flower, then the art of the *nō*, even if the foliage is slight and the tree grows old, still retains its blooms. This is the very proof that, even in an ancient frame, the Flower remains.

What has been written above constitutes the appropriate stages of *nō* training at various ages.

[5] *Ch'i-lin*, [*kirin* in Japanese] famous in ancient Chinese historical chronicles was, rather like the Greek Pegasus, a horse with the miraculous ability to travel enormous distances very quickly.

[6] Generally identified as the Sengen Shrine in the present city of Shizuoka, a little over a hundred miles south of Tokyo.

CHAPTER 2. VARIOUS ITEMS CONCERNING ROLE PLAYING

It would be impossible to describe in writing all the various aspects of Role Playing. Yet as this skill forms the fundamental basis of our art, various roles must be studied with the greatest care. In general, Role Playing involves an imitation, in every particular, with nothing left out. Still, depending on the circumstances, one must know how to vary the degree of imitation involved. For example, when it comes to playing the part of a ruler or a high official, it is extremely difficult to perform with the necessary detail, since the actor cannot know the real way of life of the court nobility, or the bearing appropriate to a great lord. Still, he can study carefully their way of speaking, observe their circumstances, and ask the opinion of those noblemen who watch the performances. Next, he must imitate down to the smallest detail the various things done by persons of high profession, especially those elements related to high artistic pursuits. On the other hand, when it comes to imitating laborers and rustics, their commonplace actions should not be copied too realistically. In the case of woodcutters, grass cutters, charcoal burners, and salt workers, however, they should be imitated in detail insofar as they have traditionally been found congenial as poetic subjects. In general, men of lowly occupation should not be imitated in any meticulous fashion, nor shown to men of refined taste. Should they see such things, they will merely find them vulgar, and the performance will hold no attraction for them. The need for prudence in this matter can be fully understood. Thus the degree of imitation must vary, depending on the kind of role being performed.

Women's Roles

In general, a young *shite* is the most suitable actor to play the part of a woman. Nevertheless, playing such a part represents a considerable undertaking. If the actor's style of dress is unseemly, there will be nothing worth watching in the performance. When it comes to impersonating high-ranking women of the court, such as ladies-in-waiting, for example, since the actor cannot easily view their actual deportment, he must make serious, detailed inquiries concerning such matters. As for items of clothing such as the *kinu* and the *hakama*, these too cannot merely be chosen on the basis of the actor's personal preference. The actor must make a proper investigation concerning what is correct. When it comes to impersonating an ordinary woman, however, the actor will be familiar with the appropriate details, and so the task will not be difficult. If the actor dresses in an appropriate *kinu* or *kosode*, that will doubtless suffice. When performing *kusemai*, *shirabyōshi*, or mad women's roles, the actor should hold a fan or a sprig of flowers, for example, loosely in his hand in order to represent female gentleness. The *kinu* and the *hakama*, as well, should be long enough to conceal his steps, his hips and knees should be straight, and his bodily posture pliable. As for his head posture, if he bends backward, his face will appear coarse. If the actor looks down, on the other hand, his appearance from the back will be unseemly. Then too, if he holds his neck too stiffly, he will not look feminine. He should certainly wear a robe with long sleeves, and he should avoid showing the tips of his hands. His *obi* should be loosely tied. The fact that an actor takes great care with his costume means that he is truly anxious to perform his role as well as possible. No matter what the role, bad costuming will never be effective, and, in the case of a woman's role, proper dressing is essential.

Old Men

Playing the role of an old man represents the very pinnacle of our art. These roles are crucial, since the spectators who watch can gauge immediately the real skills of the actor. There are many *shite* who have mastered the art of *nō* quite well, but who cannot achieve the appearance of an old man. When an actor plays a woodcutter, salt scooper, or a similar part that contains conspicuous gestures, it is easy enough for the spectators to be deceived and to make a false judgment too quickly concerning the performer's talents. But to play the part of an old man of high rank whose gestures involve no characteristic movement is truly difficult and requires the skills of a master actor. Unless an actor rehearses over the years until his art is at its peak, he cannot properly present this kind of role. Without a proper Flower, such a restrained performance can have nothing of interest about it.

In terms of stage deportment, most actors, thinking to appear old, bend their loins and hips, shrink their bodies, lose their Flower, and give a withered, uninteresting performance. Thus there is little that is attractive in what such actors do. It is particularly important that the actor refrain from performing in a limp or weak manner, but bear himself with grace and dignity. Most crucial of all is the dancing posture chosen for the role of an old man. One must study assiduously the precept: portray an old man while still possessing the Flower. The results should resemble an old tree that puts forth flowers.

Performing without a Mask

This too represents an important aspect of our art. As such roles are those representing ordinary persons, they may seem to be easy to perform, but, surprisingly, unless the highest level of skill in the *nō* is used, such a performance will not be worth watching. The actor must of necessity study the object of each role individually [since the face is visible]. Although it is not possible to imitate any particular individual countenance in performance, actors sometimes alter their own ordinary facial expressions in an attempt to create some particular effect. The results are always without interest. The performance should rather be constructed from the movements and general feeling of the person being portrayed. The actor must always use his own natural facial expressions and never try to alter them.

Roles of Mad Persons

This skill represents the most fascinating aspect of our art. In this category there are many types of roles, and an actor who has truly taken up this specialty can play successfully all types of roles. I must repeat again and again that an actor must fully commit himself to rehearse and practice continuously, as I have admonished. In general, there are various types of possessed beings; for example, those inhabited by the curse of a god, a Buddha, the spirit of a living person, or of a dead person. Therefore, if the actor studies the nature of the spirit who possesses the character, he should be able to manage the part well. On the other hand, the really difficult parts involve those characters whose thoughts have become confused because their minds have become crazed—a parent searching for a lost child, for example, a wife thrown over by her husband, or a husband who lives on after his wife. Even a relatively skillful *shite* may fail to make the distinction between them, and he will create his mad gestures in the same manner, so that no emotional response is engendered in those who watch him. In the case of characters of this sort, the actor must have as his intention the manifestation of the precise feelings that can indicate the character's emotional disturbance, and make them the core of his Flower; then, if he feigns madness with all the skill he has at his command, there will certainly be many arresting elements in his performance. If an actor possesses this kind of skill, and if he can make his spectators weep, his art will represent the highest attainment possible. Reflect as fully as possible on what I have written above.

It goes without saying that a costume appropriate for the role of a mad person is essential. Still, as the character is a mad person, the costume might, depending on the occasion, be more gaudy than usual. The actor can carry in his hand a sprig of flowers appropriate to the season.

Then again, while I have spoken in terms of acting that imitates surface realities, there is another point that must be seriously considered. Although I said that the madness of the character must be performed in terms of the being who possesses that character, when it comes to playing a madwoman possessed by a warrior or a demon, for example, the circumstances are made quite difficult for the actor. Thinking to act out the true nature of the being who possesses such a character, the actor will show masculine wrath while playing a woman, and his performance will seem quite inappropriate. On the other hand, if the actor concentrates on the womanly traits of his character, there will be no logic to the possession. Similarly, when a male character is possessed by a woman, the same difficulty arises. In sum, to avoid plays with such characters represents an important secret of our art. Those who compose such texts simply to not understand the nature of our art. A writer who truly understands the art of *nō* would never compose a text that showed such a lack of harmony. To possess this truth is another secret of our art.

When it comes to playing the role of a mad person without a mask, the performance will not be complete unless the actor has truly mastered his art. For, if the expressions on the actor's face are not properly descriptive, there will be no sense of madness conveyed. If the actor changes his face without a profound understanding of his art, on the other hand, the results will be merely ugly. The deepest arts of Role Playing are required for these paradoxical circumstances.

Thus, in important performances, inexperienced actors must participate with the greatest caution. Playing without a mask is very difficult. Acting a mad role is also very difficult. To combine these two elements into one: how difficult indeed to elevate such a role to the level of the Flower. Rehearsal and study are the only methods possible.

Roles of Buddhist Priests

Although such roles exist, they are few in number and do not require so much practice. In general, when playing a gorgeously robed cleric or a priest of high rank, the actor must use the majesty and dignity of the character as the basis for his performance. When it comes to lesser-ranking priests, such as those who have abandoned the world and practice austerities, their religious pilgrimage is of paramount importance to them, and so it is crucial for the actor to create the impression that such characters are absorbed in their religious devotions. In the end, when it comes to the materials on which to build a performance, more pains may be required than might be expected.

Shura

Here is still another type of role. Such dead warrior roles, even when well performed, are seldom arresting. Thus they should not be performed too often. Nevertheless, when it comes to events dealing with the famous Genji or Heike warriors,[7] if the various elements are knit together with suitable elegance, so that the text is a good one, such a performance can be more moving than one of any other variety. In such plays, some spectacular moment is particularly important. The wildness of the *shura* style may well lead to the kind of behavior appropriate to a demon role. Then again, such a role risks turning entirely into a dance performance. If there is a section in the play that resembles *kusemai*, it is allowable to include some appropriate dancelike gestures. As it is customary for the actor to carry with him a bow and quiver and to wear some variety of sword, the performer should undertake a careful study of how to carry and use such objects, making efforts to exhibit the essence of this type of role. The actor must take special care to avoid both those movements appropriate to a demon role on the one hand, and the use of purely dancelike motions on the other.

[7] The Genji and Heike clans were the chief rivals in the disastrous civil wars of 1185 that brought an end to the political domination by the Kyoto court. Many important *nō* texts by Zeami dealt with characters and incidents from those battles.

Roles of Gods

In general, this kind of Role Playing is related to that appropriate for the demon roles. As the appearance of such a figure is always fierce, no particular difficulties are created by playing the part in the manner of a demon, depending, of course, on the role of the god involved. However, there is one essential difference between the two types of characters. Dancelike gestures are the most appropriate for the role of a god, but they are not suitable for a demon role. Particularly in the case of a god role, the only means available to the actor to represent such a being lies in his being properly dressed, and therefore he must give particular attention to the creation of a properly noble appearance. The actor must decorate his costume correctly and adjust his clothing in an appropriate manner.

Demon Roles

These roles are a particular specialty of the Yamato school. They are extremely difficult to perform successfully. True, it is simple to play effectively the demon roles of vengeful ghosts or possessed beings, as they offer visible elements of interest that can make them arresting. The performer, directing himself toward his acting partner, should use small foot and hand motions and make his movements in accordance with the effect created by his headgear. In the case of a real demon from hell, however, even if the actor studies well, his performance is likely to be merely frightening. There are no real means to make such roles truly enjoyable for the spectators. In fact, these are such difficult roles to play that there are few actors who can perform them in an effective way, it seems.

The essence of such roles lies in forcefulness and frightfulness. Yet such qualities do not stimulate feelings of enjoyment. For this reason, the role of a demon is particularly difficult to play. Logically, the harder the actor tries to perform them, the less interesting they become. The essence of such a role is frightfulness, yet the qualities of frightfulness and enjoyment

are as different as black and white. Thus, it might be said that
an actor who can perform such a role in an enjoyable way
would indeed be a performer of the highest talent. Indeed, an
actor who strives for nothing but to play demon roles well
can never really attain the Flower. Therefore, a performance
by a young actor, even if it seems well done, will not really
be effective. Is it not then true that an actor who only strives
to play demon roles well can never actually perform them
well? This paradox must be carefully studied. For the interest
the spectator finds in the performance of a demon role is like
a flower blooming among the rocks.

Chinese Roles

As these are special kinds of characters, there is no fixed form
of practice for the actor. The element of appearance is essential. In choosing a mask—even though the character is of
course a human being just like anyone else—it is best for the
actor to wear something with an unusual appearance so as to
maintain the effect of something somehow out of the ordinary.

Such parts are effectively played by older artists with talent
and experience. Still, other than costuming, there are no special techniques required. In any case, since any attempt to
imitate the Chinese style directly, either in chant or in movement, will not in itself be effective, it is better to add just one
representative element to an ordinary performance. The selection of just such an element, slight in itself, can serve as a
means to animate the whole. Although usually such changes
are not considered appropriate, there is no way truly to copy
the style, and so such a slight change in gesture will add
something of the Chinese flavor and can give the spectators
an appropriate sensation. Such methods have been practiced
for a long time.

In general, such are the various elements of Role Playing.
It is difficult to express any finer details in writing. Nevertheless, an actor who has fully grasped the points enumerated
above will be able by himself to grasp them.

CHAPTER 3. QUESTIONS AND ANSWERS

QUESTION: Before a performance begins on a particular day, when I look out at the spectators in the theater, how can I know to what extent the performance will be successful?

ANSWER: This is an important matter. Such a judgment can only be made by one with long experience in our art. First of all, by looking at the audience, one should be able to predict whether the results of the performance will be good or bad. It is difficult to explain precisely how this can be done. Nevertheless, there are certain ways to attempt it. For example, when a performance is held for religious purposes or before the nobility, the audience will be a large one and the spectators will be slow in quieting down. On such an occasion, the performer must wait until the audience falls silent; when they find it difficult to wait any longer for the performance to begin, and when all the spectators are as one in their feeling that the performance is surely late in starting, they will look toward the greenroom from which the performer will come. The performer should emerge at precisely the proper moment and begin his *issei*. This atmosphere that is created by such precise timing will in turn be transferred to the spectators, and their emotions will fall in harmony with the actor's performance. Once this atmosphere has been established, that day's performance can already be judged a success.

Of course, the basis for the success of a *sarugaku* performance depends on the presence of the nobility. Should they arrive early, it would be inappropriate not to begin the performance at once. On such occasions the general audience may not yet have fallen silent. Some spectators will be hurrying in late, some will be sitting, some standing, and, in the confusion, the audience will not be prepared for the performance. The proper settled atmosphere will be missing. On such an occasion then, during the opening play, even when the actor appears in a certain role, he must perform his movements in a broader fashion and make his voice and his dance steps more forceful than the role normally requires, so that the atmosphere of his performance will possess a vigor sufficient to attract the audience's attention. Such a performance should silence the spectators. Nevertheless, it is crucial for the actor to perform in such a fashion so as to harmonize with the feelings of those nobility who are among the spectators. For this reason, then, a performance of the opening play under such conditions can never really be successful.

In all these matters, the essential point is to satisfy the feelings of the nobility. In any case, it is by no means a bad thing when the theater falls quiet and an atmosphere of concentration is established of itself. Only an actor of great experience has the ability to ascertain the level of intensity of the audience at a particular performance.

Another point. An evening performance presents a different situation altogether. As the performance begins at a later hour, there is inevitably something gloomy in the atmosphere. Therefore the kind of *nō* that is appropriate for the second piece in a daytime performance should be used to open a program in the evening. If the opening play of the evening creates a gloomy atmosphere, the mood of the performance will not lighten. A good *nō* performance must be brisk. In the evening, even when the audience proves noisy, the sound of the *issei* will be enough to silence the spectators. Thus in daytime performances, the later parts are the most crucial for success, whereas at night, the beginning section is the most important. If the opening section of a nighttime performance is too dispirited, it is very difficult to lift the level of the performance afterwards.

According to a secret teaching, any endeavor will meet with success at the point when the principles of *yin* and *yang*[8] are harmonized. The spirit of the daytime hours can be represented by the positive principle, *yang*. Thus to plan to play the *nō* as gently as possible provides a spirit of the complementary negative principle, *yin*. Giving birth to *yin* during the

[8] *Yin* and *yang* are two terms basic to ancient Chinese thought. *Yin* represents the passive, female cosmic principle that stands as complementary to *yang*, the active, masculine cosmic principle.

hours of *yang* produces that sought-for harmony. The creation of this harmony is the first step in producing a successful *nō* performance. Performers and spectators alike will find such a performance moving.

On the other hand, the spirit of the night is represented by the negative principle, *yin*. Therefore, the *nō* must be played as buoyantly as possible; what lifts the feelings of the audience is the positive principle, *yang*. Success comes from harmonizing the spirit of *yang* with the spirit of *yin* of night. On the other hand, if the spirit of *yang* is applied to *yang*, or the spirit of *yin* to *yin*, no harmonization can take place, and no success will be forthcoming. And without such a harmony, such a fulfillment, there will be nothing of interest in the performance.

Then too, sometimes even during the daytime, on certain occasions, for some reason or other, the audience may seem dejected and somehow sad; therefore the actors, sensing the negative *yin* principle at work, must give no impression of gloom and should perform with all their energies. Although on occasion the negative principle is operative in the daytime, it is quite unlikely that the positive principle will be effective during the evening. Therefore, in attempting to judge the audience before a performance, this principle should be observed.

QUESTION: In a *nō* performance, how are the *jo, ha,* and *kyū*[9] to be arranged?
ANSWER: This is a simple matter. Since the principle of *jo, ha,* and *kyū* is universal, it applies as well to *sarugaku*. The par-

---

[9] These aesthetic units of a *nō* drama may be roughly translated (using Malm's terminology) as Introduction (*jo*), Exposition (*ha*), and Denouement (*kyū*). These three sections move at an ever-increasing pace and form the basic dramatic, rhythmic, and melodic basis of the *nō*. A more literal translation might be "introduction" (*jo*), "breaking" (*ha*), and "rapid" (*kyū*), suggesting some of these performance elements. There is no set of English terms that can encompass all these meanings, and so they have been left in the original in the translation.

ticular artistic qualities of each play will determine the arrangement. To begin with, for the *waki sarugaku*, a play based on an authentic source should be played with dignity and grace and in an uncomplicated way, with the chant and dancing performed in a smooth and elegant fashion. Most importantly, the play must be congratulatory in nature. No matter how fine a *waki sarugaku* may be, if the play is lacking in this quality it will not be suitable for this position in the program. Even if the play is somewhat weak, if it does possess this congratulatory quality, there should be no difficulty in creating a successful performance. This is because the play itself serves as the *jo* for the whole series of plays to be performed that day. When it comes to the second and third plays in the program, which represent the *ha*, well-written plays that show off an actor's skill should be chosen. Most importantly, since the last play to be performed for the day represents the *kyū*, strenuous movements and concentrated skill are required. When a series of plays is performed over more than one day, any *waki nō* presented after the first day should be chosen with a different kind of appeal in mind. Plays that are particularly moving should be carefully placed in the middle of a series during those successive days.

QUESTION: What are the various strategies to adopt during a contest of *nō*?

ANSWER: This is a very important point. In the first place, it is important to have an extensive repertory and to perform plays with artistic qualities different from those given by the opposing troupe, so as to provide some variation. I mentioned in the opening section of this treatise the study of poetry, and it was for this reason. When the author and the actor of a *nō* are different persons, it is impossible for an actor to perform to his full satisfaction. If the actor has written his own play, however, both the text and the gestures can be performed according to his conception. One who can perform the *nō* and has some talent in writing can surely compose one without difficulty. Such is the very life of our art. For no matter how skillful an actor may be, if he does not perform his own plays, he will be no better than a great warrior on the battlefield without his weapons. The results of the actor's skill must be visible in the contest. Should the opposing troupe perform a colorful play, then the actor must alter his intent and choose a play that is quiet yet well constructed. Therefore, if an actor performs a sort of play that is different from that chosen by his adversaries, then no matter how good the play his opponents may put on, he cannot lose. And if the performance is truly well executed, the actor will surely win.

Now, as far as the *nō* performances themselves are concerned, they can be judged as high, average, and low. A play that is taken from an authentic source, shows novelty, and possesses Grace will have something of interest about it and will surely be a play of first quality. If such a play is well performed and successfully received, then it is doubtless in the first category. Even if the play is not such a good one but is constructed properly in accordance with its source and without any flaws, then, if the performance is successful, it can be considered in the second category. Even if the play is merely showy and not authentic, should the actor make proper use of the text and apply all his skill and effort to please the audience, then such a performance will be in the third category.

QUESTION: I have great doubts on one point. How can it be that, despite the artistry and reputation of an experienced performer, a young artist can win over him in a competition? Why should this be so?

ANSWER: As I wrote above, the younger performer is able to manifest the kind of transient Flower that is possible for him to possess before he reaches the age of thirty. An older actor will have lost that temporary Flower, and, at a time when his own art may seem old, a Flower that seems novel will doubtless triumph. A real connoisseur, however, will be able to make the distinction. Perhaps it amounts to a question of a battle between the spectators who have a sense of discrimination and those who do not.

Nevertheless, there are some detailed considerations that should be made. When the contest involves a truly gifted actor who, when over fifty, has still not lost his Flower, then no matter what Flower a young actor may possess he cannot win. If a well-trained older player loses, it is because he has lost his Flower. Take a famous flowering tree, for example: who will admire that tree when it is out of season and not in bloom? Think then of an unremarkable cherry tree, which manages to send out its blossoms at the beginning of the season, before the others. Surely it will attract attention. Think over this comparison, and you will understand why an actor who possesses a transient Flower may be chosen winner in a competition.

It is a cardinal principle of our art that the Flower represents the very life of our art, and an actor makes a great error should he, not realizing that he has lost his Flower, continue to depend on his past reputation. Watching the art of an actor who performs various kinds of roles without an understanding of what the meaning of the Flower might be could well be compared to one who collects and looks at flowering plants and trees out of season. The color of each flower that blooms is different; yet to those who look at them, each partakes of beauty. Even though an actor has learned only a few parts, if he has really been able to manifest his Flower in them, he will never lose his reputation when he performs them. On the other hand, even though the actor may feel in a self-righteous fashion that he possesses many Flowers, if his art is not made manifest to his audience, then his performances will be like flowers blooming in the fields or plums in the thickets, where flowers and odors go unnoticed.

When speaking of excellence in general, there are various levels of ability involved. Even a player who is considered gifted and is well known, should he fail to work to the utmost to perfect his Flower, will not be able to preserve his art, although he may manage to maintain his reputation. Yet a skillful player who does continue to perfect himself will retain his Flower, even though his skills may decline. If this Flower can be retained, then there will always remain something moving in an actor's performances. As for an artist in whom the true Flower remains, no young actor, no matter who he may be, can win over him.

QUESTION: There are various possible strong points in *nō* performances, yet performers who are in general markedly inferior will sometimes be extremely skillful in one aspect of their art. In spite of this, superior performers do not copy them. Is this because they cannot? Or because they feel they should not?

ANSWER: In any aspect of life, when it comes to special skills, there are those who have been born with them. Even a player who has been ranked as quite skillful will not be able to accomplish certain things. Such is the judgment that might be rendered concerning an ordinarily gifted player. On the other hand, an actor who has truly mastered the art and skills of the *nō* can surely manifest any aspect of his art. Of course there is only one such artist in a thousand. This is because the others have not mastered such techniques and remain self-satisfied.

In any case, even the most skillful player may show some defects, while even the most clumsy will show some good points. There are few spectators who can make these distinctions. And the actors themselves do not take cognizance of them. The skillful player, resting on his reputation and deceived by his successes, does not take notice of them. An unskilled player, as he has never learned his art, does not recognize his bad points. If, occasionally, he does something in an effective manner, he will not realize what he has accomplished. Thus all actors, skilled and unskilled alike, must consult others about their performances. In order to truly master the art and skills of the *nō*, one must know both one's own abilities and shortcomings.

No matter how unskillful an actor may be, if there is an attractive quality in his performance, a superior player should study what he has done. This is the best means to further self-improvement. Yet if the actor takes the attitude that "this player is beneath me and I do not have to think of imitating him," then he will be trapped in his own attitudes, and he will never come to an appreciation of his own weaknesses. Such is the attitude of one who is not truly devoted to mastering his art.

Then again, when an unskilled player sees bad points in the performance of a superior actor, he must realize that even such performers fall short and so understand that, as he is just a beginner, he too must have many faults; thus he will reflect on his own art, ask others about his performances, try to increase his skills, practice all the more diligently, and so will surely improve the level of his own accomplishment. Yet if such is not the case, and the actor merely thinks pridefully to himself, "I would not perform in such an unskilled fashion," then he is an actor who will never learn to recognize his own strong points. If he does not understand his own areas of strength, then he will take his defects for his virtues. He may rehearse for years but will never increase his skill in the nō. Such is the basic nature of an unskilled player.

Even in the case of a superior actor, if he is filled with pride over his mastery of the nō, his art will dwindle. And how much more so that of the poor player who takes the same attitude. The following is crucial: the skillful actor must serve as a model for the unskilled actor, and the unskilled player must serve as a model for the skilled player. Such is the very basic principle on which to proceed. A talented performer might best proceed by taking the best elements in the performance of a less skillful player and using them to expand his own art. The sight of another's weak points can act for him as an excellent model. So how much more so the strong points. This is why I wrote "rehearse with every effort; do not be overbearing with others."

QUESTION: How can the various Levels of performance be distinguished?

ANSWER: For a spectator of discernment, it is a simple matter. Usually a rise in Level requires strenuous efforts at the *nō*, but, surprisingly, sometimes even a *nō* actor of ten will show such skill that his Level will rise of itself. Yet if an actor does not study and practice, his Level, even though he may manage to maintain it, remains a useless thing. Normally an actor achieves a high degree of refinement only after many years of work. The Level that reveals a player's inborn talents is referred to as Magnitude. What is called Appeal represents something different. Many people tend to confuse the two and think that they are the same. What is called Appeal represents a grave, imposing forcefulness. Then again, it can be said that Appeal indicates a wide mastery of all the various aspects of our art. The Level involving Magnitude is quite a different thing from Appeal. For example, some actors possess an inborn quality of Grace. Such a natural quality in their art represents their Magnitude. Then again, there are players who do not possess Grace in any fashion, yet still show Magnitude. This quality can thus be said to exist without Grace as well.

Here again is something that an actor new to the art should consider. It is impossible to study and practice one's art with an express idea of elevating one's Level. Not only is such a change impossible to obtain by such means, but if an artist continues to maintain such an attitude, whatever he has gained through his practice will be lost. In the end, such things as Level and Magnitude really cannot be sought after. Still, after arduous practice, and when all the dust of artistic ostentatiousness has been washed off an actor, he may suddenly find that Magnitude arrives of itself, as it were. The immediate object of rehearsal and practice is to perfect the chant, dance, movements, Role Playing, and other similar elements of the *nō* [not as a means to achieve a higher Level]. If one thinks over the matter carefully, is the level of Grace really a question of inborn capabilities? Then again, is the rank of Magnitude something that can be created through hard work and practice? There is much to ponder in these matters.

QUESTION: What is the relation between movement and text in a *nō* performance?
ANSWER: This matter can only be grasped through intricate rehearsal. All the various kinds of movement in the *nō* involved in the performance depend on the text. Such things as bodily posture and carriage follow from this, as well. Specifically, one must project feelings that are in accord with the words being spoken. For example, when the idea of observing some object is suggested in the text, the actor performs a gesture of looking; if such matters as pointing or pulling are mentioned, then the appropriate gesture is made; when a sound is to be heard, the actor assumes an attitude of listening. As the body is used in the service of all that is suggested by the text, these gestures will of their own accord constitute the appropriate acting style. The most important aspect of movement concerns the use of the actor's entire body. The second most important aspect concerns the use of his hands, and the third, the use of his feet. The movements of the body must be planned in accordance with the chant and context expressed in the *nō* text. It is hard to describe this effect in writing. It is best to observe and learn during actual rehearsals.

When one has practiced thoroughly with respect to the text of a play, then the actor's chant and gesture will partake alike of the same spirit. And indeed, the genuine union of music and movement represents a command by the actor over the most profound principles of the art of the *nō*. When one speaks of real mastery, it is to this principle that one refers. This is a fundamental point: as music and movement are two differing skills, the artist who can truly fuse them into one shows the greatest, highest talent of all. Such a fusion will constitute a really strong performance.

Incidentally, many do not really make the distinction between a strong and a weak performance [confusing this with matters of style]. It is curious that some judge a performance

without elegance as strong and a performance that shows
Grace as weak. There are actors who, regardless of the style
adopted, never seem to give a threadbare performance. Such
are the strong performers. Those actors who, in spite of their
strength, never fail to reveal something colorful and elegant
about themselves possess Grace. After all, if an actor has
mastered the means to realize his text and to fuse music and
movement, he will have learned how to give a strong performance and how to give that performance the quality of
Grace as well. He will truly be a masterful performer.

QUESTION: In the common language of artistic criticism, the
term Bending is often used. What does the term mean?
ANSWER: The term is almost impossible to explain in writing.
No explanation can capture its beauty. Nevertheless, such an
artistic element certainly does exist. Such beauty can grow
only after the actor's own Flower is well established. If one
examines the matter closely, it can be seen that Bending is
hard to grasp through rehearsal and difficult to manifest through
any particular means of performance. To manifest Bending,
one must first grasp the extremity of the Flower.

Therefore, an actor who has truly identified one aspect of
the Flower, even though he has not mastered every form of
Role Playing, may be able to grasp the beauty of Bending.
Indeed, this quality can be said to exist at a stage even higher
than that of the Flower. Without the Flower, Bending has no
meaning. Without the Flower, the effect of Bending is merely
gloomy and grey. The Bending of a flower in full bloom is
truly beautiful. Yet how can the Bending of trees without
blossom attract any interest? The crucial element to master is
the Flower; then, on top of that, one must master the beauty
of Bending. To give an example of this quality is not easy.

An old poem says:[10]

[10] The poem, by Fujiwara Kiyosuke (1104-1177) is included in the imperial
anthology the *Shinkokinshū* (compiled 1206) in the autumn poems (no. 340).

Usugiri no	In the thin mist,
Magaki no hana no	Morning flowers wet
Asajimeri	On the bamboo hedge:
Aki wa yūbe to	Who was it who said
Tare ka iiken.	Autumn evenings are best?

Then again, there is another poem:[11]

Iro miede	Find mutability
Utsurou mono wa	In that being which alters without
Yo no naka no	fading
Hito no kokoro no	In its outward hue—
Hana ni zo arikeru.	In the color, looks, and the deceptive flower
	Of the heart of what this world calls man!

Such feelings are doubtless those that must be expressed in Bending. One must look into the heart of these poems for the meaning of such things.

QUESTION: From what has been explained here, I understand that to grasp the nature of the Flower is the most important element of nō. Yet however crucial, the concept is difficult to grasp. In what way can I come to know the Flower?

ANSWER: The Flower represents the principle that lies at the deepest recesses of our art. To know the meaning of the Flower is the most important element in understanding the nō, and its greatest secret.

Some details concerning the Flower have already been explained in the first two chapters above. The Flower of youthful beauty, the Flower of the voice, and the Flower of Grace: all these concrete virtues are qualities easily comprehensible to the spectators. Yet such Flowers, since they grow from particular techniques, just like the beauty of a live flower even-

---

[11] The poem, by Ono no Komachi (fl. 860) is included in the imperial anthology the *Kokinshū* (compiled c. 905), in the love poems (no. 797). The translation is from Brower and Miner, *Japanese Court Poetry*, p. 205.

tually come to scatter their petals as well. Thus it is that, as time goes by, the actor cannot maintain his reputation. Yet the fine actor who possesses the true Flower has at his disposal the principle of blooming and of fading. His blooming will not be short-lived. How can one come to grasp this principle? Perhaps it can be understood from what is written in the annexed Secret Teaching. These principles are surely not simple to grasp through logic alone.

First, having practiced since the age of seven, the actor will have learned through years of rehearsing the various components involved in Role Playing. He will have understood how to distinguish these various elements, will have practiced assiduously, and will have mastered the various necessary techniques. Only after this stage will he be able to grasp the principle of the Flower that does not fade. Only the character of an actor formed by such a thorough training can know the seed of the Flower. For before he can know the Flower, he must know the seed. The Flower blooms from the imagination; the seed represents merely the various skills of our art.

In the words of an ancient sage:[12]

The mind-ground contains the various seeds,
With the all-pervading rain each and every one sprouts.
Once one has suddenly awakened to the sentiency of the flower,
The fruit of enlightenment matures of itself.

In order to support our house, and because I have such a deep respect for our art, I have pondered deeply over things that my late father told me, and I am recording here those major points. I am not concerned with the criticisms of the world; I am worried rather that our art may decline, and I certainly do not intend that any outsiders should read this for their own enlightenment. I am leaving this document for the purpose of providing instruction for our family members.

[12] A quotation from Hui-neng (638-713), the sixth patriarch of Ch'an (Japanese *zen*) Buddhism. The lines are from a Buddhist hymn attributed to him. The translation is by Philip Yampolsky and can be found on page 178 of Yampolsky, tr., *The Platform Sutra of the Sixth Patriarch*.

Here ends this portion of the Teachings on Style and the Flower.

Ōe 7, [1400] 4th month, 13th day.
(signed by Zeami)

signed: Saemondayū of the
Junior Lower Fifth Rank[13]

Hata no Motokiyo[14]

CHAPTER 4. MATTERS PERTAINING TO THE GODS

The beginnings of *sarugaku* in the age of the gods, it is said, occurred when Amaterasu, the Sun Goddess, concealed herself in the heavenly rocky cave, and the whole earth fell under endless darkness.[15] All the myriad deities gathered at the heavenly Kagu mountain, in order to find a way to calm her. They played sacred music to accompany their comic dances. In the midst of this Ama no Uzume[16] came forward, and, holding a spring of *sakaki* wood and a *shide*,[17] she raised her voice and, in front of a fire that had been lighted, she pounded out the rhythm of her dance with her feet and became possessed by divine inspiration as she sang and danced. The Sun Goddess, hearing the voice of Ama no Uzume, opened the rock door slightly. The land became light, and the faces of the gods could be seen again. It is said that such entertainments marked the

[13] An artificial rank assigned to Zeami to permit his free entry into the palace.

[14] Zeami uses here the official family name Hata, showing his presumed lineage from Hata no Kōkatsu.

[15] For the source of this famous legend, see the *Kojiki*, Philippi translation, pp. 81-86.

[16] An important heavenly goddess in Shintō legend. See Philippi, *Kojiki*, p. 460.

[17] *Sakaki* (*cleyera ochnacea*) is a type of evergreen tree important in Shintō rites. A *shide* is a specially folded strap of cloth hung as a sacred offering. In later centuries, the use of paper became more common.

beginning of *sarugaku*. There are doubtless other particulars remaining about this in other secret writings.

In the country of the Buddha, a wealthy man named Sudatta had built a Buddhist place of retreat, the Jetavana Monastery.[18] At the dedication ceremonies, the Buddha preached a sermon. Devadatta[19] and a throng of unbelievers cried out and danced wildly, holding branches and bamboo grass in which they had placed *shide*, making it more difficult for the Buddha to carry out the ceremony. The Buddha then signaled his disciple Śāriputra with his eye; and Śāriputra, through the power of the master, had the idea of arranging for flute and drum music to be played at the rear entrance to the hall. Then three of the disciples—the learned Ānanda, the wise Śāriputra, and the eloquent Pūrna[20]—performed sixty-six entertainments. The heretics, listening to the sound of flute and drum, assembled at the rear entrance and fell silent observing the spectacle. During this time, the Buddha was able to continue on with the dedication service. Such were the beginnings of our art in India.

In our own country, during the reign of the Emperor Kimmei [A.D. 509-571], on an occasion when the Hatsuse River in Yamato overflowed its banks, a jar floated down in the current. A high court official picked up the jar near the cedar gate of the Miwa Shrine.[21] Inside was a young child. His face was gentle, and he was like a jewel. Because the infant seemed to have descended from heaven, the incident was reported to the emperor at the imperial palace. That very night, the child appeared to the emperor in a dream and said, "I am the reborn

---

[18] Sudatta was a rich man who devoted himself to the Buddha. He constructed the Jetavana monastery for him, where the Buddha remained for more than twenty years.

[19] Devadatta was a cousin of the Buddha who, although at first a follower, later turned against the Buddha and attempted to have him killed.

[20] Three of the "ten great disciples" of Buddha. Śāriputra was the guiding spirit of the early Buddhist monastic order, Ānanda was known for his wisdom, and Pūrna for his eloquence.

[21] One of the most sacred Shintō shrines in Japan. The site is approximately eleven miles from the city of Nara.

spirit of the emperor Shih-huang of the Ch'in Dynasty in China.[22] My destiny has a connection with Japan, and I now appear before you." The emperor, thinking this occurrence a miracle, had the child brought to serve in court. When he grew to manhood, he came to be of surpassing talent and wisdom, and at the age of fifteen, he rose to the rank of Minister. He was given the family name of Chin. Because that Chinese character is pronounced *Hata* in Japanese, he was called Hata no Kōkatsu.

Prince Shōtoku, at a time when there were disturbances in the land, asked this Hata no Kōkatsu to perform sixty-six dramatic pieces, following the precedents set down at the time of the gods and Buddhas, and the prince himself made sixty-six masks for Hata no Kōkatsu's use. Kōkatsu performed these entertainments at the Shishinden Hall at the imperial palace at Tachibana.[23] The country soon became peaceful. Prince Shōtoku then passed this entertainment on for the benefit of later generations. The word *kagura* ["god-given entertainment"] employs the character 神 樂 [which stands for the word "god" and consists of the radical 示, meaning "sacred" and the root 申, which means "to speak"]. He removed the radical 示 but left the remainder 申. As that character is pronounced *saru* and stands for one of the twelve horary signs,[24] he thus gave the name *sarugaku* to this entertainment. Then too, because of the original meaning of the root 申, "to speak," *sarugaku* also means "to speak of pleasure." This meaning comes about because part of the original character was removed [as described above].

Kōkatsu served a number of emperors, including Kimmei, Bidatsu, Yōmei, and Sushun, as well as Empress Suiko and

[22] Emperor Shih-huang (259-210 B.C.) united China under the Ch'in Dynasty. He built the Great Wall and issued the famous edict for the burning of the books.

[23] The site of the present Tachibana Temple, near Nara. The *shishinden* was the main building in the complex.

[24] Traditionally, the day was divided into twelve parts, each of two hours' duration. *Saru* (monkey) corresponds to the period from 4:00 to 6:00 P.M.

Prince Shōtoku. He passed his art on to his descendants, and then, as he himself was an apparition and thus could leave no trace of his whereabouts, he set out from Naniwa in the province of Settsu in a boat hollowed out of wood, letting the wind blow him where it would. He landed in the province of Harima, in the bay of Shakushi.[25] The people there, when they pulled the boat on shore, found a being that did not have human shape. This being haunted and cursed many and caused strange things to happen. The people began to worship this being as a god, and their province grew wealthy. They called this god Taikō Dai Myōjin, the Great Raging God. Even now his virtue is still efficacious. His True Body is that of Bishamon Tennō.[26] When Prince Shōtoku put down the rebellion of Moriya of the Mononobe,[27] he used the divine aid of this Kōkatsu in order to defeat his enemy, it is said.

When Kyoto became the capital of our country, during his reign the Emperor Murakami [A.D. 926-967] read what Prince Shōtoku had recorded about the *sarugaku*: first, that the art had originated at the time of the gods and in the land of the Buddha, then that it had come to Japan [from India] through Bactria[28] and China; second, that these "wild words and specious phrases"[29] that constitute this art will serve to praise

[25] A site to the east of Akō in Okayama Prefecture on the Inland Sea.

[26] The True Body represents the Buddhist identity of a Shintō god. Bishamon (in Sanskrit, Vaísravaṇa), is one of the Four Quarter Kings who protect the various continents. Vaísravaṇa protects the northern part of the world.

[27] Moriya (died 587) was a courtier who attempted to destroy the growing power of Buddhism in Japan. His forces were eventually defeated, and he was killed.

[28] An ancient country of southwestern Asia, now a district of northern Afghanistan.

[29] Thomas J. Harper's translation of the phrase *kyōgen kigo*, an expression derived from the phrase by the Chinese T'ang poet Po Chü-i (A.D. 772-846) in which he expresses the hope that his "wild words and specious phrases" may be transformed into a hymn of praise to the Buddha. The passage is cited in the *Wakanrōeishū* compiled in 1013 by Fujiwara Kintō (A.D. 966-1041), a poetry collection still widely appreciated at Zeami's time. For a

the Buddha and provide the means to spread his teachings, will chase away evil affinities, and will call forth happiness, so that the country will remain in tranquillity, bringing gentleness and long life to the people. Finding Prince Shōtoku's words efficacious, Emperor Murakami thought that *sarugaku* might serve as a means of supplication for the good of the nation. At this time there was a descendant of Kōkatsu who practiced his art who was named Hata no Ujiyasu. At the emperor's request, he performed sixty-six pieces of *sarugaku* in the Shishinden Hall of the imperial palace.

At that time there was a man of great talent named Ki no Gon no Kami. He was the husband of a younger sister of Hata no Ujiyasu. With him as a partner, Ujiyasu performed *sarugaku*. Later, thinking that it was too difficult to perform all sixty-six items of *sarugaku* in one day, the two decided to select three pieces, *Inatsumi no Okina, Yonasumi no Okina*, and *Chichi no Jo*. What is presently referred to as *Shiki samban*[30] doubtless refers to these three plays. These three serve as symbolic representations of the Three Bodies of the Buddha.[31] There are separate secret teachings on this subject.

Komparu Mitsutarō is a descendant of Hata no Ujiyasu in the twenty-ninth generation. He is the head of the Emman-i troupe[32] in the province of Yamato. His family possesses items handed down from Ujiyasu, including a devil's mask carved

---

discussion of this important concept, see Harper's article, "A Twelfth Century Critique of The Tale of Genji," in *Criticism in Translation* 1 (Spring 1976), 1-5.

[30] The titles of these three plays might be tentatively rendered in English as "Old Man of the Harvest," "The Old Man Heir Apparent," and "The Venerable Old Father." *Shiki samban* might be translated as "Three Ceremonial Pieces." The play *Okina* (literally, "Old Man"), which is still performed on ceremonial occasions, doubtless derives from such earlier pieces, now lost.

[31] That is, the Body of Essence, the Body of Bliss, and the Transformation Body. See Wm. Theodore de Bary, ed., *The Buddhist Tradition in India, China, and Japan*, pp. 94-95.

[32] The group later became the Komparu troupe.

by Prince Shōtoku himself, a portrait of the god of Kasuga Shrine, and bones from the Buddha's own body.

In our present generation [as concerns performances related to religious observances], when the *yuimae* service[33] is performed at the Kōfukuji temple in Nara, the service proper is held in the lecture hall, while *ennen* dances are performed in the dining hall. The dances calm those who do not believe and pacify the devils. During this time, in front of the dining hall, a lecture is given on the *Vimalakīrti sutra*.[34] This practice is based on the ancient example of the Jetavana monastery.

In Yamoto province, religious rites of the Kōfukuji Temple and the Kasuga shrines are held on the second and fifth day of the second month. Four *sarugaku* troupes perform at these ceremonies that mark the beginning of the year's religious observances. The performances serve as prayers for the peace of the whole country.

The various companies are as follows:

1. The four troupes that perform at religious functions of the Kasuga Shrine in Yamato: Tobi, Yūzaki, Sakado, Emman-i.[35]

2. The three troupes that perform at religious functions of the Hie Shrine in Ōmi: Yamashina, Shimosaka, and Hie.[36]

3. The two troupes of *shushi* that perform at Ise.

4. The three troupes that perform services at the beginning

---

[33] A seven-day ceremonial reading of the *Vimalakīrti sutra* (Japanese, *Yuimakyō*) held during October at the Kōfukuji on a regular basis since the ninth century. For details of the service, see various entries in M. W. de Visser, *Ancient Buddhism in Japan*.

[34] This sutra eulogizes Buddha's lay disciple Vimalakīrti, who, while remaining a householder, achieved a greater degree of enlightenment than others who undertook monastic discipline. See Robert Thurman, *The Holy Teaching of Vimalakīrti* (University Park: Pennsylvania State University Press, 1976).

[35] Tobi is the old name for the present Hōshō troupe. Yūzaki is the former name of the Kanze troupe. Sakado is the old name for the present Kongō troupe. Enman-i is the former name for the Komparu troupe.

[36] The three important troupes of Ōmi *sarugaku*.

of the year at the Hosshōji temple in Kyoto:[37] the Shinza, the Honza, and the Shuku troupe.[38]

These three troupes also perform for the various ceremonies held at the Kamo Shrines in Kyoto and at the Sumiyoshi Shrine in Settsu.[39]

CHAPTER 5. THE MOST PROFOUND PRINCIPLES OF THE ART OF THE NŌ

I do not intend that the various things I have written in the Teachings on Style and the Flower should be shown to the world, but rather that they might serve as a legacy for my descendants. Still, I do have one quite definite purpose in writing this account. For these days, those who carry on the *nō* seem uninformed with respect to our art and put their efforts into everything except the true path; and when on rare occasions they do manage to achieve an acceptable level of artistic performance, they seem to lose themselves in the foolish praise of a night, or in some sort of temporary recognition. They have forgotten the wellsprings of our art and the traditions that flow from them. I deeply regret the fact that our art already seems in a state of decline. Still, if an actor loves the art of the *nō* and studies its precepts seriously, he will surely find, if he refuses to treat his art in a self-serving manner, that he will accrue the merit due him.

[37] The Hosshōji was an important temple built under the sponsorship of Emperor Shirakawa (1053-1129). Due to natural disasters, it fell into ruin later in the medieval period. The ceremonies mentioned here were held for several days at the beginning of each year as a plea to the Buddha to bring peace and abundant crops.

[38] The Shinza was also known as the Enami troupe. Zeami locates the troupe in Kawachi (an area in present-day Osaka Prefecture). The Honza was resident in Tamba (part of Kyoto Prefecture) and was sometimes referred to as the Yata troupe. The Shuku troupe was located in Settsu, the present-day Hyōgo Prefecture.

[39] The two Kamo shrines in Kyoto held festivals during the sixth month in order to bless the crops grown on their sacred lands. Sacred rice planting ceremonies were held at the Sumiyoshi Shrine, located in what is now a part of Osaka Prefecture.

Even though it might be said that our art consists of passing on the principles inherited from earlier generations, still there is much in a successful performance that comes from an actor's individual creativity on a particular occasion, so that written explanations themselves are not satisfactory. The real Flower derives from a mastery of the principles handed down from our predecessors, passed on by absorption from soul to soul. For this reason I have named this account "Teachings on Style and the Flower."

In our art, the styles of Ōmi and Yamato differ. In Ōmi *sarugaku*, the area of Grace is principally emphasized, and Role Playing is given a lesser place, since the creation of an elegant beauty of form is the main aim. In the Yamato style, on the other hand, Role Playing is considered the central element; still, while the various kinds of Role Playing are developed to the fullest, an attempt is made to add the beauty of Grace as well. A truly fine artist must master both possibilities and let nothing slip away. An actor who seeks to master only one of these two facets of the art can never become a truly great player.

On the whole, a majority seem to think that the basis of the Yamato style of acting rests on an emphasis on Role Playing and plot, stressing Magnitude, fierce movements, and such things. It is true that our training chiefly emphasizes these elements, but when my late father Kan'ami was at the height of his popularity, he was particularly renowned for his performances in such plays as *Shizuka ga mai* or *Saga no dainembutsu no onna monogurui*. He won fame everywhere for his performances of these roles and was widely appreciated. Thus it can be said that he achieved a peerless level of Grace in his performance.

It is a commonly held opinion as well that *dengaku* represents quite a different form of art from our own and that it cannot be judged on the same principles as *sarugaku*, yet I understand that recently Itchū of the Honza troupe, who is considered a peerless master of the form, has, among his various types of roles, chosen to perform the parts of demons and gods, and furthermore, that such fierce roles reveal his limitless skill. Indeed, my late father said, and quite correctly, that Itchū's work served as a means of instruction for the development of his own art.

It seems, in fact, that many an actor, based on his own selfish prejudices, may, because there is some aspect of his art in which he is not proficient, attempt to master only one part of the whole, and, without making any effort to understand those other aspects of the *nō*, will merely despise the skills shown by actors in other troupes. Such a dislike is, in fact, not founded on any real judgment. Rather it represents a prejudice on the part of those who do not possess such skill themselves. And because an actor has not mastered these abilities, even though he may gain a temporary reputation for a certain kind of skill, his Flower will not be of long duration, and he will lose his popularity. A truly great artist who enjoys the genuine approbation of his audience will be able to perform in all styles and make each of them enjoyable. Styles of acting and the basic forms of art may differ variously, but what is effective about each is common to all. This moving quality is the Flower. It is recognized as crucial to Yamato and Ōmi *sarugaku* and to *dengaku* as well. If an actor cannot manage to possess this quality, whatever his affiliation, then he cannot receive the public's support.

Then again, even if an actor has not mastered every style but has learned, let us say, seven or eight out of ten, and is determined to make his areas of greatest skill into the fundamentals of his art, and he truly learns to do so, he will certainly earn the respect of his audiences. Nevertheless, if an actor has not fully mastered every aspect of his craft, then he will not be able to please his audiences, city and country, nobility and commoner, on every occasion.

There are various circumstances that permit an actor to earn fame. A good player will find it difficult to please an audience that is not discriminating. A bad actor cannot please any audience that displays artistic judgment. Thus, while it is true that an untutored audience may not be able to grasp the elements that make a performer good, and thereby learn to appreciate him, nevertheless a truly gifted player, if he really makes use of all his artistic skill, should be able to move even an undiscriminating audience. An actor who has truly mastered such skills and the real secrets of his art can be said to have achieved his Flower. One who has reached this rank, no matter what his age, will never be found inferior to an actor who merely displays the temporary Flower of youth. An actor at this higher level of proficiency will be respected everywhere, even by those in the countryside and in the far-off provinces. Such a player will be able to perform ably in the style of Yamato and Ōmi *sarugaku*, and even in the style of *dengaku*, depending on the wishes of his audience. It is in order to make those principles clear that I have written this account.

On the other hand, if an actor is inattentive concerning the fundamental principles relating to his own basic style of acting, then how can his performance possess any genuine life of its own? Such an actor will be a weak and unreliable player. An actor who has a sure sense of his own fundamental style, however, will understand the other styles as well. An actor who thinks to know every style without mastering his own will not only fail to grasp the fundamentals of his own proper art but will certainly fail to understand any of the others. He will be a weak performer and will not maintain his Flower for long. Failing to maintain the Flower can thus be compared to having no deep knowledge of any style. That is why I wrote previously that only after an actor "will have practiced assiduously and mastered all the necessary techniques . . . will he be able to grasp the principle of a flower that does not fade."

Certain Additional Secret Observations

It can be said that the purpose of the art of the *nō* is to serve as a means to pacify people's hearts and to move the high and the low alike, which brings prosperity to all of us and promotes a long life. Any act, when pursued to its highest level of attainment, can have the effect of increasing longevity and happiness. In our art in particular, when the highest reaches have been obtained, one who leaves behind a great name is one who has gained recognition everywhere. Thus is longevity and happiness prolonged for our troupe.

There is still one crucial point to be considered. In the case of those spectators who have real knowledge and understanding of the nō, there will be an implicit understanding between them and an actor who has himself reached his own level of Magnitude. Yet in the case of a dull-witted audience, or the vulgar audiences in the countryside or in the far-off provinces, spectators will have difficulty in reaching a proper level of understanding in order to appreciate such a level of accomplishment. How should an actor behave in such a case? In our art, the greatest good fortune for the development of any troupe is to bring happiness and earn the respect of their audiences. Thus, if the level of the performance is too demanding, the actor will fail to obtain the praise of his spectators. Therefore, an actor should remember the easy style of performance he used when a beginner, and when the location or the occasion demands, and the level of the audience is low, the actor should strive to bring happiness to them by performing in a style which they truly can appreciate. When one thinks over the real purposes of our art, a player who truly can bring happiness to his audiences is one who can without censure bring his art to all, from the nobility to audiences in mountain temples, the countryside, the far-off provinces, and the various shrine festivals. However gifted a player, if he does not win the love and the respect of his audiences, he can hardly be said to be an actor who brings prosperity to his troupe. As my late father said, in no matter what out-of-the-way country place, an actor must perform so as to keep always in mind the feelings of his audience and the customs of the place.

Hearing all of this, a beginner may wonder that such a level of mastery can be achieved, and he may certainly feel discouraged. Yet if he takes to heart the various points discussed here and learns little by little the ideas behind them, he will come to grasp them and his own strength will grow with his understanding, so that eventually he will achieve real skill.

Actually, those particular points I have made are really of more importance to an actor who has already gained some skill in his art than they are to a beginner. And I much regret the fact that there are so many relatively gifted players who have too high an opinion of their accomplishments and are taken with their own reputations. They pay no heed to such principles, and they lack the ability to bring happiness to others but only depend on those reputations. Even when an actor has grasped the deepest principles of his art, this knowledge will be of no use if he does not make them a part of his true skills. If the actor does grasp the principles and is able to incorporate them into his art, it will be as though he bears not only a flower but the seeds of new blooms, as well. For example, even when an actor has received approbation from his audiences, he may unexpectedly enter a period when he is no longer in favor, because of some situation over which he has no control. Yet even so, he can perform in the countryside and in the far provinces, be appreciated there, and thereby retain his Flower, so that his art will not suddenly disappear. And if he can maintain his art, then there will come a time when he will meet with approbation again.

One speaks of the principle of increasing longevity and happiness, yet the fact that many actors become wholly involved in worldly attitudes and give in to vulgar desires remains the first cause for the decline in our art of the *nō*. If prosperity is made the end in itself, then the art of the *nō* will decay. And if the art declines, then the artist's prosperity itself will decline. If only one remains honest and open, such an attitude will serve as a means to create a delicate Flower that will show every virtue to the world at large.

What I have written in all the various sections in this treatise does not come from my own strength or my own talents as an artist. From the time I was a small child, I received guidance from my late father, and so for more than twenty years, I have followed his teachings on the basis of what I have heard and seen, and so I have written all this not for any personal benefit but for the sake of our art and our house.

Ōe 9 [1402], 3rd month, 2d day
(signed) Zeami

CHAPTER 6. TRAINING IN THE FLOWER

Writing texts for the *nō* represents the very life of our art. Even if a person is not possessed of extraordinary learning, still, if he has attained a certain level of technique, he can create a good *nō* play. The general style is described in the section on *jo, ha* and *kyū.*

First of all, in the opening play, the source for the text should be authentic [based on legends or the classics], and the play composed in such a way that from the opening speech on the audience can recognize the subject matter. It is not necessary to compose the text in any complex artistic fashion, but the general effect should be smooth and gentle, while giving a colorful impression from the beginning. On the other hand, when it comes to the plays that make up the rest of the program, they must be composed with the greatest care given to the words and to the general style to be employed. For example, if a play involves a location famous in history, or an ancient spot of interest, it is wise to collect and write into the key passage of the play some poetic phrase the words of which are well known to the audience. The writer should not include such crucial material in a play at a moment when the *shite* is not chanting or performing some important moment in his role. After all, as far as the audiences are concerned, they will only give their undivided attention to the most gifted players. Thus if the spectators find reflected in their eyes the speech and gestures of a company's great actor, those who see and hear will be touched and will react with emotion. This, then, is the first important rule in composinng *nō* drama.

In this regard, it is best to choose poetic quotations that are elegant and quickly recognized by the audience. If an actor makes use of such elegant expressions, his demeanor will of itself, surprisingly enough, seem to possess the artistic qualities of Grace. Words that give a stiff impression make a performance difficult. Still, although such stiff speeches may be hard for an audience to follow, there are times when they can be effective. The situation depends on the nature of the central character in the play. Proper usage will depend on distinctions in the story concerning the characters involved, be they Chinese or Japanese. In any case, any vulgar expressions will make a play lose its artistic merit.

To repeat: a successful play of the first rank is based on an authentic source, reveals something unusual in aesthetic qualities, has an appropriate climax, and shows Grace. A play of the second rank may not possess any unusual aesthetic qualities, but it will not be overly complex, will be simple to comprehend, and will possess some moments of real interest. Roughly, such is the means by which plays can be ranked. Still, whatever the level of the play itself, as long as it exhibits a particular atmosphere that the actor can use as the basis for his performance, there will be something noteworthy in the results. When performing a play again and again, or on occasions when performances continue on for several days, then even if the text is not a good one, the play will appear to be of interest as long as a way can be found to renew the conception and make it more colorful in performance. Therefore, the success of *nō* depends as well on the occasion when it is performed and on its place in the program. An actor should not abandon a text merely because he does not find it effective. Everything depends on the care taken by the *shite*.

One caution, however: there are certain kinds of plays that are altogether unsuitable. Even though one may say that any kind of Role Playing is possible, there are certain situations that are unplayable, such as incidents in which nuns, old women, or venerable priests are portrayed as deranged or excessively angry. Then again, a character who is to show rage cannot be portrayed in the style of Grace. Such plays represent truly improper *nō*, and these works can be said to misrepresent the art. This point has already been taken up in the section on Role Playing.

Another point: in all things, without a sense of balance and symmetry, no genuine achievement in the *nō* is possible. When a play with a good subject is performed by a skilled player and the results are effective, such a balance has been achieved. Most spectators assume that if a good play is given a fine performance, the results will be successful, yet surprisingly enough such a performance may not succeed. A discerning audience will be able to realize that the performer is not to be blamed, but the majority of spectators will regard the play as bad and the player without much talent. Yet why, when a performer is skillful, are the results unsuccessful? Reflecting on this matter, it seems there are several possibilities. For example, on such an occasion, perhaps there is a lack of harmony in the *yin* and *yang* that exists between the stage and its surroundings. Or again, perhaps the actor has not striven to achieve the proper Flower. Still, there remains something difficult to account for in this situation.

Again, there is another point that a playwright should strive to grasp. Some plays stress only one aspect of the art of the *nō*. For example, a play may be based on an altogether quiet subject [that emphasizes only the musical elements of a performance]. Or, on the other hand, a play may involve a great deal of gesture and dancing. Such plays involve only one aspect of the whole and so are comparatively easy to compose. But a truly fine play involves gesture based on chanting. The existence of just such a combination is the crucial element. It is this combination that creates a real sense of interest and emotional response on the part of the audience. In order to compose such a play, the writer must choose words and phrases that, when heard, can easily be understood and combine them with elegant and appropriate melodies, with a suitable flow between the two. Then too, he must also provide a climax that will play well. If these various elements can be properly blended together, then all those who see the play will truly be moved.

There is another point that must be understood in some detail. If the actor bases his chanting on his movements, he shows himself as a beginner. For an artist of experience, movement will grow from the chant. The audience hears the text and watches the movements. In any aspect of life it can be said that our intentions give rise to the various aspects of our behavior. It is through words that these intentions are expressed. In the case of the *nō* too, therefore, the chant provides the substance of which the movements of the actor serve as a function. This is because functions grow out of substance and not the other way around. Thus, at the time of an actual performance, the actor stresses the importance of the chant. In this fashion, a performer will be able through experience to blend chant with gesture, and the dance with the chant, so as to become the kind of accomplished player who has within himself every element of his art. The fact that he can do this is due ultimately to the playwright's art.

In the *nō*, there are the complementary terms strong and Graceful, as opposed to rough and weak. These may seem simple to understand, as such differences can of course be manifested in performance, but there are many players who, because they do not know how to make these distinctions, merely perform in a weak or rough way. First of all, if the proper conception of a particular role being performed is not fully realized, there will be areas of false expression that will result in roughness or weakness. To make these distinctions properly, even with skill and experience, is a difficult matter. A great deal of deep reflection on this matter is required.

If a part that should be weak is played in a strong way, there will be a false element introduced, and the results will be classed as rough. If a role that is meant to be strong is played in a strong fashion, the results will be properly strong and not rough at all. On the other hand, if what should be strong is performed with an attempt at Grace, the results will merely be weak, as elements proper to the role are not realized. Therefore, insofar as the actor can concentrate in order to depict his real object and unite himself totally with it, there will be no danger of a rough or a weak performance. On the other hand, if a strong performance is made too strong, this strength will degenerate into roughness. And, in a performance demanding Grace, if an attempt is made to play in too gentle a fashion, the results will merely appear as weak.

In considering carefully these various distinctions, a person risks going astray if he believes that strength and Grace have an existence separate from the object of a performance. Both are inherent in the substance of that object [and are realized on the stage in a particular character]. For example, stage characters such as Ladies-in-Waiting, or women of pleasure, beautiful women, or handsome men, all show alike in their form, like the various flowers in the natural world, the quality of Grace. On the other hand, roles such as those of warriors, brave men, or demons and gods show in their form the quality of strength, like pines and cedars in the natural world.

If an actor does his best to create truly such varied characters, then a role that involves Grace will produce an atmosphere of Grace, and a role demanding strength will of itself appear strong. If such distinctions are not observed, however, and an actor merely decides to attempt to create a sense of Grace directly, the performance will be crude and cannot realize its object. The actor who does not realize that he has failed to obtain that object but thinks he has created an atmosphere of Grace will give a weak performance. Rather, if the actor can imitate perfectly a woman of pleasure, a handsome man, and so forth, then the Grace will be created of itself. The actor must simply think to represent his character as skillfully as possible. Again, if the actor truly imitates those who are strong, then the strength of his performance will be born of itself.

In this connection, however, there is one important point to keep in mind. Unfortunately, as our art is based on the desires of our audience, successful performances depend on the changing taste of each generation. Therefore, when performing in a strong fashion before an audience that admires Grace, which has become so popular these days, the actor must depart to some extent from a strict representation of that forceful quality and shift his performance in the direction of Grace. The playwright as well must keep this situation in mind. In other words, the writer must think carefully and choose materials that will create the sensation of Grace and so make the spirit and the text of his play as beautiful as he can. If this is done as faithfully as possible, then the actor performing the play will seem to have created the feeling of Grace quite naturally. Thus if the fundamental principles of what constitutes Grace are firmly grasped, then the principles of a strong performance will be clear as well. If an actor carries out his representation of a properly conceived text, his audience will feel at ease and not on edge. Such a quality assures a strong performance.

Then too, the slight differences in the sounds of words in the text are most important: for example, words such as *nabiki* (waving or fluttering), *fusu* (to lie down), *kaeru* (to draw back), *yoru* (to come close), and so forth have a soft sound and seem of themselves to create a sense of gracefulness. On the other hand, words like *otsuru* (to fall down), *kuzururu*, (to crumble), *yabururu* (to break), *marobu* (to knock down) have a strong sound and require forceful gestures. Thus it can be understood that the qualities referred to as strength and Grace are not totally distinct and separate but rise from a fidelity to the object of the role being portrayed, while weakness and roughness indicate a divergence from that ideal.

Keeping these principles in mind, the writer, when composing his opening lines, the *issei*, or the *waka* section should, because of the nature of the role being created, attempt to create an atmosphere of Grace and suggestiveness; he will make an error if he attempts to introduce any harsh words, odd expressions, Sanskrit words,[40] or words to be pronounced in the Chinese fashion.[41] If such words are accompanied with

---

[40] That is, vocabulary taken from the sutras or mystical Buddhist incantations (dhāraṇi).

[41] That is, the pronunciation of Chinese characters in a fashion using a Japanese version of Chinese pronunciation used during the Han Dynasty (202

gestures on the stage, the portrayal of the character will not be accurate. Nevertheless, a highly trained performer can comprehend these contradictions and through unusual means manage his performance smoothly. Such are the arts of a great actor. But the playwright's mistakes in such a case should not be overlooked. Then too, even if the playwright composes with the proper principles in mind, should the actor perform without making use of them himself, any success is out of the question. Such are the essentials concerning this matter.

Within the repertory of the *nō*, there are certain plays that should be enacted in a broad style without any over-meticulous attention to plot or dialogue. Such a play should be chanted and danced in a simple fashion, and performed in a gentle and easy manner. To present such a play in an intricate manner would show poor artistry. It is clear that to continue such performances would lower an actor's skill. On the other hand, fine dialogue and emotional subtlety are needed in the case of a play that requires a plot and a powerful climax. In the case of a simple *nō*, however, even if an elegant and refined character is provided with somewhat stiff words to chant, the play will be successful if the sentiments expressed in the chant are steadily maintained. Indeed, it should be understood that such plays represent the essence of our art. As I have said again and again, these various points must be fully mastered and given fluent and easy expression; otherwise, the results will not be in accord with the precepts of our house.

Determining the worth of a play requires an understanding of the close reciprocal relationship between the text and the level of skill of the performer. There are a number of plays of high standing that do not depend on any literary or artistic

---

B.C.-A.D. 220). This system of pronunciation, being less familiar than the pronunciation systems normally employed, tended to sound stiff and foreign. For a discussion of the various kinds of sounds employed in spoken Japanese when Chinese characters were pronounced, see Roy Andrew Miller, *The Japanese Language* (Chicago: University of Chicago Press, 1967), pp. 102-112, and George Sansom, *An Historical Grammar of Japanese* (London: Oxford University Press, 1928), pp. 30-31.

atmosphere but are uncomplicated yet based on authentic sources. In the case of plays of this sort, the pleasure of watching them does not come from observing the details of the performance. For that reason, even a very skilled player may not perform them properly. Even the most suitable performer of the highest abilities may not achieve any success until he performs before a discerning audience in a large playing space. Success can only be assured when various elements are properly matched—the level of the play, the skill of the performer, the discernment of the audience, the performing area, and the occasion itself.

On the other hand, there are some rather slight plays that, although they do not depend on any important source, do nevertheless possess the quality of Grace and reveal a suitably delicate quality. Such plays are most appropriate for players in the early stages of their careers. Such plays are naturally suited for performances at country shrines or evening performances. Yet both actors and spectators can make errors of judgment: although they are accustomed to finding such plays successful of themselves in the countryside or in a small playing space, they may find them without appeal when performed in a large, imposing playing area, before the nobility, or at a specially sponsored exhibition performance. As a result, a player will hurt his reputation and the sponsors will be embarrassed as well.

Unless an actor is one who is able to perform without falling prey to such conditions—the type of play being presented, or the place of performance—he cannot be said to have truly mastered the Flower. If an actor can perform well in any location, then there can be no room for argument.

It seems there are certain actors who, although they are quite skillful, do not grasp the real nature of *nō*. Then again there are those who understand the essence of the *nō* better than their level of skill might seem to indicate. An actor who does not truly understand the *nō*, therefore, may bungle his performance and show himself unnecessarily meticulous when performing before the nobility or in a large and important playing space. On the other hand, an artist with limited artistic training who has not achieved such a variety of techniques— a beginner at his art, let us say—can perform in a large, important space without losing his Flower, gradually win the praise of his audiences, and so appear unblemished. This happy situation arises because he understands the art of the *nō* to a greater degree than he can exhibit with his skill.

As for such players, there will be various opinions concerning which type is the more likely to succeed. Certainly, an actor who can succeed in performances on significant occasions or in important playing spaces will continue to develop a growing reputation. Therefore it would seem that, rather than a skillful player who does not grasp the essence of the *nō*, a player who may lag in skill but who understands the *nō* would better succeed at establishing a troupe and running it. A *shite* who understands the essence of the *nō* will know the limitations of his own abilities. On the occasion of an important performance, he will allow for what does not suit him and so will only appear in plays that show him in his proper light. As such performances will be successful, he will certainly earn the praise of his audience. As for those areas in which an artist may feel deficient, it is best for him to develop his skills in small playing areas or in performances in the countryside. Through such practice, he will doubtless become gradually and naturally more proficient in these aspects of his art as time goes by. During this time, then, his art will become more secure, his imperfections will fall away, and the time will come when his reputation will be great and his company will prosper. He will surely keep his Flower until the end of his career. This comes about because the artist has understood the real meaning of *nō* since his earliest beginnings as an actor. If a performer has a real desire to understand the deep meaning of *nō* and expends every means to do so, he will surely come to understand what is the seed that produces the Flower.

As to which is more important, an understanding of theory or a concentration on practice, views will differ widely among various persons. This is perhaps a matter that each should decide for himself.

Chapter 7. A Separate Secret Teaching

In this secret teaching, I wish to explain how to understand of what the Flower consists. First of all, one must understand the conception that, just as a flower can be observed blooming in nature, the flower can be used as well as a metaphor for all things in the *nō*.

When speaking of flowers, in all their myriad varieties, it can be said that they will bloom at their appointed time during the four seasons; and because they always seem fresh and novel when they bloom at that appointed season, they are highly appreciated. In performing *sarugaku* as well, when this art appears novel to the spectators, they will be moved to find it attractive. Flower, charm and novelty: all three of these partake of the same essence. There is no flower that remains and whose petals do not scatter. And just because the petals scatter, then, when the flower blooms again, it will seem fresh and novel. An understanding of the principle of the Flower explains why in the *nō* there does not exist that stagnation that results from the monotony of any single means of expression. As the *nō* does not always remain the same, various new aesthetic qualities can be emphasized, bringing a sense of novelty.

However, one note of caution is necessary. When one speaks of "novelty," the term does not necessarily refer to some means of artistic expression that never existed before. After thoroughly mastering all the various principles that have been set down in these *Teachings on Style and the Flower*, an actor, thinking to perform a play, can show as the occasion demands the various arts that he has mastered. To cite again the example of flowers, among all growing things, there are no special flowers that bloom out of their appointed seasons. In the same way, if an actor masters the various elements of *nō* that he has learned to remember, he can show his art, basing it on the taste of the moment and the kind of plays that his audiences appreciate. His performance can thus be compared to looking at a flower that blooms at the proper time. The concept of a flower suggests a seed grown from a flower of years before. The *nō*, too, includes artistic elements seen before; but if all aspects of our art are practiced to the utmost, a considerable span of time will be required before they are exhausted. Seen after a lapse of time, elements of our art look fresh again. Then, too, the taste of audiences differs, and as interest in chanting, movement, and Role Playing varies, no artistic elements can be neglected. Thus an actor who has mastered every aspect of his art can be said to hold within him the seeds of flowers that bloom in all seasons, from the plum blossoms of early spring to the chrysanthemums of the fall. As he possesses all the Flowers, he can perform in response to any expectations on any occasion. Yet if an actor has not mastered various aspects of his art, there will be occasions when he will invariably lose his Flower. For example, suppose that the flowers of the spring are finished and the occasion has come when it seems appropriate to admire the summer grasses. If an actor can only show his audience the spring flowers, how can it be said that he matches himself to the flower of the season? From this example, my point should be clear.

A real flower is the one that seems novel to the imagination of the spectator. This is what I meant when I wrote earlier that only after an actor "will have practiced assiduously and mastered the various necessary techniques will he be able to grasp the principle of the Flower that does not fade." Indeed, the Flower is not something special unto itself. The Flower represents a mastery of technique and thorough practice, achieved in order to create a feeling of novelty. When I wrote "the flower blooms from the imagination; the seed represents merely the various skills of our art," I had the same principle in mind.

In the section on demon roles in the chapter on Role Playing, I also wrote that an actor who strives only to play demon roles will never come to understand what is really of interest about them. An actor who has mastered every technique and occasionally plays a demon role, will create the Flower, because his portrayal of the role will be unusual and so will be of interest to his audiences. On the other hand, an actor who thinks to play only demon roles and possesses no other art may appear to perform his part well, but there will be no sensation of novelty, and those who observe him will experience no Flower. I wrote that a good performance of a demon role was "like a flower blooming in the rocks," because the only appropriate style of acting for such roles calls for strength, fierceness, and a frightening manner. This particular art represents the rocks. And the Flower? It comes when an actor gifted with Grace and who can play in a variety of styles performs a demon role, contrary to the public's expectations, and so creates a real sense of novelty. This is the Flower. On the other hand, an actor who only thinks to play demon roles possesses merely the rock, but not the Flower.

A certain secret teaching on details of performance reveals the following: chanting, dance, gesture, expressive movement—all of these require the same spirit of novelty. On an occasion when the audience believes that a performance will consist of the same movement and chanting as usual, they imagine that they know what to expect. An actor can carry out his performance in a different fashion, however, so that, for example, even if the play being performed maintains fundamentally the same appearance, he will attempt to play his role in such a way that he infuses it with a more delicate level of feeling than before; or, in the case of his chanting, even though he changes nothing, he will use anew all his old arts, color the music and his voice in a skillful manner, using a level of concentration he has never felt before, and show exceptional care. If such a successful performance is achieved, those who see it and hear it will find it more novel than usual and they will praise it. This effect is surely what constitutes the feeling of novelty felt by the audience.

So it is that even when the usual play is chanted and the

same gestures are involved, a fine actor will bring something novel to the performance. An unskilled performer, even if he does remember all the proper musical notations, will not approach them with any original conceptions. A gifted performer is one who will truly grasp the essence of the "inner music." This "inner music" is the Flower that lies behind the chant itself. Even for players of equally great ability, with the same Flower, the player who has studied his art to its furthest reaches will come to know the Flower that lies within the Flower. In general, the melody is fixed in the chant, but the "inner music" can only be captured by a gifted performer. In the dance as well, the various patterns can be learned, but the emotions engendered from them come from the performer.

In the art of Role Playing, there is a level at which imitation is no longer sought. When every technique of Role Playing is mastered and the actor has truly become the subject of his impersonation, then the reason for the desire to imitate can no longer exist. Then, if the actor seeks to enjoy his own performance to its fullest extent, how can the Flower not be present? For example, in imitating an old man, the psyche of a truly gifted player will become altogether like that of a real old man, who, perhaps, dresses himself up for some procession or temple entertainment, thinking to dance and make music himself. Now since the actor has already himself assumed the personality of an old man, he actually "becomes" the old man and can have no wish to imitate one. Rather, he will think only of the part he, the old man, will play in the entertainment.

According to the teaching about creating the Flower when playing the role of an old person, it is important, first of all, to make no attempt merely to imitate the external attributes of old persons. When speaking in general of dance and movement, it can be assumed that these will be performed in time to the rhythm of the music, and that the stamping of the feet, the motions of the hands, and the actor's gestures and movements will be attuned to that mutual rhythm. In the case of an old person, however, when the beat sounds from the *taiko*, the chant, or the *tsutsumi*, his feet will be just a bit slow in responding, and his gestures and movements as well will follow an instant after. Such movements surely represent the best way to show the character of an old person. Keeping this concern in mind, the role must otherwise be performed with the kind of expansiveness that an old man would wish to show. It can be said that, above all else, an old person wants to appear young. Yet he can do nothing about the fact that his limbs are heavy and he is hard of hearing, so that, although he may still be quick of spirit, his physical movements cannot keep pace. Knowing this principle represents true Role Playing. One should basically play the role in a youthful manner such as that which an old person would wish to assume. In this way the actor can show through his performance the envy the old feel for the young. An elderly person, no matter how youthfully he wishes to dance, will not, in principle, be able to keep up with the beat of the music. Here, for the spectator, the sense of novelty comes from the fact that an old person dances like a young one. This is a flower blooming on an ancient tree.

An actor must absorb all styles of acting. An actor who can manage all styles of expression will require a certain time before he can perform them all, and he will thus be able to create a continuous impression of novelty. One who has truly grasped the various styles can summon up his art to color them and expand upon them a hundredfold. An actor should plan to repeat himself only once in a three- to five-year period, so as to create a sense of novelty for his audiences. This technique will give an actor a great sense of ease. In addition, during the course of the year, the actor must keep in mind the plays appropriate to each season. Also, in a sequential performance of *sarugaku* that extends over several days, the various styles of acting must be alternated and colored not only on each day but throughout the whole program. Thus if one concentrates naturally on all apsects of our art, from the most fundamental principles to the smallest details, there will be no danger of losing the Flower throughout one's career.

Then too it has been said that, more important than learning the myriad styles of expression, an actor must not forget the Flower that he has established at various phases of his career. These various Flowers, past and future, make up the various elements of one's acting style. By "past and future" I mean that the various styles that an actor has naturally mastered at various times, such as his presence as a child actor, his art as a young adult, and his elaborate skill as a mature actor, as well as his technique as an older performer, should all form a part of his art. Sometimes it should appear as though his performance were that of a child, sometimes of a youth; then again, on occasion like that of an actor at the height of his power, or again, like an actor who has in his maturity thoroughly mastered his art. In other words, the actor must perform so that it appears as though he were not the same person in each role. That is, he must hold to the idea that, within his accomplishment at any given time, there must lie an art ranging from that of a child to that of an old man. So it is that one can speak of a Flower drawn from past and future.

However, no one has ever seen or heard of such a supremely gifted artist from the beginnings of our art down to the present day. Perhaps only my father Kan'ami, during the vigor of his youth, played in the kind of polished style capable of giving his spectators that kind of satisfaction, or so I have heard. I myself witnessed his performances when he was about forty, and I have no doubt about it. In performing the play *Jinen Koji*, when he played one particular scene on a dais, people who saw him at the time were convinced that he had the appearance of a youth of sixteen or seventeen: such was his reputation. As many said that this was true, and as I myself witnessed his performances, I can say that he really did achieve this level of excellence. Yet how rare is the actor who, in this way, can learn as a youth the styles of acting he would later use, and who, as a mature artist, never manages to forget the styles he mastered as a youth. I have never seen or heard of another.

Again, an actor must never forget the aspects of his art that he has learned from his beginnings as an actor, so that, in response to varying circumstances, he may make use of them. If a young artist studies the style appropriate for an older actor, and if a mature actor retains the art of his vigorous period, will each not be able to create a sensation of novelty in his spectators? So it is that, as a performer grows more skillful, he will surely lose the seed that produces the Flower if he should abandon the styles of acting that he has already mastered. If those various Flowers have not themselves produced seed, they will represent nothing more than a broken branch of flowers. But if there is a seed, then a flower will form in consonance with every season as it arises. To repeat again, an actor must never forget what he has learned as a young performer. Quite ordinarily he hears it said of a young actor that "he has quickly risen to high accomplishment," or, "he already seems mature," while it is said of an older actor that "he seems youthful." Such remarks illustrate the importance of novelty. If an actor embellishes the basic styles, he can color them a hundredfold. Then, if an actor can incorporate into his accomplishments at any given moment all the past and future aspects of his art, then what a flowering that would represent.

When performing *nō*, there are endless matters that must be kept in mind. For example, when an actor plans to express the emotion of anger, he must not fail to retain a tender heart. Such is his only means to prevent his acting from developing roughness, no matter what sort of anger is expressed. To appear angry while possessing a tender heart gives rise to the principle of novelty. On the other hand, in a performance requiring Grace, an actor must not forget to remain strong. Thus all aspects of his performance—dance, movement, Role Playing—will be genuine and lifelike.

Then too, there are various concerns in connection with using the actor's body on the stage. When he moves himself about in a powerful way, he must stamp his foot in a gentle way. And when he stamps his feet strongly, he must hold the upper part of his body quiet. This matter is difficult to describe in words. It is better to learn this directly from a teacher. (This technique is explained in more detail in a section of the *Ka-shū*.)[42]

Over and above this, it is important to know that a Flower blooms by maintaining secrecy. It is said that "when there are secrets, the Flower exists; but without secrets, the Flower does not exist." Understanding this distinction is the most crucial aspect of the Flower. Indeed, concerning all things, and in any aspect of artistic endeavor, each family maintains its secrets, since those secrets are what make its art effective. However, when these so-called secret things are revealed openly, they often appear to be nothing special. Those who say that there is nothing to such secrets, however, have not yet grasped the principle of the efficacy of such teachings. For example, even in terms of what I have written here, should everyone come to know that the principle of novelty represents the nature of the Flower, then the spectators coming to watch a performance would expect just this quality. Before such an audience, even if the performance did contain something novel, those who watched would not be disposed to accept it as such. The Flower of the actor is possible precisely because the audience does not know where that Flower may be located. The spectators merely know that they are seeing something unexpected and quite skillfully performed, but they cannot recognize the Flower as such. Thus the technique can represent the Flower of the actor. The Flower provides the means to give rise to a sensation of the unexpected in the hearts of the audience.

To give an example from the military arts, a skillful commander will, through his plans and stratagems, find an unexpected means to conquer a powerful enemy. Indeed, in such a case, has not the loser been vanquished because he has been taken in by the use of this principle of novelty? In all things, in all arts, there is the element of achieving victory in a contest. As for the strategy itself, once the affair is over, and once the loser realizes the scheme that has been used against him, he

---

[42] This sentence was originally a note, calling attention to a discussion in the *Kashū* (Learning the Flower) (compiled in 1418), the text of which was later incorporated into *The Mirror of the Flower*, dated 1424.

will be more careful afterwards. After all, he lost because he did not know the means used against him at the time. Thus, I want to pass this matter along as one important secret teaching to our family. Knowing this, the following will be clear as well. It is not enough to keep from revealing a secret; an actor must not let others know that he is one who even knows a secret. For if others know his heart, then his opponents will not remain careless but will be circumspect and so will be on guard against their enemy. On the other hand, if their caution is not aroused, then he will easily win over them. And is it not by making use of this principle of novelty that he can put the others off their guard and so defeat them? Thus, in our house, by refusing to tell others of our secret teachings, we will be the lifelong possessors of the Flower. When there are secrets, the Flower exists; without secrets, the Flower does not exist.

You must also know the Law of Cause and Effect with respect to the Flower. This principle holds great significance for our art. Indeed, in all things, the Law of Cause and Effect is in operation. In the case of *nō*, the skills an actor has gained since his early days constitute the Cause. To master the *nō* and achieve distinction represent the Effect. Thus if an actor is negligent in practice, which is the Cause, the proper Effect will be difficult to bring about. This is a principle an actor must truly take to heart.

Then too, an actor must pay due heed to the movements of fortune. He must understand the idea that, if blossoms have been profuse in times past, there may be none this season. Time can be divided up into moments of good luck and bad luck. Thus with regard to the *nō* as well, when there is a period of good luck, then there must inevitably follow a period of bad. Such is the inevitable process of Cause and Effect.

If an actor really understands this principle, then when it comes to a performance that he feels is not such an important one, he need not commit himself so completely to winning the contest; therefore, he should not overextend his efforts. He will not be too concerned about losing and, holding back some of his skill, he will perform with a certain restraint. His audience, thinking that this is all he has to offer, may lose interest. Yet for a really important performance, he will summon up all his skills, and, choosing a play that shows off his special strengths, he will put forth all his energies and so move and surprise those who watch him. Thus, in a really important contest, he will doubtless gain a victory. Such is the vital efficacy of novelty. And so, after a bad period, the Law of Cause and Effect brings about good in the end.

For example, on the occasion of a three-day series of performances, an actor may be expected to perform perhaps three times. On the first day, he should not overextend his energies and should hold himself back; but, when he believes that he knows which is the crucial day for him, he should expend every effort to perform a good play that shows off his special talents. Even in the course of a single day's performance, when participating in a contest, the moment may come when the actor faces a period of bad luck. At this moment, he should perform with restraint, so that at the moment when the luck of the opposing troupe turns from good to bad, he can himself press forward with a fine play. On such an occasion, if his performance goes well, he will surely win the day.

In the matter of good luck and bad luck, in every contest there inevitably comes a time when the performance becomes more colorful and more relaxed, and so the situation improves. An actor should look on this moment as one of good luck. In the case of a contest that continues on for a considerable time, then luck will of its own accord change hands again and again from one side to the other. It is written that "both the god of victory and the god of defeat are always present to decide the outcome of any contest. Such is a crucial secret in the military arts."[43] Therefore, in a contest of *nō*, if the opponent is doing well, the actor must realize that the god of victory dwells on the enemy's side and be awed accordingly. However, these gods decide the Cause and Effect for only a

---

[43] The source of this quotation has not been identified.

short time, so that fortune switches again and again from one side to the other; thus, if an actor is convinced that his turn will come, he will be able to perform with confidence. Such is the Law of Cause and Effect in performance. An actor must never be remiss in pondering over this truth. Remember the expression "to him who believes accrues virtue."[44]

If the matter is examined thoroughly, however, it can be said that, after all, the Law of Cause and Effect or a good or bad occasion can be reduced to the matter of novelty or a lack of novelty. If a spectator sees the same actor in the same play for two days in succession, what he found effective the day before will now seem uninteresting. This is because the spectator has a memory of something novel, which, since he does not find it again on the second day, makes him feel the performance is unsatisfactory. Later, however, on another occasion, he will go to the play with the memory of an unsatisfactory performance, and as he will now discover something new, he will find the performance successful.

Thus, when an artist masters our art to the highest degree, he finds that the Flower as such does not exist as a separate entity. When all the secret mysteries of the *nō* have been penetrated, it can be seen that Flower exists only to the extent that the actor has a firm self-understanding of the principle of novelty in all things. As the sutra says, "good and bad alike are undifferentiated; wickedness and righteousness are the same."[45] It is not true that, fundamentally, there is nothing fixed concerning good or bad? Rather, depending on the occasion, what is useful is good, and what is not useful is bad. Our art depends on the taste of the audience at a particular time and place and will be produced in response to the general taste of the time. Such is the Flower that is truly useful. Here, one kind of performance is appreciated; there, another sort of acting is welcomed. The Flower thus must differ depending

[44] No particular source is cited for this maxim.

[45] Scholars have not agreed on the exact source for this quotation, which appeared in other Japanese medieval texts as well. Similar sentiments are expressed in the Vimalakīrti sutra.

on the spirit of the audience. Which of those Flowers then represents the true one? The nature of the Flower truly depends on the occasion on which it will be employed.

This separate secret teaching concerning the art of the nō is crucial to our family and should be passed down to only one person in each generation. For example, even where the rightful heir is concerned, should he be without the proper abilities, this teaching must not be given to him. It is written that "a house does not mean merely lineage. Carrying on the line correctly defines a house. Succession is not a question of being born into the family, but of a real grasp of the art."[46] This teaching can provide the means to come to truly master that exquisite Flower that permits the understanding of a myriad virtues.

I have previously passed along these teachings to my younger brother Shirō, and I have given them as well to Mototsugu,[47] who is also a gifted player. They should only be passed on as an important secret.

Ōe 25 [1418] the first day of the 6th month.

(signed) Ze

[46] The exact source of the quotation is unknown. Similar ideas are expressed in the *Sasamegoto* (Whisperings) of the priest and *renga* poet Shinkei (1319-1406). Zeami, with his interest in *renga* poetry, may well have known the work.

[47] Modern scholars tend to agree that the name Motosugu refers to another name for Motomasa, Zeami's eldest son. The reference, however, is unclear.

The True Path to the Flower
(Shikadō)

1. Two Basic Arts, Three Role Types

There are various important elements to be mastered in our art. Among them, an actor who is beginning his training must not overlook the Two Basic Arts and Three Role Types. By the Two Basic Arts, I mean dancing and chanting. By the Three Role Types, I refer to the human forms that constitute the basis of role impersonation [an old person, a woman, a warrior].

A beginning actor must follow his teacher and study dancing and chanting as thoroughly as possible. From the ages of ten to seventeen, however, it is not necessary to study the Three Role Types. The young actor may perform any sort of role using his natural, childlike appearance. He need not wear a mask, nor attempt any actual Role Playing; even if he does assume various roles in name only, he should retain his own youthful appearance. In the case of *bugaku* dances as well, the same procedure should be followed—in such dances as *ryōō* and *nasori*,[1] the child should perform them in name only, preserve his natural appearance, and wear no mask. Following such a method of avoiding any banality will insure that, at a later stage in the development of the actor's art, his basis for creating Grace will be established. In *The Great Learning*, it says that "it cannot be, when the root is neglected, that what should spring from it will be well ordered."[2]

---

[1] *Ryōō* and *nasori* are two ancient court dances in which masks were employed. Both are derived from Chinese models. For details, see various entries in Inoura Yoshinobu, *A History of Japanese Theatre I* and Eta Harich-Schneider, *A History of Japanese Music*.

[2] The quotation, slightly altered in Zeami's text, occurs in *The Great Learning* (*Ta Hsüeh*). For a translation of the whole passage, see James Legge, *The Chinese Classics*, I, 359.

From the time that an actor comes of age and his appearance becomes that of a fully grown man, he can wear a mask and should begin to change his appearance in order to perform in various roles. Although he may perform a wide variety of parts, his only successful beginning must lie in his study of the Three Role Types if he wishes to succeed in creating an acting style of the Highest Fruition. These three are: the old person, the woman, and the warrior. An actor must master the study of what is required for the imitation of an old man, a woman, and a man of strength. Then, adding to this what he has already learned as a youth concerning the Two Basic Arts of chanting and dancing, he can create the specifics of any particular role; if he can manage this, no other method of study will be required.

As for the various other kinds of roles, all of them grow naturally out of the Two Basic Arts and the Three Role Types, and therefore, the actor will have them at hand. The style of acting appropriate to a quiet and solemn god is adapted from the style of the old man; roles requiring great taste and elegance come naturally from the style of women's roles, and roles requiring powerful body movements and foot stamping grow from warrior roles. Therefore, whatever the actor's artistic intentions, he will be able to find a means to manifest them in his performance. Then too, even if he does show some shortcomings in his artistic abilities and cannot produce the technique appropriate to certain roles, his mastery of the Two Basic Arts and Three Role Types, if he has attained it, will still make him a superior actor. In sum, the Two Basic Arts and Three Role Types provide the proper means to achieve the correct style in acting.

Observing the method of training used for *sarugaku* players these days, however, it seems clear that the actor's basic training does not begin with the Two Basic Arts and Three Role Types; rather, all kinds of roles are studied, as well as techniques not central to our art. Thus the actor's style does not seem assured, and his performances are insecure and lack interest. Indeed, it seems that artists of the first rank are no longer performing. To repeat again, those who do not begin their training with the Two Basic Arts and Three Role Types will only succeed in committing themselves to the creation of mere scattered elements in their Role Playing, trees and leaves without any trunk. Yet the elegant beauty of the child performer does remain in the Three Role Types of the mature performer, and the skill arising from a mastery of the Three Role Types can permit the actor to manifest his own vision, no matter what the play.

2. An Art That Remains External

In terms of the *nō*, art that remains External is to be despised. This point must be fully understood. First, if an actor is born with the proper natural character, and gifted with talent, he can surely become a master. As he polishes and practices his art, his natural abilities will manifest themselves of their own accord.

In terms of dancing and chanting, an actor has not yet achieved a fluent mastery at the stage when he is still imitating what he has learned from his teacher. On the surface, the imitation may be effective, but he will not yet have assimilated the art unto himself, his artistic powers will be insufficient, and his real skill in *nō* will not increase—such is the actor who remains at the level of Externalization. A real master is one who imitates his teacher well, shows discernment, assimilates his art, absorbs his art into his mind and in his body, and so arrives at a level of Perfect Fluency through a mastery of his art. A performance by such an actor will show real life. An actor who adds strength to his natural abilities through constant practice and rehearsal, understands quickly, and puts himself totally into the object of his role is one who can truly be said to have achieved Internalization. To repeat again, a performer must truly grasp the distinction between true mastery and its opposite. "To do something is not hard; but to do it well is very difficult indeed."[3]

[3] Zeami's text attributes the text to Mencius, where it does not appear. A

3. Perfect Freedom

It happens in our art that an actor who has mastered every secret and has attained the pinnacle of artistic maturity does occasionally perform in an unorthodox manner, and young actors may attempt to copy this style of performance. Yet a style that grows out of true mastery is no simple matter to imitate. Why should they try to do so?

The art that achieves Perfect Freedom requires thorough practice of the elements of the *nō* appropriate to the actor's whole career, from his beginnings as a young actor through his period of full maturity; the actor must assemble all these elements, remove their impurities, and achieve self-mastery. Such attainments are revealed in performance through the force of the actor's skills. The actor can accomplish this by mixing in his performance some of the impure elements that in years past he has learned to exclude from his art through training and practice. It may be asked why a skillful player should introduce such elements of improper style into his performance. Certainly, such means constitute a strategy available only to the most experienced actors. Generally, all that remains for such actors are the pure and orthodox techniques. As there are no novel elements in a perfect performance, then on those occasions when the audience has become accustomed to an actor's art, the actor who is truly a master may include something unorthodox, in order to introduce again the element of novelty. Thus, in this manner, bad art can indirectly serve the cause of good art. The power of the artist's personality can thus transform impurity into purity, and so make such art exciting for his audiences.

Beginning actors, of course, only see this technique as out of the ordinary and think of it as something that can be imitated; but when they do so, since their own technique is naturally insufficient, the mixing in of these unusual elements

---

similar phrase occurs in the *Book of Documents* (*Shu ching*) and was quoted and paraphrased in a variety of texts circulated in Japan before and during Zeami's time.

in an art based on such immature foundations is like adding brushwood to the fire of error. Such young actors doubtlessly believe that Perfect Freedom is a matter of mere technique, rather than something that grows out of the artistic maturity of the master actor. This is a matter that must be thoroughly considered. The master actor can use such techniques with the knowledge that they are impure; but insofar as the novice mistakes them for true art and imitates them, these two ways of thinking will remain as different as black and white. And without a long development of self-mastery, how can a beginner hope to achieve a level of Perfect Freedom? Thus, when a beginner tries to imitate an actor who has reached a level of true proficiency, he will merely copy what is incorrect and will never improve. As is written in Mencius, "to achieve what one wants by following one's own desires, rather than following the Way, is like climbing a tree to find a fish." And Mencius says as well, "as for climbing a tree to find a fish, no great harm is done. But it is a great loss to follow one's will rather than the Way."[4]

The art of an actor who has attained the highest level, by turning bad art into good, will allow him to manifest his precise meaning. A clumsy actor does not have the ability to do this. An unskilled actor, performing with the amount of artistic skill he has available to him, thinks to emulate the strength of a performance that lies beyond him. He will fail absolutely. This situation is just the same as [the saying of Mencius that] it is dangerous to try to accomplish something by using merely the means you yourself choose. Thus, if a young actor wishes to copy something beyond his ability and yet which lies within the realm of true art, there will be no great harm done even if he fails in his attempt. This is merely to climb a tree to try to find a fish. To repeat again, one must not copy the performance of an actor who has attained the highest mastery and who performs in an unorthodox fashion.

---

[4] For this passage in context, see W.A.C.H. Dobson, *Mencius* (Toronto: University of Toronto Press, 1963), p. 12.

Such a practice serves only as a means to seek out failure. Take careful note of this.

Rather, a beginner must follow his teacher, ask concerning what he cannot grasp, and make every effort to achieve an understanding appropriate to the level of his own art. And, even though he sees the art of one who has mastered its secrets, he must first strive himself in order to master the fundamental elements of the Two Basic Arts and the Three Role Types. As the Lotus Sutra says, "be careful of those who say that they have attained what they have not."[5]

4. Skin, Flesh, and Bone

In the performance of *nō* there are three basic elements: Skin, Flesh, and Bone. The three are almost never found together in the same actor. In the art of calligraphy, it is said that the three have never been found together except in the work of Kūkai.

When it comes to explaining the elements of Skin, Flesh, and Bone in terms of the *nō*, then what can be described as Bone represents that exceptional artistic strength that a gifted actor shows naturally in his performance and which comes to him of itself through his inborn ability. Flesh can doubtless be defined as that element visible in a performance that arises from the power of the skills of the actor that he has obtained by his mastering of the Two Basic Arts of chant and dance. Skin, on the other hand, may be explained as a manner of ease and beauty in performance that can be obtained when the other two elements are thoroughly perfected. To put it another way: when considering the art that comes from Sight, the art that comes from Sound, and of the art that comes from the Heart, it can be said that Sight should be equated with Skin, Sound with Flesh, and the Heart to the Bone. Within the category of the chant itself, these three qualities can be

[5] A slightly altered version of a phrase from *The Lotus Sutra*, Book II. For the passage in context, see Leon Hurwitz, tr., *Scripture of the Lotus Blossom of the Fine Dharma* (New York: Columbia University Press, 1976), p. 29.

seen to exist. The beauty of the voice of the actor represents the Skin, the interest of the melody is the Flesh, and the techniques of breathing employed represent the Bone. The same principle applies to the dance. The beauty of the actor's appearance represents the Skin, the artistic patterns of the dance represent the Flesh, and the richness of the emotions manifested by the dance represents the Bone. These are matters to be pondered over with great care.

On this point, when I look at the artists who are performing today, I find that not only are there no artists who can truly manifest these three principles in performance, but indeed there are none who even know that such conceptions exist. My father taught me such things privately, and I have taken his lessons to heart. From what one can observe in the performances of actors these days, they are only able to manage certain elements of Skin. And yet such is not the true Skin [which has behind it the Flesh and the Bone]. It is only the Skin that they attempt to imitate. Such actors have not gained a fluent mastery.

Then again, even if an actor should manage to possess all three of these qualities, there is still more that he must understand. Even if he possesses them (the Bones, his naturally inherited talent; Flesh, his acquired skills in chant and dance; and Skin, the elegance of his outward appearance on stage), these three have, of themselves, no greater significance than each of these individual qualities may possess. It is difficult to describe the qualities of an actor who has truly fused them together. To speak of such a level of achievement involves, for example, a true mastery of those artistic principles that have already reached a high degree of perfection, to a level where the artist moves beyond his means of expression to produce a performance of profound ease. The spectators, witnessing his performance, will be caught up in his mastery and will forget themselves; only afterward will they reflect on the performance, realizing that they found no weak spots whatsoever. Such, for the audience, represents the sensation of having seen an actor whose years of training have added to the Bone of his natural skills. Secondly, they will find in him one whose art, no matter how often it is observed, will seem inexhaustible. Such is the effect of the Flesh of an artist who exhibits the mastery of the skills that are highly developed to the point of rare mastery. Thirdly, the audience will always find the actor elegant. This quality derives from his attainment of the skills represented by Skin. When the actor himself can naturally reflect those emotions felt in mutuality with the audience, it can be said that he is one who has truly blended Skin, Flesh, and Bone.

5. Substance and Function

One must know the elements of Substance and Function in the *nō*. If Substance can be compared to a flower, then Function can be compared to its odor. The moon and its light make a similar comparison. If the concept of Substance is fully understood, then the nature of Function will be naturally comprehensible of itself.

When it comes to observing the *nō*, those who truly understand the art watch it with the spirit, while those who do not merely watch it with their eyes. To see with the spirit is to grasp the Substance; to see with the eyes is merely to observe the Function. Thus it is that beginning actors merely grasp the Function and try to imitate that. Although they do not understand the real principle of Function [that is, the fact that it derives from Substance], they attempt to copy it. Yet Function cannot be imitated. Those who truly understand the *nō*, since they grasp it with their spirit, are able to imitate its Substance. Thus in a performance, Function comes of itself from a successful attempt to assimilate Substance. Yet those who do not understand this principle try to master Function and imitate it as a principle of their art; they do not realize that as they do so they rob Function of its proper role. And since Function can never become Substance, the art of *nō* therefore becomes broken and confused, possessing neither

Substance nor Function. Under such circumstances, there is no proper path for the *nō*, and our art has no meaning.

Substance and Function may seem to represent two independent elements. But in fact, without Substance there can be no Function. Therefore, there are no means with which to imitate it directly [as it cannot exist independently]. Thus it is foolish for an actor, thinking that there is something there to be copied, to attempt to imitate it. One must understand that it is precisely by attempting to reproduce substance that the actor can manage to create naturally the appropriate Function. To repeat again, if one truly comes to understand the principle that the imitation of Function cannot become an end in itself, he will evolve into an actor able to truly grasp this crucial distinction between the two. It has been said that "everyone wishes to resemble a master actor, yet no one should try to imitate him."[6] Here, imitation refers to Function, resemblance to Substance.

In previous times, such attention was not given to these various theoretical terms. Among those performing before, in the older style, however, there were quite a few who managed of themselves to gain high artistic power. At that time, the nobility and the people of high rank took note only of what was good in various performances, but they did not make it a point to observe the defects. These days, however, their eyes are highly skilled and so audiences have come to observe even the slightest fault, so that if a presentation is not as elegant as a polished gem or a bouquet of flowers, it cannot meet the expectations of a cultured group of spectators. Therefore, there are few artists who are considered to have attained the highest level of success. Because the *nō* is entering into a period of decline, I am concerned that if our training loses its rigor, our art will cease to be, and it is for this reason that I have written here an outline of my own understanding of our art. As for the rest, it will depend on the intelligence and artistic skills

---

[6] Doubtless an expression current at the time. No source has been located.

of the individual actor and should be transmitted directly through oral teaching.

Ōe 27, [1420] the Sixth Month
Zeami

In the *Analects* it is written that, "not to talk to one who could be talked to, is to waste a man. To talk to those who cannot be talked to is to waste one's words."[7] Then again, the *Book of Changes* says, "if suitable changes are given to those who are not suitable, the hatred of Heaven will be aroused."[8]

When the art of *sarugaku* is refined to a high level, and when Substance is fully manifested in its Function, the differences between the two will disappear altogether, and a truly gifted performer will be able to make all styles his own. He will surely achieve a remarkable art that will lie beyond description. Then, there is still another kind of artistic elegance called Mood, and its precise location cannot be found. This quality flows like a breeze from the Substance of an actor's art. Mood is fostered through Substance and can be sensed in a performance through Function.

Cannot the beauty of Grace be compared to the image of a swan holding a flower in its bill, I wonder?

[7] The translation is by Arthur Waley. For the passage in context, see Arthur Waley, tr., *The Analects of Confucius*, Book XV, No. 7, p. 194.

[8] The quotation does not appear in this source and has not been located. It is cited again in *A Mirror Held to the Flower*.

A Mirror Held to the Flower
(Kakyō)

1. Pitch, Breath, Voice Production

First Teachings concerning Music. Correct pitch is based on sustaining the proper breath. While listening carefully to the pitch of the accompanying instruments [flute, etc.] that precede him, the actor must align the increasing intensity of the pressure of air in his chest to this pitch, close his eyes, and draw in his breath, so that, when he projects his voice, his first sounds will automatically be produced at the proper pitch. If he merely listens to the pitch but does not align himself with it [by preparing the proper amount of air in his chest], then when he produces his first sounds he will by no means find it simple to enter on the proper pitch level. Because proper pitch is regulated by the intensity of the pressure of air used to produce the voice, it can be said that the proper order involves, first, determining the pitch, second, preparing the breath, and third, producing the voice.

Another point. As pitch depends on the breath that the performer sustains, he must be careful to move his lips in such a way as to produce clearly the proper sounds, syllable by syllable. In a passage so subtle that the musical notation cannot be sufficiently precise, the problem of vocal shading can doubtless best be properly handled by facial movements. An actor should try as much as possible to grasp these concepts and incorporate them into his technique.

There is a fixed relationship of upper and lower between tones such as *kyū* and *shō*.[1] When sound achieves an orderly

[1] For a discussion of these terms and their Chinese antecedents, see William Malm, *Japanese Music*, p. 66, and Eta Harich-Schneider, *A History of Jap-*

pattern, it can be called tone. *Kyū* represents the *yin* principle, as does Earth, the *ryō* pitches, and the inhalation of breath. *Shō* represents the *yang* principle, as does Heaven, the *ritsu* pitches, and the exhalation of breath.

The *ryo* and *ritsu* pitches as well combine in sound with a fixed upper and lower relationship. Thus it can be concluded that sound which achieves a pattern divides into a series of five tones and establishes as well a gamut of twelve pitches, six of which are *ryo*, six of which are *ritsu*.

2. What Is Felt in the Heart Is Ten; What Appears in Movement Seven

The expression "when you feel ten in your heart, express seven in your movements" refers to the following. When a beginner studying the *nō* learns to gesture with his hands and to move his feet, he will first do as his teacher tells him and so will use all his energies to perform in the way in which he is instructed. Later, however, he will learn to move his arms to a lesser extent than his own emotions suggest, and he will be able to moderate his own intentions. This phenomenon is by no means limited to dance and gesture. In terms of general stage deportment, no matter how slight a bodily action, if the motion is more restrained than the emotion behind it, the body will become the Substance and the emotion its Function, thus moving the audience.

3. Violent Body Movement, Gentle Foot Movement; Violent Foot Movement, Gentle Body Movements

The conception behind this teaching is similar to the preceding. If the body and the feet are moved in the same fashion, the effect will seem rough. If, however, the body is moved

---

anese Music, pp. 134-138, as well as various entries in Kenneth J. DeWoskin, *A Song for One or Two*. In this system, *kyū* represents the first note of the scale and *shō* the second.

violently, yet the feet are moved with restraint, the effect will be wild but not rough. When, on the other hand, the feet are stamped but the body itself is moved gently, the sound of the feet will be powerful, yet as the body itself remains still, there will be no effect of roughness.

The actor must try to put in proper consonance the art of body movement, which is for the eyes, and the technique of stamping, which is for the ears. They should not merely be performed in unison. In general, learning how to move the feet when performing does not begin with learning dance steps. Rather, the actor must first learn this technique from other elements of movement and Role Playing.

4. Communication First by Hearing, Then by Sight

All of the arts of Role Playing are guided first by the words chanted on the stage and then by the actions that accompany them. However, sometimes gestures and lines are performed at the same time; or it sometimes occurs that the gestures actually precede the words concerned. Thus the proper order is reversed.

Actually, the audience should first hear the chant, then see the appropriate gesture afterwards, so that when they see what they have already understood, the satisfying sensation of a genuine union between the two images will be created in the moment of transition from one to the other.

For example, in the matter of weeping, the actor should first allow the audience to hear the word "weeping," and then, just afterwards, bring the sleeve up to the face and so complete the total action with this gesture. If the audience sees the motion of the sleeve before the concept of weeping is settled in their minds, however, the words will somehow seem left over, and the entire action will appear to be reduced. The action will already seem to have been consummated, and the total image will lack intensity. Since any action should be completed by a movement, not by the words, the principle of "first communicate by ear, then by sight," comes into being.

5. First Truly Become the Thing You Are Performing;
Then Find the Skill to Imitate Its Actions as Well

The expression "first truly become the thing you are performing" represents a principle that applies to every variety of Role
Playing in *sarugaku*. When performing the part of an old man,
for example, as such a character will naturally have an aged
posture. The actor must bend at the hips, walk in a frail
fashion, and use small gestures when moving his hands. After
having truly assumed this kind of posture, the actor's dancing,
stage deportment, and chant will seem to emanate from within
the character itself. When performing a woman's role, the
actor should slightly bend the hips, hold his hands high, sustain the whole body in a graceful manner, feel a softness in
his whole manner of being, and use his physique in a pliant
manner. It is from within the province of this kind of general
stance that an actor must bring forth his particular skills [for
the role], from dance and chant to movement and gesture.
When it comes to roles requiring anger, such as in demon
roles, the actor must assume a strong attitude, set his body
in a firm stance, and then carry out his movements. Indeed,
for any part involving Role Playing, an actor must learn to
truly "become" the object of his performance. After this, he
can use his skills to depict the role.

6. The Basis of the Dance in the Voice

If [what is expressed in] the dance is not based on [what is]
sung, no emotion will be engendered. At the moment when
the fragrance of the actor's song moves past that boundary
into the dance itself, a strange power of beauty is created. The
end of the dance as well should blend its overtones into the
atmosphere of the music that follows.

It has been said that the fundamental properties of dance
and song have always arisen from the Buddha-nature that is
stored in all sentient beings. There are five "storages"[2] and

---

[2] Traditionally, the heart, lungs, spleen, liver, and kidneys. The "five notes"

the breath that comes from them, and, dividing according to the the five colorings, becomes the "five tones" and "six modes." Three of these modes fall in the *ritsu* pitches and are referred to as *sōjō, ōshiki,* and *ichi kōchō,* whereas *hyojō* and *banshiki* represent the two that lie in the *ryo* pitches. *Mujō* is a combination of *ryo* and *ritsu* pitches.

When the voice is produced on the basis of these five "storages," the entire body begins to move, and this movement itself becomes the genesis of the dance.

The so-called "modes of cosmic change" are divided into the four seasons. There is also another method by which these rhythms are broken down into the twelve hours for the day and for the night, with a mode (*sō, ō, ikotsu, hyō, ban*)[3] appropriate for each. Then again, it has also been said concerning these "modes of cosmic changes" that on the occasion when the angels in heaven sang and danced and the sense of this heavenly rhythm was conveyed to earth, the name "modes of cosmic change" was given to them. There is no reason why heaven should not have established such things, and so both versions concerning the origins of these modes may be said to be in accord. In connection with the matter of the angels in heaven, the origin of the dances of Suruga[4] might also be

---

(*kyū, shō, kaku, chi,* and *u*) were thought to correlate with breath movements depending on the five internal organs. For the complex relationship between the five notes and the six modes, see Harich-Schneider, *A History of Japanese Music,* pp. 136-137. For certain details on classical Chinese practice on these matters, see Joseph Needham, *Science and Civilization in China,* Vol. 4, part 1, section 26, p. 163ff.

[3] According to traditional designations, the *sō* mode was associated with spring and the hour of the Snake (10 A.M. to 12 A.M.), the *ō* mode with summer and the hour of the Sheep (2 P.M. to 4 P.M.), the *ikotsu* mode with midsummer and the hour of the Rat (midnight to 2 A.M.), the *hyō* mode with autumn and the hour of the Tiger (4 A.M. to 6 A.M.), and the *ban* mode with winter and the hour of the Dog (8 P.M. to 10 P.M.).

[4] These dances formed an important part of the so-called *azuma asobi* or "dances of the Eastern Provinces," performed at celebrations held at Shintō shrines and other locations under imperial patronage since the ninth century. According to ancient legend, an angel descended to earth and first performed these dances at the beach of Uze in Suruga (the present Shizuoka Prefecture).

mentioned. From the time when the heavenly angel originally came down from heaven and left behind her dance and her music, this secret musical tradition has existed in our country. As there are so many details that exist concerning these matters, I refrain from recording any more detailed explanations here.

In any case, the point to keep in mind is the fact that, if the musical strength of the chant is insufficiently powerful, a dance cannot give rise to any emotive stimulus. Even in the case of a very familiar dance, when an actor dances to the music of a *kusemai*, he has the advantage of dancing to a familiar piece of music and so will experience no special difficulties. Of course, without the flute and the rhythm of the drum, it is difficult indeed to dance in a proper fashion. Indeed, dancing is truly impossible without the strength of sound behind it.

Next I would like to discuss the Five Skills of dancing. The first is the Skill of Self-Conscious Movement. The next is the Skill of Movement beyond Consciousness. The third is the Skill of Mutuality in Balance. The fourth is the Skill of Mutuality in Self-Conscious Movement. The fifth is the Skill of Mutuality in Movement beyond Consciousness.

a) The Skill of Self-Conscious Movement, which involves establishing the technical form of the dance and can be learned, begins with the actor pressing his palms together, as though in reverence, placing the various elements of the body into motion, moving the hands in appropriate gestures, controlling the performance so that it will fall into the proper structure of *jo, ha*, and *kyū*, and, in sum, carrying out a performance in consonance with a thorough mastery of all the various principles involved. This represents what is referred to as the Skill of Self-Conscious Movement.

b) Movement beyond Consciousness. Although the Skill of Self-Conscious Movement concerns the movements of the dance as well, in this second skill the handling of the actor's hands and feet are not involved; rather, this skill is concerned with the creation of an appearance that can bring about the proper feelings inherent in the dance itself. It is the creation of an atmosphere central to that method of performance in which the appearance of the actor can go beyond mere techniques and concrete forms. Such a performance resembles a bird that opens its wings and trusts itself to the movement of the winds. Such is the meaning of the Skill of Movement beyond Consciousness.

c) The Skill of Mutuality in Balance involves blending the Skill of Movement with the *jo, ha*, and *kyū* that result from the Skill of Control. The Skill of Control produces an art of design; the Skill of Movement produces an art beyond external pattern. When these two can be combined together in an art of mutuality, the results will reach a culmination of artistic skill. The spectators, for their part, will then find such a performance truly moving. When an actor can perform with those two principles in mind, the term Skill of Mutuality in Balance can truly be applied to his performance.

d) The Principle of Mutuality in Self-Conscious Movement arises when, after the Skill of Mutuality of Balance is mastered, the Skill of Self-Conscious Movement is made the basis for an artist's conception, and the Skill of Movement beyond Consciousness is made subordinate to it in a particular performance. I call an understanding of this principle Mutuality in Self-Conscious Movement.

e) Mutuality in Movement beyond Consciousness, on the other hand, places the Skill of Movement beyond Consciousness in the center and makes the Skill of Self-Conscious Movement subordinate to it. This combination produces an art beyond any mere appearances.

Now, when applying those principles to the matter of the Three Role Types, the principle of Mutuality in Self-Conscious Movement is doubtless more appropriate for men's roles [such as the old man and the warrior]. For the women's roles, the principle of Mutuality in Movement beyond Consciousness is more suitable. In any case, the actor must be careful to choose the correct style of dance in order to create properly the role he is performing.

Again, as concerns the dance, it is said that "the eyes look ahead and the spirit looks behind." This expression means that the actor looks in front of him with his physical eyes, but his inner concentration must be directed to the appearance of his movements from behind. This is a crucial element in the creation of what I have referred to above as the Movement beyond Consciousness. The appearance of the actor, seen from the spectator in the seating area, produces a different image than the actor can have of himself. What the spectator sees is the outer image of the actor. What an actor himself sees, on the other hand, forms his own internal image of himself. He must make still another effort in order to grasp his own internalized outer image, a step possible only through assiduous training. Once he obtains this, the actor and the spectator can share the same image. Only then can it actually be said that an actor has truly grasped the nature of his appearance. For an actor to grasp his true appearance implies that he has under his control the space to the left and to the right of him, and to the front and to the rear of him. In many cases, however, an average actor looks only to the front and to the side and so never sees what he actually looks like from behind. If the actor cannot somehow come to a sense of how he looks from behind, he will not be able to become conscious of any possible vulgarities in his performance. Therefore, an actor must look at himself using his internalized outer image, come to share the same view as the audience, examine his appearance with his spiritual eyes and so maintain a graceful appearance with his entire body. Such an action truly represents "the eyes of the spirit looking behind."

To repeat again, an actor must come to have an ability to see himself as the spectators do, grasp the logic of the fact that the eyes cannot see themselves, and find the skill to grasp the whole—left and right, ahead and behind. If an actor can achieve this, his peerless appearance will be as elegant as that of a flower or a jewel and will serve as a living proof of his understanding.

The expression, "the fool who carries a board can only see

in front,"[5] has universal application: in dance and movement as well, the actor must come to master the right and the left, the front and the rear.

7. Matching the Feeling to the Moment

In the performance of *sarugaku*, when the actor first appears there is one particular instant when the opening speech should properly begin. It must not begin too soon. Nor must it come too late. First the actor leaves the green room, stops as he approaches the stage from the bridge, takes cognizance of the audience, and then, just when the spectators think that he is to begin his opening speech, he must commence at exactly that instant when his feelings match those of his audience. The principle of chanting at precisely the high point of the audience's expectations can truly be called matching the feeling to the moment. If this moment comes even a bit too slowly, the audience's expectations will weaken, so that, when the actor begins, he will no longer be able to match them. This moment should come just at the highest point of the spectator's feelings of anticipation. This instant when the feelings of the audience reach the proper level of tension must be grasped intuitively by the *shite*. It is the moment when the experienced actor can absorb the concentration of the audience into his own performance. This moment is, in fact, the most crucial one in the entire day's presentation.

In general, when crossing the bridge the actor should stop a third of the way across and perform his entrance song. The latter half of the song should be performed at the end of the bridge, close to the stage. At this moment the actor should face that part of the audience in the best seating area yet not concentrate his gaze directly on the spectators. In general, the actor should direct his performance toward the nobles seated in the audience. In the case of indoor performances or per-

[5] A Chinese expression often quoted in Zen texts of the period, used as a term of abuse for a fool.

formances at banquets, the actor should play to the most important members of the audience but never look fixedly at them. As for the hand positions in the dance, since the hand motions are carried out in harmony with the angle of the head, the actor's performance in relation to his audience should involve a smooth coordination of all parts of the presentation, whether the hall is large or small. The same principle holds true when the performance is held at a banquet. It is crucial that the actor strike this balance.

When entering the stage space, the actor should remain two-thirds of the way back from the front of the stage, closer to the area occupied by the musicians. In the case when a dance is performed, the actor should both begin and finish a third of the way back from the front edge of the stage. Again, when *sarugaku* is performed in a large playing space, the performer must take care to make the distance from the nobility seem as short as possible. On the other hand, when the performing space is restricted, a sense of distance should be created between the actor and the nobility. This principle is even more important to observe when the performance is held indoors.

Again, in a case where the chant is performed indoors, the actor must find the proper moment to seize the attention of the audience. It is bad to begin either too quickly or too slowly. When the actor hears in his inner ear that instant of silence when the audience waits in expectation, thinking "ah, now he is going to sing!" he must begin. He must sing using the principles in pitch, breath, and voice production that have been discussed above.

8. *Jo, ha, and kyū*

Since the term *jo* means "beginning," the *waki sarugaku* that begins a day's performance should be a play that reveals the authentic nature of our art. Such a play should have a simple source, be constructed without any complex detail, be felicitous in nature, and have a plot that is easy to follow. Song and dance should be the main elements in such a play. *Nō* dramas that are performed on the second place on the program have a quality different from that of the *waki nō*. Their sources are quite specific and they are quite powerful emotionally, although very dignified in conception. Although they differ artistically from the *waki nō*, they are not so complex and do not require enormous efforts in performance; therefore, they too may be included among plays in the *jo* category.

Plays that occupy the third place on the program fall into the *ha* category. Whereas plays in the *jo* category concentrate on a simple and straightforward manner of presentation, plays in the *ha* category place an emphasis on complexity of expression. Plays in the *jo* category are quite natural in conception and are gentle and simple to understand. On the other hand, from the third play onward, *nō* plays require great artistic efforts on the part of the actor and are of a style that involves the use of Role Playing. Plays in this category form the central element in the day's entertainment. And indeed, as plays in the fourth and fifth place on the program are also included in the *ha* category, various artistic efforts must be expended [to perform them properly].

Kyū has the same meaning as the term *ageku* [in *renga*],[6] that of "ending." *Kyū* represents the last memento of the day, a play appropriate for such an ending. The term *ha* requires breaking the mood of *jo*, and is an art that brings complexity and great artistic skill to the performance. *Kyū*, on the other hand, extends the art of *ha* in turn, in order to represent the final stage of the process. In this fashion *kyū* brings on powerful movements, rapid dance steps, as well as fierce and strong gestures, in order to dazzle the eyes of the spectators. Agitation characterizes this final stage of the *nō*.

On the whole, in previous times no more than four or five plays were normally performed at a time. Thus the fifth play was inevitably in the *kyū* category. However, these days, the number of plays performed on a program changes indiscrim-

---

[6] *Ageku* is the last stanza in a *renga* or linked verse sequence, an important poetic form developed during the medieval period. See Earl Miner, *Japanese Linked Poetry*, p. 61.

inately; therefore, if the level of *kyū* is reached too quickly, the appropriate pace cannot be sustained. A program of *nō* can best be performed with the longest span of time devoted to the plays in the *ha* category. Various arts of the *nō* can be exhibited in these plays, and only one play in the *kyū* category should be added. Nevertheless, when performing in conformance to the wishes of noble patrons, some irregularities in the planned program may arise. Even in such an instance, however, the performance can be planned with care, so that, even if a piece is left over that still must be performed—as for example when another *kyū* piece is requested—the play can still be presented with careful restraint and with its excitement controlled, with the emotions cut back by a third, so that some margin is held in reserve during the performance.

There is one important matter concerning this situation that needs to be mentioned. It may happen by chance that, during a performance of *nō*, when the *ha* and the *kyū* sections have already been attained, some noble members of the audiences may arrive late. Thus, while the performance itself will already have reached the stage of *kyū*, the emotional responses of those noblemen as they enter will be merely at the stage of *jo*. In such a case, when the spectator watches the *kyū* stage in a performance with an emotional reaction appropriate to *jo*, he will not be able to match his emotions with the performance. And in addition, those others as well who have been watching the performance since the beginning will, because of the late arrivals, also find their emotions becoming subdued. These changes will result in the creation of an inappropriate atmosphere, and the spectators will find themselves back at the emotional level appropriate to *jo*. In such a case, there is no way that the performance can go well. For their part, the actors may feel that it would be better to go backwards and perform a play in the *jo* category, but this decision too would result in an unsatisfactory performance. The danger here is very great. Therefore, on such an occasion, the actor must choose a play from the *ha* category that seems as appropriate as possible, then try to inject into the performance some of the elements appropriate to *jo*; he must play in a gentle and relaxed manner, so as to capture the emotions of the nobility present. If their feelings can be drawn into the play in this fashion, the actor can use all the traditional efforts at his disposal to pull all the spectators back into the more amiable atmosphere of *ha* and *kyū*. Still, even with such efforts, it may be difficult for an actor to make the performance succeed completely.

Then again, the occasion may arise when a performance is unexpectedly demanded for a gathering, or perhaps for a large banquet, when the actors will be hastily summoned. In such an instance, the emotional level of the spectators will already be at the level of *kyū*. The *nō* to be performed, on the other hand, will be at the level of *jo*. Such a situation also presents a crisis. In a *sarugaku* performance held under such circumstances, it is best, while playing at the level of *jo*, to begin to introduce some of the feeling of *ha*, performing in a light and agreeable manner, so as to move the atmosphere along to the level of *ha* and *kyū* as rapidly as possible. Such is the fundamental procedure to follow. Played in this fashion, the performance should be a success.

For a small informal entertainment, the same concerns will apply. Knowing ahead of time that such an occasion will take place, the actor should prepare his own emotions, so that, from the opening tap of the fan and the short song of greeting,[7] he will have prepared himself for every part of the program and should be able to carry it out as he had planned. Should some of the noblemen attending arrive late at the banquet, the actor should adopt the same kind of concern expressed above and try to bring the *kyū* section more into the spirit of *jo*, following the fundamental principles of our art. But, if he finds the audience is already at the level of *kyū* when he begins, then, using the basic principles explained above, he can work

---

[7] On such an occasion the tap of a fan was meant to replace the sound of the drum at the beginning of a performance, followed by a short greeting, before the actual presentation began.

to move the atmosphere of *jo* along as quickly as possible toward an atmosphere of *kyū*.

Therefore, one must have a real understanding of the proportionment of *jo*, *ha*, and *kyū*, from large formal performances of *nō* to performances at official entertainments, down to impromptu informal performances.

9. *Understanding the Proper Meaning of Learning Our Art*

An actor must not only rehearse thoroughly with his teachers but he must learn through practice to imitate their peerless performances. Indeed, it is precisely because the art of these great performers has been brought to the highest levels of training that they can present in their acting an appearance of total mastery and ease, thus fascinating their audiences. If a beginner wishes merely to imitate this level of accomplishment, he may seem to achieve its semblance, yet there will be nothing moving in his performance. A truly great artist has for many years succeeded in training both his body and his spirit; he can hold back much of his potential in reserve and perform in an easy fashion, so that only seven-tenths of his art is visible. If a beginner tries to perform in this fashion, without the proper practice, he will only imitate what he can observe, and so his spirit and his performance cannot reach beyond that seven-tenths he can grasp. What is more, his own progresss will be blocked.

Therefore, when a student is learning his craft, the teacher should show not his own high level of ability [in which there is a reserve of artistry], but, as he did when he too was a beginner, indicate to his pupils how to use fully both their minds and bodies. After such lessons have been absorbed, the students will gradually reach a level of mastery and attain a level of ease in their own performances, understand how to hold in reserve a certain amount of their own physical energy, and grasp of themselves the principle that "what is felt by the heart is ten, what appears in movement seven."

In general, a performance of Perfect Fluency cannot be imitated. And if an actor makes an attempt to imitate it, the very effort involved in the attempt will produce a tension that cannot be a part of Perfect Fluency. Only something that is meant to appear difficult can actually be imitated. "The truth and what looks like it are two different things,"[8] it is said. Thus, could there be any way to imitate the truth of the master actor's easy performance? Indeed, ease and difficulty are two aspects of the same thing. There is a separate teaching on this matter. The means by which a student learns from a teacher are well known, and so no special comment is needed here. However, the teacher's official certification of the student must be based on a thorough examination of his capacities and devotion; otherwise, certification should not be given. If the student's basic abilities are insufficient, no certification is possible. Should certification be given when talent is lacking, a level of accomplishment is suggested that cannot actually be matched. The certification will be fraudulent and the results meaningless; therefore, it should not be given. In the *Book of Changes* it is written that "if suitable teachings are given to those who are not suitable, the hatred of Heaven will be aroused."[9] In order that such a suitable person can be created, three conditions must be present. First, he must possess himself the requisite talent. Secondly, he must adore his art and show a total dedication to the path of *nō*. Thirdly, he must have a teacher capable of showing him the proper way. If these three conditions cannot be met, the candidate will not be suitable. A suitable person is one who has the capacity to achieve the highest reaches of his art, to be recognized himself as a teacher.

When I observe the artistic abilities of young performers now, it appears that "skipping"[10] has become commonplace. This situation comes about because they imitate without study.

---

[8] A popular saying found in many texts circulated in this period.

[9] The quotation as recorded here does not appear in the *Book of Changes* (I ching).

[10] "Skipping" (*tendoku*) was a term originally used to mean "turning the *sutras*," chanting the first few lines and then skipping the rest to save time, as a kind of devotional exercise. Zeami of course uses the term ironically.

An actor must begin by studying the Two Basic Arts and the Three Role Types, continue to practice all that is appropriate for his age, and carry on his studies in the proper sequence, so that he will reach a stage of mastery in all the arts of the *nō* that can permit him to perform in any artistic style. To learn only by imitation and so only manage a temporary resolution seems indeed to represent a kind of "skipping." For example, when studying the Two Basic Arts, one must not study the Three Role Types. When the time comes to study the Three Role Types, one must put off for a certain time the study of military roles [as they demand intense physical effort]. When an actor does come to study the military roles, then the demon roles in both the Delicacy within Strength and Rough styles of movement should be put off for a certain time, since there is an appropriate moment to learn them as well. To attempt to learn all these roles at once—what a terribly difficult thing it would be. And the degree of difficulty would be unexpectedly high. Therefore, even if by "skipping" a young performer manages to fool the public into thinking that he is a master, he will achieve a momentary Flower. And as such an artist grows older, his art will decline. And even should his art not decline, it would be impossible for him to achieve true renown. This point must be firmly kept in mind.

Concerning "skipping," there is another matter to consider. If an actor is inordinately fond of new plays, and should he come step by step to abandon the older repertory he performed in the past, he can never master the art of *nō* and will only be "skipping." Rather, the actor must fix a repertory of standard plays at which he excels and then mix new plays in with them. If he plays only fresh pieces and neglects the plays to which he is accustomed, the results, in terms of the art of the *nō*, will be a disgraceful "skipping" indeed. Besides, if only unusual pieces are performed, then that procedure of itself loses its novelty. If a mixture of old and new is achieved, then both the old and the new alike will seem novel. Such becomes the undying flower. As Confucius said, "He who by reanimating the Old can gain knowledge of the New is fit to be a teacher."[11]

10. Having a Real Understanding of Skill

If an actor has become fully proficient at music and dance, he may be called skillful. If he has not become fully accomplished, there will be no denying his shortcomings. On the other hand, there is a kind of real skill based on still different considerations. For example, there are actors whose abilities in dance and chant show no shortcomings, yet who have not achieved a high reputation. Then again, there are actors whose voices are not attractive and whose mastery of dancing and singing show defects, yet who are widely thought of as accomplished performers. The reason for this is that both dancing and gesture are external skills. The essentials of our art lie in the spirit. They represent a true enlightenment established through art. Thus, if an actor knows how to create interest and can perform from an understanding of this spirit, he will gain a reputation as a fine actor even if he has not mastered every aspect of his craft. Such being the case, if an actor really wants to become a master, he cannot simply depend on his skill in dance and gesture. Rather, mastery seems to depend on the actor's own state of self-understanding and the sense of style with which he has been blessed. Real discernment of the nature of the differences between external skill and interior understanding forms the basis of true mastery. Thus it is that an actor who has merely perfected his technique will have little of interest to show. Other actors, from the beginning of their careers, can fascinate their audiences. So it is that an actor, from the time he is young until he masters seven-tenths, eight-tenths, even all of his technique and reaches the level of a master, will continue to interest others for quite separate considerations.

Still higher than the level of interest, there is a level of skill

[11] See Arthur Waley, *The Analects of Confucius*, Book II, no. 11, p. 90.

that will simply make the audience gasp, without reflection, in surprise and pleasure. This level will be termed one of a pure Feeling that Transcends Cognition. The response to such a performance is such that there is no occasion for reflection, no time for a spectator to realize how well the performance is contrived. Such a state might be referred to as "purity unmixed."[12] In the *Book of Changes*, when the Chinese character for "feeling" (*kan* 感) is written, the element that stands for "mind" (*kokoro* 心) is eliminated [and the character is written as 咸] in order to illustrate the fact that when true feeling is involved, there is no room in the concept for reflection as a function of the mind.[13]

Thus it is that the actor comes to possess various levels of artistic skill. If a beginning actor continues on through all the various stages of his training, he will be called a good actor, but not necessarily anything more. Yet there is still a higher level where real mastery is possible. If the spectators are truly fascinated with an actor's performance, he can be said to have reached the level of a master. If, in addition, he possesses the ability to create for his audience an intensity of pure feeling that goes beyond the workings of the mind, he will have achieved the level of greatest reputation. Thus an actor should pursue his study of *nō* through these various levels, develop his skills, and through his own spiritual understanding, bring his art to the highest possible level of fulfillment.

11. Shallow and Deep

Concerning *nō* performance, there is one matter that must be given particularly serious consideration. If a performance is given without sufficient attention to detail, it will be without interest. On the other hand, if too much attention is given by

---

[12] A term sometimes used to indicate the high level of excellence in *waka* poetry. The term is probably of Zen origin.

[13] For a translation into English of this section of the *I ching*, see Richard Wilhelm, tr., *The I Ching or Book of Changes*, pp. 122-125. The interpretation of the passage is evidently Zeami's.

the performer to details, the whole performance risks to shrink in scale. Then again, if the actor thinks to play his part as liberally as possible, the opportunities for the audience to witness his skill will be fewer, and there will be a tendency for his performance to become slow and monotonous. An understanding of this distinction is of the greatest importance. An actor might, on first reflection, think that the parts of the play requiring intricate skills should be played in as complex a fashion as possible, while those moments requiring a more general approach should be played as broadly as possible. Yet in fact this kind of distinction cannot be made unless an actor knows the art of *nō* very well indeed. A student must question his teacher closely on such matters, so that these distinctions become clear. There is, however, one general principle that can be kept in mind. For the chant, the dance, and the various sorts of gestures that will be employed, the actor's spirit should be as delicately attuned as possible, but, at the same time, his physical stance should be as relaxed and broad as possible. An actor must comprehend these principles and stick to them.

In general, it can be said that, in the case of the *nō*, an art that is based on general and flexible principles can be made subtle and detailed. But a *nō* that is merely meticulous in conception cannot easily develop on a large and relaxed scale. After all, the small can be contained in the large, but not the large in the small. A great deal of skill needs to be given over to this matter. A *nō* that possesses both these qualities will truly be full and rich. Indeed, when ice formed during the deep cold melts, the ice formed during a brief chilly spell will melt as well.

12. Entering the Realm of Grace

The aesthetic quality of Grace is considered the highest ideal of perfection in many arts. Particularly in the *nō*, Grace can be regarded as the highest principle. However, although the quality of Grace is manifested in performance and audiences give it high appreciation, there are very few actors who in fact possess that quality. This is because they have never had a taste of the real Grace themselves. So it is that few actors have entered this world.

What kind of realm is represented by what is termed Grace? For example, if we take the general appearance of the world and observe the various sorts of people who live there, it might be said that Grace is best represented in the character of the nobility, whose deportment is of such a high quality and who receive the affection and respect not given to others in society. If such is the case, then their dignified and mild appearance represents the essence of Grace. Therefore, the stage appearance of Grace is best indicated by their refined and elegant carriage. If an actor examines closely the nobility's beautiful way of speaking and studies the words and habitual means of expression that such elevated persons use, even to observing their tasteful choice of language when saying the smallest things, such can be taken to represent the Grace of speech. In the case of the chant, when the melody flows smoothly and naturally on the ear and sounds suitably mild and calm, this quality can be said to represent the Grace of music. In the case of the dance, if the actor studies until he is truly fluent, so that his appearance on stage will be sympathetic and his carriage both unostentatious and moving to those who observe him, he will surely manifest the Grace of the dance. When he is acting a part, if he makes his appearance beautiful in the Three Role Types, he will have achieved Grace in his performance. Again, when presenting a role of fearsome appearance, a demon's role for example, even should the actor use a rough manner to a certain extent, he must not forget to preserve a graceful appearance, and he must remember the principles of "what is felt in the heart is ten," and "violent body movements, gentle foot movements," so that his stage appearance will remain elegant. Thus he may manifest the Grace of a demon's role.

An actor must come to grasp those various types of Grace and absorb them within himself; for no matter what kind of role he may assume, he must never separate himself from the virtue of Grace. No matter what the role—whether the character be of high or low rank, a man, a woman, a priest or lay person, a farmer or country person, even a beggar or an outcast—it should seem as though each were holding a branch of flowers in his hand. In this one respect they exhibit the same appeal, despite whatever differences they may show in their social positions. This Flower represents the beauty of their stance in the *nō*; and the ability to reveal this kind of stance in performance represents, of course, its spirit. In order to study the Grace of words, the actor must study the art of composing poetry; and to study the Grace of physical appearance, he must study the aesthetic qualities of elegant costume, so that, in every aspect of his art, no matter how the role may change that the actor is playing, he will always maintain one aspect in his performance that shows Grace. Such it is to know the seed of Grace.

However, it may well happen that an actor will put such an importance on his impersonation of the particulars of his role, regarding this aspect of his performance as the highest of his art, that he will neglect to maintain the beauty of the stance he has properly assumed. Thus he will fail to enter the world of Grace. And if he does not enter into the world of Grace, he cannot approach the level of Highest Fruition. And unless he reaches this highest level of accomplishment, he will never be recognized as a great actor. There are indeed few masters who have attained those heights. Thus an actor must rehearse with the utmost diligence on this critical point of the representation of Grace.

This Highest Fruition of an actor represents precisely the appearance of this deeply beautiful posture. I cannot repeat too often that an actor must rehearse with the need for the proper preparation of his body always in mind. Thus it is of crucial importance that, beginning with the Two Basic Arts down to the specifics of any role that may be played, the stance of the actor be attractive so as to represent this Highest Fruition in every circumstance. If the actor's posture is unattractive, his art will invariably appear vulgar. In any case, whatever gestures may be seen or music may be heard, however great the variety, the fact that the actor's stance is beautifully assumed represents the true attainment of Grace. An actor may be said to have entered the world of Grace when he has of his own accord studied these principles and made himself master of them. If an actor does not work to fulfill them and thinks that, without mastering every aspect of his art, he can still try to attain this Grace, he will, in fact, never know it during his entire lifetime.

13. Paying Heed to the Accumulation of Skills

Studying the art of the *nō*, having the reputation of a superior actor, and rising in merit as the years pass by depends on a proper accumulation of skills. Yet the nature of such an accumulation will differ depending on where the actor lives and performs. Even if he earns a reputation as a fine actor, if the praise he earns is not from those who live in the capital, it can have little significance for him. Even an actor who has earned genuine praise in the capital, should he return to his native place and continue to perform in the countryside, will merely expend his energies in attempting not to forget those means of expression that he learned in the capital, and because of his false sense that he still remembers how to perform properly, he will little by little slacken in his persistence in maintaining his beauty of performance. The result will be an accumulation of bad experiences. Such a stagnation of experience must be shunned.

In the capital, on the other hand, the actor will be performing before discerning spectators so that, should he become careless concerning any element in his art and so fail to progress, he will soon notice a response from his audience; then too, as criticism and comment come to him, he will eventually disregard the unsatisfactory elements in his art, accumulate only positive artistic experiences, and discover that his art has become polished. Of its own accord his skill will become as burnished as a jewel. There is a saying that "sagebrush, which has the ability to bend, even should it grow up among flax plants, will come out straight, without correction, while white sand, when mixed with earth, will become black like the rest."[14] Thus by living in the capital, an actor is in the proper environment, and the insufficiencies in his art will naturally disappear. This gradual lessening of error is in itself the accumulation of good experience. There is no way that an artist can simply set out to pile up these experiences of his own accord. Rather, let me repeat again and again a warning that, if an actor does not take cognizance of his good experiences, they will stagnate and turn into an accumulation of bad experiences.

So it is that even a skilled performer as he grows older will come to depend on his increasingly old-fashioned art, which has become so through an accumulation caused by his own stagnation. Although audiences may dislike his performances, he thinks only that he has been recognized as an artist of great merit for a long time. Thus he does not recognize the real feelings of his audiences. He therefore loses the chance to make his final appearances on the stage successful—such an important opportunity in an actor's career.

All of this is the result of piling up of such bad experiences. The greatest caution must be taken against this.

14. Connecting All the Arts through One Intensity of Mind

It is often commented on by audiences that "many times a performance is effective when the actor does nothing." Such an accomplishment results from the actor's greatest, most secret skill. From the techniques involved in the Two Basic Arts down to all the gestures and the various kinds of Role Playing, all such skills are based on the abilities found in the actor's body. Thus to speak of an actor "doing nothing" actually signifies that interval which exists between two physical ac-

---

[14] An expression widely circulated during the medieval period in various forms, probably originating in the writings of Tseng Ts'an, one of the most important disciples of Confucius.

tions. When one examines why this interval "when nothing happens" may seem so fascinating, it is surely because of the fact that, at the bottom, the artist never relaxes his inner tension. At the moment when the dance has stopped, or the chant has ceased, or indeed at any of those intervals that can occur during the performance of a role, or, indeed, during any pause or interval, the actor must never abandon his concentration but must keep his consciousness of that inner tension. It is this sense of inner concentration that manifests itself to the audience and makes the moment enjoyable.

However, it is wrong to allow an audience to observe the actor's inner state of control directly. If the spectators manage to witness this, such concentration will merely become another ordinary skill or action, and the feeling in the audience that "nothing is happening" will disappear.

The actor must rise to a selfless level of art, imbued with a concentration that transcends his own consciousness, so that he can bind together the moments before and after that instant when "nothing happens." Such a process constitutes that inner force that can be termed "connecting all the arts through one intensity of mind."

"Indeed, when we come to face death, our life might be likened to a puppet on a cart [decorated for a great festival]. As soon as one string is cut, the creature crumbles and fades."[15] Such is the image given of the existence of man, caught in the perpetual flow of life and death. This constructed puppet, on a cart, shows various aspects of himself but cannot come to life of itself. It represents a deed performed by moving strings. At the moment when the strings are cut, the figure falls and crumbles. *Sarugaku* too is an art that makes use of just such artifice. What supports these illusions and gives them life is the intensity of mind of the actor. Yet the existence of this intensity must not be shown directly to the audience. Should they see it, it would be as though they could see the strings

[15] A saying attributed to a priest of the Rinzai sect of Zen Buddhism in Japan, Gettan Sōkō (1316?-1389).

of a puppet. Let me repeat again: the actor must make his spirit the strings, and without letting his audience become aware of them, he will draw together the forces of his art. In that way, true life will reside in his *nō*.

In general, such attitudes need not be limited to the moments involved in actual performance. Morning and night alike, and in all the activities of daily life, an actor must never abandon his concentration, and he must retain his resolve. Thus, if without ever slackening, he manages to increase his skills, his art of the *nō* will grow ever greater. This particular point represents one of the most secret of all the teachings concerning our art. However, in actual rehearsal, there must be within this concentration some variations of tension and relaxation.

15. The Moment of Peerless Charm

The character *myō* in the term *myōsho* [Peerless Charm] means "exquisite" or "delicate." But it also has the meaning of an appearance that transcends any specific form. Such a transcendence of form represents an expression of this Peerless Charm.

When one speaks of such moments in terms of the *nō*, this Charm should exist in every aspect of our art, from the Two Basic Arts to gesture. Yet precisely where can it be located? It seems to be found nowhere. If an actor can possess this arresting power, he must be a performer of surpassing skill. However, if an actor is truly blessed with great talent, he will show from his beginnings some shadow of this Charm. The actor will not himself be conscious of it, but spectators of discernment will always find this quality within him. Ordinary spectators, on the other hand, will merely find that his performances are enjoyable in some mysterious fashion. And indeed even in the case of an actor of the highest skill, he will at best have come only to the realization that he somehow does possess this skill. Still, he will have no consciousness that he is practicing it at any given moment. An actor will possess this quality precisely because he does not recognize it; if such a moment could in any way be put into words, this Charm could no longer exist.

When one ponders carefully the substance of this Peerless Charm, can it not be said that an artist may approach it when he has truly learned his craft and attained Perfect Fluency, when he has transcended all stages of his art to the point where he performs everything with ease and exhibits every skill without care, thus achieving a selfless art that rises above any artifice? When an actor manages to ascend to the aesthetic level of Grace, will he indeed not be somewhat closer to this power of beauty? These matters must be pondered deeply.

16. Judging the Nō

When it comes to making crucial judgments concerning the nō, people invariably have different ideas. It is difficult indeed for any particular nō to match the tastes of everyone. Thus the basis of judgment should be made on the strength of the performances of accomplished actors who enjoy a wide reputation.

First of all, one should look and listen with great care during actual performances so as to understand why some plays succeed and why others do not. Plays that succeed possess three qualities: Sight, Sound, and Heart.

As for the nō that succeeds through Sight, the stage atmosphere will be colorful from the beginning, the dancing and music will have an attractive air, the spectators, noblemen and commoners alike, will be spontaneous in their praise, the atmosphere brilliant. Such is the nō that is effective to the eye. It goes without saying that such a performance will please the discriminating; even those who know nothing of the nō will find such a performance enjoyable. However, concerning such performances, there is one point that an actor must keep in mind. If the performance passes by altogether too well and with too much appeal, and if every aspect seems enjoyable, then the feelings of the audience will tend to become over-stimulated, and their sensibilities in appreciating the details of the acting will be coarsened. For his part, an actor may be impetuous and, since he wants to exhaust every aspect of his art, will make no allowance for a slackening of pace, either for himself or for the audience. In an attempt to make every aspect of the performance successful, a surface brilliance is achieved, but the end results may be unsatisfactory. This kind of abuse arises when the play goes too well. On such an occasion, the play should be performed in a more restrained manner, all the artistic appearances made more moderate, and the eyes and ears of the spectators given some surcease, so that they can have an occasion to rest and breathe easily and the audience can be given the quiet necessary to observe the really skillful elements in the performance. Then, if the results are successful, the plays that follow will seem stronger, so that, whatever the number of plays that may be staged, their fascination for the audience will never be exhausted. So it is that an effective *nō* performance can be said to succeed through the art of Sight.

Nō that can be said to succeed through Sound shows from the very beginning a serious atmosphere. The music and text are chosen in accord with the season [and the time of day], thus creating a gentle, relaxed, and enjoyable effect. Above all, it is the chant that should create the main impression. Only a peerless artist of highest experience can achieve this effect during a performance. However, the kind of sober flavor engendered by such a performance cannot be understood by country audiences and the like.

This kind of *nō*, when performed by a peerless actor, can give rise through his spiritual resources to various aesthetic qualities that make the play become more and more enjoyable as it goes along. In the case of an artist of the second rank, however, whose art has not fully matured, he will cause the day's performance to lag if he decides to follow such a presentation by a famous actor with one of his own in a *nō* that is also of this particular variety. When such a player follows the kind of performance that has successfully created a cool and quiet atmosphere, as he continues on he will only create a gloomy mood in the succeeding plays. An actor must be aware of this difficulty and put his energies into his perform-ance in order to begin to increase the number of stimulating moments in the play, so as to bring an element of surprise to his audience. Of course, as a truly peerless player has naturally a wide repertory and is highly trained in body and mind, his art will be effectively manifested in his dance and chant, so that his performance will naturally progress in an enjoyable manner. A player of the second rank, however, must take great care so that, as the performance continues, the atmos-phere does not go dead. Concerning this point, when thinking to keep up the atmosphere of his performance, the actor must not reveal his methods to the audience. The spectators must merely feel that the performance is enjoyable. Such is the actor's secret, based on long-mastered precedents as to how to perform successfully. All I have written above can explain how a *nō* can succeed through Sound.

When it comes to the *nō* that succeeds through the Heart, a truly gifted actor of *sarugaku*, after he has mastered the whole repertory, will have the ability even when performing a play of no particular distinction in terms of chant, dance, gesture, or plot, to create even in the midst of a certain dullness a particular poetic quality that can move the hearts of his audience. This level of attainment is not usually grasped even by connoisseurs; how much more beyond any imaginings of a country audience must be such an art. Indeed, such a quality must seem to represent the propitious manifestation of an actor of the highest abilities. Such a performance can be termed a *nō* that succeeds through the Heart, a *nō* that surpasses technique, a *nō* that transcends outward manifestion.

An actor must learn to discriminate between the kinds of artistic qualities that display those various differences. There are spectators of discernment who do not really understand the art of the *nō*. On the other hand, there are those spectators who possess a true grasp of the essential nature of the *nō* but who cannot observe subtle differences. Those who have both a practical and a theoretical understanding of *nō* represent the highest level of spectator. For example, there are occasions when a fine performance does not meet with success, and times when an unskilled performance pleases, but no one must use these exceptions as a basis for one's general judgments. For example, truly gifted players customarily have success with outdoor and other large-scale performances, while lesser actors perform profitably at smaller playing areas at country fairs or on other such occasions.

An actor who understands how to make his performance attractive to his audience brings good fortune to the *nō*. Then too, a spectator who understands the heart of the actor as he watches a performance is a gifted spectator. The following might be said concerning making judgments: forget the specifics of a performance and examine the whole. Then forget the performance and examine the actor. Then forget the actor and examine his inner spirit. Then, forget that spirit, and you will grasp the nature of the *nō*.

17. The Matter of Mastering the Chant

There are two aspects to the study of the chant. The person who composes the text should know the principles of music and how to make the words flow together in a euphonious fashion. For his part, the performer who sings must know how to fit the melody to the words and to chant the syllables and words in a clear and correct manner. Since the beauty of the chant derives from the syllables and the words performed, the melodies must be composed in such a way that the pronunciation is always correctly represented, and the linking between the phrases smooth and flexible. When the chant is performed, if the singer has mastered these principles and really knows them well, both the composition and the performance will reinforce each other and produce an enjoyable effect. As this is true, a standard should be established by which the melody is attached to the chant. The flow of the phrases must be attractive, and the sound characteristics of the text must be in harmony with the melody, so that the results will of themselves be musical. That is, the melody provides the basic frame for the musical composition, and the artistic effect derives from the spirit of the performer, who shades the melody in terms of the flow of the phrases. Thus an actor has various elements of music that he must muster—the physical problems of using the breath, the development of his own emotional concentration in order to direct it properly, and the understanding of the melody, as well as the music that lies behind the melody. In terms of practicing the musical aspects of *nō*, the following should be taken to heart: forget the voice and understand the shading of the melody. Forget the melody and understand the pitch. Forget the pitch and understand the rhythm.

In learning the art of musical performance, there is a proper order to be followed: first, the words of the text must be learned thoroughly; then the melody must be mastered; then the actor must learn how to color the melody; finally, he must learn how to apply the proper pitch accent. After all these steps are taken, the actor must concentrate on how to bring his performances to flower. At every stage, an emphasis must be placed on the rhythm. When practicing the voice, miss no occasion to obtain this kind of training, so beneficial to personal development.

Then there is the matter of accent in musical performance. In the case of auxiliary words or particles, the problem is not a serious one. However, mistaken accents on such substantive words as nouns, verbs, and adjectives[16] are harmful. Understanding the importance of this distinction is crucial. Serious study must be given to this point. When speaking of mistaken accents on these substantive words, I refer to pronunciations with improper pitch accent, which affect the meaning of the words. In the case of particles and auxiliary words, the problem has to do with the voicing of such sounds as *te, ni, ha,*

---

[16] That is, independent, uninflected words usually written with Chinese characters.

and the like. Concerning correct pronunciation for these sounds, when the flow of words in the course of the singing moves effectively, even if the pronunciation becomes altered to some extent, so long as the rhythm is correct, the problem is not a serious one. It is said that words that make a heavy or a light effect, that are clear or complex in sound, depend on the forward flow of the text. In addition, there are various customs and rules concerning sound changes when words are juxtaposed together. Study the transmitted teachings carefully on this matter. As concerns particles that come at the end of phrases, such as *ha, ni, no, o, ka, te, mo, shi,* and so forth, even if there should be some deviation in their pronunciation, there will be nothing disagreeable in the sound as long as the melody is tasteful. In other words, the movement of the melody should be supported by these various particles. In the chanting, every syllable must not simply be pronounced in a flat manner, with an equal length and emphasis given to all of them. Those sounds which represent substantive words should be pronounced briskly, so that their meaning remains clear, while the sound of the auxiliary syllables can be rather freely regulated—slow or fast—in order to make the melody more colorful.

[Remember that] the principle of using four basic tones is used [in Chinese].[17]

In *The History of the Former Han* by Pan Ku,[18] it is written [concerning the legendary origin of the melody] that "as for the origins of the twelve-pitch gamut, a man [named Ling Lun] climbed Mount Kun-lun and, hearing the voice of the

[17] Zeami doubtless wished to stress the importance of proper pitch accent for substantive words in Japanese, usually written in Chinese characters, by this reference to the Chinese language. For a concise description of the function of tones in classical Chinese, see James J. Y. Liu, *The Art of Chinese Poetry*, pp. 21-22.

[18] Pan Ku's history was the first of the so-called dynastic histories of China. For a general description of the text and its subject matter, see Burton Watson, *Early Chinese Literature*, pp. 103-109. Zeami's quotation contains minor errors. For an explanation of the significance of the passage in the history of Chinese music, see Kenneth J. DeWoskin, *A Song for One or Two*, pp. 59-61.

male and female phoenix, created the six *ryo* pitches and six *ritsu* pitches of the twelve-pitch gamut." *Ritsu*, since it is derived from the voice of the male phoenix, represents the principle of *yang*. *Ryo*, which imitates the voice of the female phoenix, represents *yin*. *Ritsu* represents the kind of sound that goes from high to low, and the breath is inhaled. *Ryo* represents a sound that goes from low to high, and the breath is exhaled. Breathing appropriate to *ritsu* is produced through a state of tension; *ryo* is produced in a state of ease. Then too, *ritsu* can be considered as appropriate to Non-Being, *ryo* appropriate to Being. Thus, a thin, high voice [a "vertical" voice] is appropriate for *ritsu*, while a thick, low voice [a "horizontal" voice] is appropriate for *ryo*.

In the *Analects*,[19] it is written that "the hides of the bear, the tiger, and the panther are used as targets [for the hunter's] arrow. The tiger is the prince's target, the panther the nobleman's target, and the bear the target of the officers of state." If this sequence is followed, it would doubtless be correct to write "tiger, panther, bear." But for the sake of euphony, the order is changed to "bear, tiger, and panther."

18. The Ultimate Keys of Our Art

The contents of this work have now all been set forth. There is nothing to learn in addition to what has been set down here. Indeed, there is nothing else involved but to "understand the *nō*" with one's very being. If this fundamental principle is not observed, the various matters discussed here will serve no purpose. If an actor really wishes to master the *nō*, he must set aside all other pursuits and truly give his whole soul to our art; then, as his learning increases and his experience grows, he will gradually of himself reach a level of awareness and so come to understand the *nō*.

First of all, an actor must deeply believe what his teacher

---

[19] No such passage appears in the *Analects*, but a somewhat similar one does appear in the *Chou li* or *Rites of Chou*. Both this passage and the preceding section on *The History of the Former Han* were added to Zeami's text in the form of notes, and may not be by his hand.

tells him and take those instructions to heart. The numerous teachings involved are contained in the various points discussed in this book, but the actor must truly master them and engrave them on his heart, so that, when he is actually in a performance, he can try out in practice the various things that he has learned. Then, as a result, he will value those principles, and, as he comes to revere the art of *nō*, he will as time passes come to understand the real secret of success in our art. In whatever artistic pursuit, one studies and then understands, studies and then understands, so that he will know how to carry out his art in actual practice. In *sarugaku* as well, one must study and learn, so that these various principles can be put into practice.

All these secret teachings can be summed up by saying that an actor must continually earn mastery through constant practice, from his apprenticeship through his old age. When I speak of studying through old age, I refer to the fact that from the time of an actor's apprenticeship until the peak of his maturity there are various arts that must be mastered. It is only from the time that an actor passes forty that he can slowly begin to make use of restraint in his physical performance. In other words, he must learn the means of artistic expression appropriate for an actor of his age. When the actor passes fifty, then he can begin to use the technique of "doing nothing." This represents a crucial stage in an actor's career. The first thing to learn at this point is the necessity to limit the kinds of plays in the actor's repertory. His musical performance now becomes the center of his style of performance, his acting style becomes simpler, and his dancing and gestures grow more restrained. He should only give a hint of his former colorful appearance. In fact, the art of music remains the one area in which an actor at this age can excel. This is true because an older voice will have exhausted its natural and untrained qualities, and the voice that remains will be highly polished, in whatever style of vocal production the actor may wish to use; thus whatever music is chanted, the results will always be enjoyable. This is a sure means to achieve a successful performance. Thus an older actor should learn carefully to make his age serve his own artistic purposes and work all the harder to train himself appropriately.

Concerning roles that can be played by older actors, old men and women are doubtless the most appropriate. However, depending on the strong points of a particular actor, he may not necessarily be limited to these two. Still, an actor who wishes to create an atmosphere of serenity in his performance will find the roles of older characters best suited to him. If his special strength lies in roles demanding energetic movement, however, those will not be suitable for the aesthetic qualities appropriate to the art of older actors. In any case, within these limits, he should perform his dances and gestures while limiting himself to six-tenths or seven-tenths of the energy he put forth before, following the principle of "what is felt by the heart is ten," so as to perform in a manner appropriate to his age. Such is the means to master the art suitable for the older actor.

In our Kanze school, there is one phrase that is of infinite value concerning the fundamentals of any artistic accomplishment: an actor must never forget the experiences he has undergone as a beginning artist. In the transmitted teaching, there are three explanations provided for this. Accordingly:

—he must never forget the fresh experiences he first went through as a young performer.

—at each level of accomplishment, there are new levels of fresh experience that the actor must encounter for the first time, as though he were a beginner, and then never forget.

—after the actor becomes older, there are still new stages of fresh experience that must never be forgotten.

Here are the teachings contained in these maxims in more detail.

Concerning the maxim that "he must never forget the fresh experiences he first went through as a young performer," it can be said that, if the actor retains the feelings he had at that time, he will profit from them in many ways as he grows older. As the expression has it, "an understanding of errors in the past will turn them into advantages in the future." Or, "seeing the cart in front turn over serves as a warning to the cart that follows." Forgetting the arts one has learned as a beginner amounts in fact to forgetting the skills an actor may possess at a later point in his career. The fact that his art has been perfected and his reputation has been made can only be the result of the development of his own skill. But if he does not take cognizance of how his skills have improved, he will unknowingly revert to the level he possessed as a beginner. Such a reversal means that his art is actually degenerating. His ability to maintain a sense of his present level of accomplishment shows that he has not forgotten the skills learned as a young performer. I cannot stress this principle too strongly: if an actor loses his memory of his unmatured skills, he will be forced to revert to them. On the other hand, if he does not forget them, his later accomplishments will be genuine. And, if they are genuine, his abilities, as they increase, will insure that his art can never retrogress. Thus, this truth can serve as a distinction between truth and error.

Young actors must therefore take cognizance of the current level of their accomplishment, realize that they are still only beginners, and understand that they must not lose sight of their own skills that still remain to be developed. In this way, they can truly work to lift the level of their art. To lose consciousness of the level of one's ability is to forget how to advance in the art; under such circumstances, an artist's skill will not increase. Therefore, young artists must never lose their perceptions of their actual level of ability.

Secondly, there is the principle that "at each level of accomplishment, there are new levels of fresh experience that the actor must encounter for the first time, as though he were a beginner, and then never forget." This means that, for the actor, from his beginnings through the height of his career and into his old age, there are always various suitable means of expression he must practice and learn. On all these occasions he can be seen as a beginner. Therefore, if at each stage he abandons and forgets what has come before, he will only possess the artistic ability that matches what he is doing at that particular moment in his career. If, on the other hand, he has managed to maintain in himself all the skills that he has previously mastered, so that he can still make use of them, then he can perform in an ever-increasing variety of styles. These "new skills" refer to those he has learned for the first time at every successive stage in his career. Maintaining them all and combining them together at one time means that he has forgotten none of them. It is just through such efforts that a *shite* becomes an artist of wide-ranging abilities. Thus one must never forget what he has learned at each stage of his career.

Finally, "after the actor becomes older, there are still new stages of fresh experience that must never be forgotten." Truly, although there are limits on a human life, the *nō* never comes to an end. If an actor has mastered every technique appropriate to each stage in his career, then when it comes time to learn what is correct for an older actor, he will still be able to enjoy a new experience even at this late stage in his career. If an actor still possesses this attitude when he reaches this high level, his art will still contain everything about the *nō* that he has managed to learn before. When he passes the age of fifty, as I have said, an actor need have no other plan than to "do nothing special." To face the challenge of having no other technique than to "do nothing special"—is the art of an older actor really so different than that of a beginner?

So it is that if an actor manages to live his whole life without forgetting how and what he has learned at any one time in his career, the level of his art will steadily increase during his last years, and his abilities will never degenerate. To live one's life without ever exhausting the depths of the *nō* represents the most profound principle of our school, a principle that must be passed on from child to grandchild, generation to generation as a secret teaching of our house. Passing on the importance of these attitudes I have described above will serve as a means to develop the artistry of all generations to come. On the other hand, if an actor forgets this "experience of a beginner," he will surely not be able to pass the conception along to others in later generations. An artist must not forget this "experience of a beginner," but must convey it to those who follow, for countless generations.

In addition to what I have written here, another who studies the *nō* may, depending on his own abilities and discernment, be able to discover still other truths.

All of the *Teachings on Style and the Flower*, beginning with the chapter called "The Practice of the *Nō* in Relation to the Age of the Actor" down to the "Separate Secret Teaching," is a secret document that makes clear the *nō* by using the metaphor of the flower. That text represents an account of various elements in the art of my father Kan'ami, set down twenty years after his death, and serves as a record of what I learned from him. The present treatise, on the other hand, represents discoveries that have occurred to me from time to time concerning the *nō* over a period of forty years, down to the time of my own advanced age. Summing them up, I have written out my observations in six sections and twelve parts,[20] which I leave behind as a memento of my art.

Ōe 31 [1424], 1st day of the 6th month
Zeami

This teaching was passed on by Zeami himself for the succeeding generations of his house and should not be shown to actors from other troupes. Luckily, thanks to the Will of Heaven, which knows that my heart reveres the art of the *nō*, this manuscript has come into my hands. This secret teaching forms the very core of the art of our school, and it has been written down to guide the art of our family. It is a text of fearsome power. Thus it must not be shown carelessly to others.

Eikyō 9 [1437], 8th month, 8th day
Komparu Zenchiku[21]

[20] The indication of twelve parts suggests that the manuscript was originally arranged in some different fashion.

[21] Komparu's signature is an attribution; the identity of the writer is not altogether certain.

Disciplines for the Joy of Art
(Yūgaku shūdō fūken)

In *The Book of Songs*, there is the following line of poetry: "The jeweled, tailed *liuli* bird."[1] Both adjectives employed suggest "small" and the term *liuli* refers to the species of bird.[2] According to one commentary,[3] the meaning of the line is as follows: "The officials of Wei at first appeared effective, but upon maturing, they accomplished little of note. They were just like the *liuli* bird." The *liuli* bird is an owl.

The suggestion therefore is that the owl is beautiful while still a young bird but eventually takes on a ridiculous appearance. In the same way it can be said that, in the development of any human art or skill, if this art is already fully developed when the person is still young, the chances are strong that his accomplishments will decline as he grows older. This is because in all the arts, the skills that are learned must suit the physical development of the performer in order to produce truly good results. In general, only an art that finds consonance with the personal circumstances of the artist can be said to be truly fulfilled. What, then, is the kind of deportment that corresponds to the level of development of a young actor? It is indeed fitting for an actor at such a stage of development to perform imperfectly, without any full un-

[1] The poem is in Book Three of *The Book of Songs* (Shih ching) (Mao #37). For a full translation, see Arthur Waley, *The Book of Songs*, No. 123, p. 114.

[2] Here Zeami cites the meaning assigned to the line by the Mao commentary, the earliest systematic commentary on the poems, compiled around 150 B.C. See Burton Watson, *Early Chinese Literature*, pp. 207-208.

[3] Here Zeami refers to a later commentary on *The Book of Songs* by Cheng Hsüan (A.D. 127-200). See Watson, *Early Chinese Literature*, pp. 212-213.

derstanding, still lacking a full range of techniques. Then, as he grows older and continues to mature, his range of skills can be extended, and his ripened art will be appropriate to the level of an adult in his prime. Thus, can it not be said that the deportment of a young actor who can already exhibit the full range of skills is not a suitable one for his age? Because this is so, his artistic development cannot proceed in the proper fashion. It is precisely because his skills are childlike and incomplete that, as he develops to maturity, his abilities will increase in a natural fashion appropriate to his growth and so create an impression of correspondence. Thus one can apply the meaning of this line of poetry from *The Book of Songs* to our art as well: the young owl may be beautiful in its nest, but as it inevitably must grow, it will become ungainly.

It is by no means appropriate to teach any kind of Role Playing as part of the skills needed by a younger performer. Rather, he should be taught to master the Two Basic Arts of song and dance. Those might be described as the vessel into which the actor's art can later be poured. Song and Dance are truly the skills that unite every performing art. Their usefulness is not limited to our art alone. These Two Arts form the fundamentals of the *nō*. If an actor has truly mastered them, then gradually, as he grows to adulthood, his range of skills will develop, and the time will come for him to undertake the Three Roles. On that occasion, the fact that in whatever role he undertakes his chanting will be full of feeling and his dancing enjoyable will be due to the virtue of his having accumulated and held onto the fundamentals of his art. Let me repeat again, one must think of the Two Arts as fundamental vessels of our art. The art of performing particular roles must be based in turn on them.

When one examines more closely the curious fact that a young performer who seems enjoyable will later seem inadequate, the following becomes clear. If the various skills of the young performer include an ability to play a variety of roles, the spectators will be astonished and will soon come to the conclusion that he is some sort of prodigy; therefore they will come to regard him as an already accomplished actor. However, this assumption results from the fact that the young actor merely has a colorful appearance; thus there is every reason to think that his reputation cannot continue. [There are several factors involved in this.] First of all, those who see the young actor may overestimate his abilities, since they are surprised to see that, although so young, he is already skilled in so many arts. The naturally lovely appearance of a child represents another factor. The charming sound of a youthful voice represents still another. Yet these are all merely beauties that must disappear with time. They cannot continue on. The final result of the spectators' reaction to the young performer as a prodigy will be that, when the actor does reach maturity, they will no longer find anything novel in his performance. Nothing of the beauty of his youthful figure will remain once he becomes a man. His voice will change and its sounds will no longer be the same.

Indeed, while a well-drilled performance may be fully achieved by a young performer with a childlike physique, after he reaches maturity he will have no new resources, his artistry will become insufficient, and the very Substance of his performance will change, so that he will not be able to master its Function in performance. The Substance of a youthful actor's colorful performance must naturally be largely lost; the effect will seem like a landscape in which the trees have lost their leaves and flowers and stand bare, as in winter. Therefore it is not surprising that when many actors become adults, their artistic performances excite no enthusiasm at all.

Concerning this point, as I said before, a young actor must be thoroughly trained in the Two Arts to the point of mastery. Instruction should not be given in arts related to Role Playing; this element of the training should be left incomplete. Then, as the actor grows to adulthood, the appropriate time will come for him to learn the Three Role Types, so that, as he gradually accumulates these various skills, his art, which grows along with his physique, will show that he can truly extend his mastery. Chant and dance serve as fundamentals for all the performing arts and occupy a crucial position for a beginner or an experienced player, old or young, child or adult actor alike. Role Playing, on the other hand, is limited to the art of the *nō*, so that if a performer concentrates on it completely, his level of skill can never be properly broad. A child actor whose body has been overtrained on a small scale will only achieve what is possible at his age and cannot continue to make progress. Even if he is seen as a wonder because of the roles he can play at such an age, his flower will only bloom for a certain time. He will be like the *liuli* bird, that owl that is only beautiful when small.

It is written in Confucius that "there are shoots whose lot it is to spring up but never to flower; others whose lot it is to flower, but never bear fruit."[4] There is much to ponder here concerning the appropriate steps in an actor's training, arranged in terms of *jo, ha,* and *kyū* throughout his life.

When the actor is still a child and is learning the fundamentals of the Two Arts, if he is naturally blessed with a pleasing skill in movement and an ability to chant in a moving fashion, it can be said that he has already reached the stage of the seedling. Yet, how ought seedlings to grow? If well watered, they will grow naturally by themselves, it seems. Then, when the seedlings have grown firm, they will be transplanted; and eventually, as their roots grow longer, the weeds will be pulled out, the plants will be watered, they will wait for the rain, and, finally, they will reach the stage of development when rice stalks appear. When it comes time for those stalks to ripen, they will already have taken on the appropriate coloring, they will no longer require the rain water they had waited for, and they will now await the sun in order to dry in its strong rays. Through these various means, the plants will be fully ripened.

In terms of practicing the art of the *nō*, an actor at the beginning of his career might be considered a seedling that, nurtured by the Two Arts, has already begun to blossom, so

---

[4] See Arthur Waley, tr., *The Analects of Confucius,* p. 143.

that even as he reaches his maturity, he will have mastered his art to a level that will permit no decline. He will be prepared as well to realize that his art may still show imperfections as yet unapparent to him [but which his audiences may recognize] so that, when he becomes an older actor, his ability to move his spectators will always increase. Such a training represents a consciousness of true ripening on the part of the actor.

In Buddhist teaching, there is the admonition that to receive the law is easy, but to keep it is difficult. This difficulty comes from the fact that there are occasions when we are all led astray through a stubborn adherence to our own ideas. Let me repeat again, an actor must always be ready to consider the existence of faults of which he himself may not be conscious. If an actor is not aware that such faults exist, then through negligence, his art may alter and lessen. Such an actor resembles a plant that, although it has grown steadily, is beaten down by the wind and rain and so does not ripen but only rots and decays. The three stages of growth—from seedling to a first flowering to a final ripening—all of these, as I have said, can be compared to the actor's level of training throughout his life, which can be represented as well by the stages of *jo, ha,* and *kyū.*

In the Heart of Wisdom Sutra it is written that "Form is no other than Emptiness, Emptiness is no other than Form."[5] In all the performing arts, both Form and Emptiness can be said to exist. In the case of the *nō,* once the stages of the seedling, the first flowering, and the true ripening have occurred, and the actor has reached the stage of Perfect Fluency in his performance, he will subjectively feel himself at the level where any appropriate skill can be summoned of itself for any sort of performance. He will truly have reached the level where "Form is no other than Emptiness" [when the actor's uncon-

[5] A crucial passage from the opening passage of the *Prajñāpāramitā hṛdaya sūtra* (Jap. Hanna shingyō) [Heart of Wisdom Sutra], a text widely circulated and studied in Japan at Zeami's time. See D. T. Suzuki, *Essays in Zen Buddhism,* 3rd Series, p. 192.

scious intensity of mind produces spontaneously all effects of performance that can consciously be recognized]. On the other hand, if such an effortless art is regarded as the highest level of perfection attainable, then what of the remaining "Emptiness [that] is no other than Form," which is actually an even higher level of accomplishment? Could this represent the case of one who thinks he has obtained enlightenment and has not? After all, the danger of an artistic error that lies beyond the subjective evaluation of the artist is ever present, even at the level where "Form is no other than Emptiness." Still, if a truly superior actor no longer has fears about any possible faults that may lie beyond the bounds of his own sense of himself, he will be able to act in any kind of performance with ease and confidence. His art may be unorthodox, yet it will nevertheless be enjoyable, lying as it does outside the real of "right" or "wrong," "good" or "bad;" his accomplishment might be described as that art that exists when "Emptiness is no other than Form." As his errors themselves are effective, they can no longer be termed errors. Such an actor need not concern himself then over errors that lie outside his consciousness.

In the art of poetry as well, one is warned against the error of repeating the same word in a poem. Still, in the Preface to the *Kokinshū*, there is the following verse.[6]

Naniwazu ni	In Naniwazu
Saku ya kono hana	*It must be blooming, that flower:*
Fuyugomori	After being closed up all winter
Ima wa harube to	Now that it is spring
Saku ya kono hana.	*It must be blooming, that flower.*

This poem shows a particularly conspicuous example of repetition, yet it is a fine poem and achieves an artistic level where

---

[6] The *Kokinshū* (Collection of Ancient and Modern Times) was compiled about A.D. 905 and was the first imperial anthology of Japanese *waka*. Ki no Tsurayuki (A.D. 884-946), who wrote the Japanese preface, cites there the poem quoted by Zeami as an early example of *waka*.

such criticism no longer applies. Indeed the poem has come to be regarded as a prototype of *waka* poetry.

Then again, there is a famous poem of Fujiwara no Teika.[7]

Koma tomete	Stopping my horse,
Sode uchi harau	There is no shelter
Kage mo nashi	Where I can brush my sleeves—
Sano no watari no	The crossing at Sano
Yuki no yūgure.	In the snow at dusk.

The poem is very well known, and of course when we hear it we are touched; yet it is difficult to point out precisely what the elements are in this poem that make it so moving. It seems merely to concern itself with a scene in which a traveler finds himself in a snowstorm during his journey and searches for a shelter to which he can repair. As I myself am not an adept in the study of poetry, I wondered if the poem had some other nuance of meaning. I asked the opinion of one who knows the art of poetry well, but he simply replied that the art of this poem rests on the surface. If that is the case, the feeling we get from the poem is evidently not one that records the poet's appreciation of the snowy scene but only seems to express in a simple fashion the poet's feelings as he stands by a mountain river and can neither see where he is nor find suitable shelter; the poem is merely a travel scene. Therefore, as concerns the skill of a truly great artist such as Fujiwara Teika, there must exist some profound and undefinable quality in his art [that is nevertheless deeply moving]. There is a teaching in Tendai Buddhism that says, "cut off all verbal expression, transcend thought, and enter the Realm of Peerless Charm."[8] Can we say that this "Realm of Peerless Charm" is represented in Teika's poem? In our art as well, when a perfected level of accomplishment has been reached, then, just as in this poem by Teika, there will seem to be no artistic

[7] The poem is No. 671 in the *Shinkokinshū* (New Collection of Ancient and Modern Times), completed in A.D. 1206. Fujiwara Teika (A.D. 1162-1241) was one of the compilers and the supreme poet of his generation.

[8] The source of this quotation has not been identified.

craft involved, no concern over theatrical effect; rather, the actor is able to transmit an emotional state to his audiences that cannot be articulated in words. As a result, his troupe will be praised everywhere, and the actor himself will be one who has truly attained a Peerless level in his art.

In the *Analects*, it is written as follows:[9]

> Once Tzu-kung said, "If I were to be compared with something, what might that be?" Confucius replied, "You might be compared to a vessel." (According to the explanation of K'ung An-kuo[10] this means, "you are a man of capacity.") When Tzu-kung asked, "what kind of vessel?" Confucius replied, "A *hu lien* vessel." (According to the explanation of Pao Hsien,[11] this means a sacrificial, sacred vessel.)

Now, how does this example of the vessel apply to our art of the *nō*? First of all, the actor who has gone on from the Two Arts and Three Role Types to master every variety of skill may be said to be just such a "man of capacity." One who has mastered every style of performance and has developed within himself the ability to manifest a wide range of Role Types is such a man. One whose art can give rise to sights and sounds of beauty through the Two Arts and Three Role Types, extending to all aspects of his art, and whose artistic skills are without limit—such is the "man of capacity," who is a true vessel of our art.

As for the principle of Being and Non-Being [expressed in the doctrines of Buddhism], Being might be said to represent an external manifestation that can be seen with the eyes. Non-Being can be said to represent the hidden, fundamental readiness of mind that signifies the vessel of all art [since a vessel

[9] The quotation is from Book V, Section 3. For the passage in context, see Arthur Waley, *The Analects of Confucius*, p. 107.

[10] K'ung An-kuo (2nd century B.C.) was traditionally regarded as the compiler of an important commentary on the *Analects*. The work is not now considered by his hand. See ibid., p. 71.

[11] Pao Hsien (6 B.C.-A.D 65) helped compile an important commentary on the *Analects*. See ibid.

itself is empty]. It is the fundamental Non-Being that gives rise to the outward sense of Being [in the nō]. For example, quartz represents a completely transparent substance that of itself is clear, without color or design; yet from it, fire and water can be born.[12] If elements so different in character as fire and water can issue from this colorless matter, what chain of cause and effect can bring this about?

There is a certain poem,[13] as follows:

Sakuragi wa	Break open the cherry tree
Kudakite mireba	And look at it:
Hana mo nashi	There are no flowers,
Hana koso haru no	For they themselves have bloomed
Sora ni sakikere.	In the spring sky.

[So it is with the nō.] What gives the actor the seeds for endless flowering in every aspect of his art is that interior spiritual power that lies within him. And, just as pure quartz gives birth to fire and water, and just as the cherry tree gives birth to flowers and fruits of a different nature from itself, so a truly gifted actor carries out his interior artistic intentions in myriad ways through his artistic performances, and may truly be called a "man of capacity," the vessel of our art.

Indeed, in the meritorious, life-sustaining art of the nō, there are many elements of nature—flowers, birds, the wind, the moon—that adorn it. The world of nature is the vessel that gives birth to all things, alive and inert alike, in all the four seasons—flowers and leaves, snow and the moon, mountains and seas together. To make all this multitude of things an adornment for our art, an actor must become one in spirit with the vessel of nature and achieve in the depths of the art of the nō an ease of spirit that can be compared to the boundlessness of that nature itself, thus to achieve at last the Art of the Flower of Peerless Charm.

[12] The source and precise significance of this statement have not been determined.

[13] A similar poem can be found in a collection compiled by the Zen Buddhist priest Ikkyū (A.D. 1394-1481), but the author has not been identified.

Notes on the Nine Levels
(Kyūi)

The Flower of the Upper Three Levels

1. The art of the flower of peerless charm "In Silla, in the dead of the night, the sun shines brightly."[1]——The meaning of the phrase Peerless Charm surpasses any explanation in words and lies beyond the workings of consciousness. It can surely be said that the phrase "in the dead of night, the sun" exists in a realm beyond logical explanation. Indeed, concerning the Grace of the greatest performers in our art, there are no words with which to praise it, [as that Grace gives rise to] the moment of Feeling that Transcends Cognition, and to an art that lies beyond any level that the artist may have consciously attained. Such surely represents the level of the Flower of Peerless Charm.

2. The art of the flower of profundity "Snow covers a thousand mountains; why is there one peak that is not white?"[2]——In ancient days, someone said that "because Mount Fuji is so high, the snow there cannot melt." A man of T'ang [China] reproved him, saying, "it is rather because Mount Fuji is so deep." Indeed the greatest heights are equivalent to great depths. There are limits to heights. Yet the depths cannot be measured. Thus, cannot the image of depth conveyed by the

---

[1] A phrase often cited, in a slightly different form, in a variety of texts by Zen priests of the period, such as Musō Kokushi (A.D. 1275-1351).

[2] Another Zen saying that appears, in various versions, in a number of texts circulated at this time in Japan, among them the Hsü-t'ang ho-shang yü (Jap. *Kidō oshō goroku*) [The Sayings of Preceptor Hsü-t'ang]. Hsü-t'ang (A.D. 1185-1269) was a priest of the Ch'an [Jap. Zen] sect. The passage is located in Book 2.

one snowless peak amid a thousand mountains covered with snow serve to convey the sense of the Flower of Profundity?

3. The art of the flower of tranquillity "Piling up snow in a silver bowl."[3]——Piling snow in a silver bowl, the hues that derive from the pure, clean white light, an appearance that gives rise to a real sense of gentleness—can it not be said that such represents the Flower of Tranquillity?

The Middle Three Levels

4. The art of the true flower "In the bright mists the sun is setting, and all the mountains become crimson."[4]——In the blue heavens, a spot of bright light: as far as the eye can see, the countless mountains stand revealed in utter clearness— such is the way of the True Flower. This level is superior to the way of Broad Skill and represents the moment when the actor begins to enter into the Realm of the Flower.

5. The art of broad mastery "To describe fully the spirit of the clouds on the mountains, the moon on the sea."[5]—— When the essence of mountains ringed by clouds and the moon shining on the sea, indeed when all that the eye can absorb of the vast panorama of the green mountains can be fully recounted, then the stage of mastery appropriate to the Art of Broad Mastery has been achieved. At this level, the actor can move either forward or backward: the crossroads are here.

6. The art of early beauty "What the world calls the Way

---

[3] A passage found in Section 13 of the *Pi-yen lu* (The Blue Cliff Records) compiled by Yüan-wu (A.D. 1036-1135) and widely circulated in Japan as the *Hekiganroku*. For a translation of the passage, see R.D.M. Shaw, tr., *The Blue Cliff Records*, pp. 65-67.

[4] The precise source of this quotation has not been determined.

[5] The phrase is adapted from *The Blue Cliff Records*, Section 53. See R.D.M. Shaw, pp. 177-178.

is not the True Way."[6]——While first walking the True Way, the actor must follow the various other Ways as well. If he does so, he can show the beauty he has achieved since the beginning of his training. Thus, the Art of Early Beauty provides the first means to begin to master the nine levels.

The Bottom Three Levels

7. The art of strength and delicacy   "The shadow of the metal hammer moving; the cold gleam of the sacred sword."[7]—— The moving shadow of the metal hammer represents an artistic appearance of strong movement. The cold gleam of the sacred sword represents a cold and restrained performance in which a certain delicacy also plays a part.

8. The way of strength and crudeness   "Three days after its birth, a tiger wants to eat an ox."[8]——A tiger three days after its birth can be said to show an energetic and forceful spirit. On the other hand, to eat an entire ox is merely coarse.

9. The way of crudeness and leadenness   "The five skills of the flying squirrel."——Confucius[9] said, "The flying squirrel has five skills. He can climb trees, swim in the water, dig holes, fly, and run. Yet in none of these talents does he exceed his lowly station."[10] In an art that does not show some Delicacy within Strength, the results will be coarse and leaden.

---

[6] That is, what the world calls the Way of *nō* is Role Playing, yet the True Way represents the Two Basic Arts. The phrase is an adaption of the opening of Section One of the *Tao Te Ching* of Lao Tzu. See Arthur Waley, tr., *The Way and Its Power*, p. 141. Zeami has slightly changed the emphasis of the original.

[7] A similar passage appears in Section 12 of *The Blue Cliff Records*. See R.D.M. Shaw, *The Blue Cliff Records*, pp. 59-60.

[8] A similar phrase appears in Section 27 of the *Shih-men wen-tzu ch'an* (Jap. *Sekimon moji zen*) [Zen of the Stone Gate Inscription], compiled by the Chinese Ch'an priest Hui-hung (A.D. 1071-1128).

[9] The phrase does not originate in Confucius but in the writings of the Confucian scholar Hsün Ch'ing (Hsun-tzu), c. 300 B.C. See note 10.

[10] See Homer H. Dubs, tr., *The Works of Hsüntze*, p. 35.

The Order in Which to Study the Nine Levels

It is commonly said that one should study first the middle three levels, next the upper three, and finally the lower three.

As a beginning toward learning the art of *nō*, the various aspects of the Two Arts must be thoroughly practiced, so as to achieve the level of Early Beauty. When this level has been thoroughly mastered through study, and when the actor has in turn developed the beauty he has gained since the beginning of his training, he is already in the realm of Broad Mastery. At this stage, all kinds of roles are studied thoroughly, and the actor broadens his art in every direction while still keeping the True Way [of the Two Basic Arts], so that all comes to fruition at the level of the True Flower. Thus, this level can be said to serve as the turning point at which the actor expands his mastery to the Three Role Types. This level is also the crucial crossroad where the actor attains the Flower of Perfect Fluency, and his enlightenment concerning the Way of his art can be manifested in his appearance. At this level, the actor can look below him at the levels of mastery he had previously achieved; now he occupies a position of the Highest Fruition, an ease that represents the Flower of Tranquillity.

Then, above this level still, the actor achieves the peerless art of Grace, and his performances can manifest that beauty that surpasses the difference between the adorned and the unadorned; such is the level called the Flower of Profundity. Then, still above this, exists that level that no words can describe, where the workings of the spirit and their manifestation in performance can no longer be divided: such is the Art of the Flower of Peerless Charm, which represents the highest reaches of our art.

In general, the point of departure for all three upper levels of our art rests in the Art of Broad Mastery. This level provides the basis for all the skills of the *nō* and serves as a means to nurture the seed of every artistic Flower, be it broad or delicate in scale. This level represents the crossroads from which these broad and delicate skills may either develop or wither away.

Those who grow to gain real Flower will achieve the level of the Art of the True Flower. Those who cannot achieve this will sink down to the lower three levels.

The lower three levels represent the rapid currents of theatrical art; they can be divided from the rest and do not constitute an important element in our training. On occasion, when an actor has acquired the three middle levels and has gone on to master the upper three as well, and has achieved the level of Perfect Fluency and the Flower of Peerless Charm, he may then reverse himself and sometimes for his own amusement select the manner of the lower three levels; and should he perform on these levels of skill, something mild and approachable will be found in his performance. However, from the beginning there have been artists of great ability who, while they have mastered the upper three levels of the Flower, have declined to descend to make use of the lowest three levels in their own performances. Their choice might be likened to the old expression, "an elephant does not amuse himself by walking the path of a rabbit."[11] I know of no one other than my late father Kan'ami who was able to perform in all styles, from high to low. Apart from him, among all the heads of the various troupes, there were many who studied to achieve the level of Broad Mastery but were not able to ascend to the level of the True Flower, and so sank back to the three lowest levels of skill, thus never finally gaining a reputation in the capital. Indeed even today there are those who begin their study at the lower three levels in order to achieve their art. Such is not the proper way to proceed. So it is that many actors can never enter at all into the nine levels.

It can be said, therefore, that as a means to enter into the three lower levels, three possibilities are available. In the case of the superior actor who begins by learning his art at the middle levels, then proceeds to the higher levels and finally

[11] The phrase is based on one from the *Cheng-tao ke* (Jap. *Shōdōka*) [The Song of Enlightenment] by the Chinese priest Yung-chia (A.D. 665-713) of the T'ien-t'ai (Jap. Tendai) sect. For a translation of the passage, see D. T. Suzuki, *Manual of Zen Buddhism*, p. 121.

descends to the lower levels, he will give a superior performance by using the techniques of the three lower levels as well.
An actor who begins at the level of Broad Mastery in the
middle level and then descends to the lower levels can only
exhibit the artistic strength appropriate to the Art of Strength
and Delicacy, or Strength and Crudeness. In addition, those
who vainly attempt to begin at the lower three levels can
hardly be said to have entered into the nine levels in any
fashion, as their art does not follow the proper path and
cannot even be said to have a name. Such men, even though
they yearn for the art of the three lower levels, cannot even
achieve the skills appropriate to them. It is unthinkable that
such actors could even reach the middle three levels.

Finding Gems and
Gaining the Flower *(Shūgyoku tokka)*

1. QUESTION: Concerning the presentation of *saru-gaku*, suppose that an actor has rehearsed and learned his art in accordance with his own development and has studied his art in every detail, and, with the value of long experience, has reached the limit of his capacities. Why is it then that, although he neglects nothing, it may well occur that some of his particular performances are successful and some are not? What is the reason for this?

ANSWER: In the case of any artistic endeavor, not just in the *nō*, there are elements that give rise to successful and unsuccessful performances. Indeed it may be said that there are occasions when human strength seems of no avail. Even if an actor has truly practiced his art and has achieved a level of real fluency, why is it that he cannot know the reasons that brought forth success or failure? It might seem that such reasons may have to do with deficiencies in rehearsal or with negligence; yet why is it that, although the same artist is presenting the same performance, what succeeded the day before will, for some reason or other, fail the day after? Somehow this seems a mysterious riddle, but those of us who practice this life-lengthening art of the *nō*, borrowing the beauties of nature as our means, must find a way to manage, even when the situation is not easy; it is naturally our wish that a means can be found to deal with these difficulties.

The reason that the same actor who performs with the same highly developed skill will achieve different results from different performances may well be because, depending on the occasion, the balance between *yin* and *yang* may not be in harmony [with the rhythm of his performance]. Conditions vary because of the four seasons, day and night, morning and evening. The nature of the audience itself changes. Sometimes it is made up of the nobility, sometimes commoners. The playing spaces, too, range from large to small. If the first sound made by the actor after sensing this changing atmosphere is inappropriate, or if the pitch of the music is not suitable, the performer and the audience will not be in harmony. Therefore, the actor must put himself thoroughly in accord with the atmosphere of the occasion so that his chant will suit the situation and cause the spectators to issue cries of appreciation. Such is the way to begin a harmonious performance.

Then again, there are variations due to warm and cold weather, day and night, morning and evening. The sound of the music must harmonize with those factors for good results. Cold weather is related to *yin*, and warm weather to *yang*; appropriately, therefore, bright music should be performed to balance cold weather, and melancholy music played to counteract the warm weather. Concerning the matter of harmonizing bright and melancholy, if the atmosphere at the place of performance is gloomy, because of the weather, and the mood seems somehow forlorn, the actor should grasp the precise nature of this condition and use a bright voice, which might be described by the following poem:[1]

> The moon is serenely reflected on the stream,
> The breeze passes softly through the pines,
> Perfect silence, reigning unruffled—
> What is it for?

He should blend it with a relatively easy and lengthy melody, so as to obtain a proper vocal synthesis. He can thus bring about a regulation of the atmosphere, and when this is achieved, actor and audience share the same feelings. When this musical atmosphere is reflected in the visual aspects of the performance as well, the audience will be stimulated to find the performance

---

[1] These lines are taken from the *Cheng-tao ke* (Jap. *Shōdōka*) [The Song of Enlightenment] by the Chinese T'ien-t'ai (Jap. Tendai) priest Yung-chia (A.D. 665-713). For a translation of the text, see D. T. Suzuki, *Manual of Zen Buddhism*, p. 112.

truly moving. When the musical elements can completely unite the feelings of an actor and audience, the presentation will achieve genuine success.

On the other hand, when the atmosphere of the performance seems basically bright, the breath used in the actor's vocal production should be well controlled, and he should choose as the basis for his performance a dark voice, which might be described by the following poem:[2]

> In the midst of the night
> The raven, tinged with snow,
> Flies off.

He will thus achieve a mutual harmony and appeal to the feelings and senses of the spectators, thereby demonstrating the effectiveness of his musical art. On an occasion when the performance is held on a fall evening, or during the winter, although the sun may be bright and the assembled audience remains excited and bustling and does not quiet down, the actor should use a voice containing both bright and dark elements so that the immediate mood of the spectators can be matched. The musical atmosphere created by the *shite* will come to move the audience and reinforce the visual aspects of the performance. As the actor continues to chant, the spectators will be drawn to the performer's physical appearance, producing a powerful effect. If the audience is as one person in praise of the beauty of the emotions shared with the actor, an ideal performance will truly have been achieved. The fundamental principle for such a success involves the transfer by the actor of the musical atmosphere that he first creates to the visual aspects of his performance. In *A Mirror Held to the Flower*, I stressed the principle of "Communication first by Sound, then by Sight." This conception is closely related to what I have explained here.

---

[2] The line can be found among various Zen texts included in the Sung Dynasty compilation, the *Wu-chia cheng-tsung ts'an* (Jap. *Goke shōshū san*) [Praising the True Teaching of the Five Sects]. The line is attributed to the monk Liang-shan, a disciple of the famous monk Yün-chü (died 902).

Circumstances may vary. A particular performance may be given for the nobility or for a general audience. The playing space may be large or small, inside or outside. The performance may even be a simplified one given on an informal occasion. In all cases, however, the particular circumstances will determine how the arrangements made for the performance should vary. For Subscription Performances, or other presentations that take place in large spaces, the atmosphere will be affected by the elements of the weather, the place, and the audience; in small-scale performances such as those given in gardens or interior spaces, the human element is the most important in determining the atmosphere of the performance, and the weather remains of less concern. Thus keep in mind that at any particular presentation, depending on the attention given by the actor to the atmosphere, the play may or may not succeed.

(The heretic spoke to the Buddha. "Yesterday, what kind of law did you preach? The Buddha replied, "yesterday I preached the Definite Law." The heretic asked again, "What kind of law will you preach today?" The Buddha replied, "I will preach the Indefinite Law." The heretic asked, "Why do you preach the Indefinite Law today?" The Buddha responded, "Yesterday's Definite Law is today's Indefinite Law.")[3]

2. QUESTION: Now I can certainly understand that the success or failure of a performance depends on the atmosphere of the occasion. In our art, I can see that in the case of an artist who has practiced for many years and has finally reached a level of wide fame, he can present a performance that moves his audiences on the basis of his long experience. On the other hand, a beginner who has merely learned the Two Arts can excite the interest of his audience as well through the charm of his childlike appearance. Can it be said that the nature of

---

[3] A similar passage can be found in Section 73 of the *Shōbōgenzō* (Treasury of Knowledge of the True Law) by the Zen priest Dōgen (A.D. 1200-1253), founder of the Sōtō sect in Japan.

this fascination the audience finds in a mature performer is the same? I am unclear about this.

ANSWER: I have written about this matter elsewhere. I have compared the nature of this artistic attraction to a Flower, which gives rise to a sense of profound novelty. The knowledge of this process at its highest development means to "know the Flower." This is described in the *Teachings on Style and the Flower*.

In general it can be said that a flower shows its beauty as it blooms and its novelty as its petals scatter. A certain person once asked, "What is the spirit of Transiency?" The answer was, "scattering blossoms, falling leaves." Then came another question. "What is the meaning of Eternity?" The same answer, "scattering blossoms, falling leaves" was returned. Indeed there can be different interpretations of one single moment that are of profound interest.

One who can create such feelings of enjoyment in any of the performing arts is truly gifted, and if he can sustain this ability to create interest during a long career, he is truly a master. The fact that an actor can develop and maintain this skill to the end of his career can be likened to the constancy of "scattering blossoms, falling leaves." Then again, there are artists who merely manifest an ordinary level of talent. Now, as concerns the Nine Levels, it goes without saying that the Flower is manifested in the upper three levels, yet in the middle three and lower three levels of our art as well, insofar as they possess elements of interest, there are appropriate Flowers for them as well. For example, if farmers and rural people find the flowers of wild trees beautiful, then such is the viewpoint of uneducated persons. Those who are moved by the three highest levels share the viewpoint of those who are highly cultivated. Actor and spectator alike will show a level of discernment depending on their own level of cultivation.

Let me attempt to explain what I mean. Let us imagine two general categories, the fundamental Changeless Flower and a second, its manifestation, the Changing Flower. The Changeless Flower represents the upper three levels of the *nō* and can be compared to the cherry. Such is the level appropriate to a highly cultivated audience. The highest level of the middle rank can be referred to as the True Flower and can be represented as the cherry also. Still, a bloom on this level can be compared not only to the cherry but to the plum, the peach, or the pear. The red and white appearance of the plum in particular is especially elegant. Sugawara Michizane himself was very attracted to the sight.

Then too, it is important to remember that our art is based on the ideal attraction felt by all kinds of people. True, the enjoyment of the three highest levels of artistic accomplishment stands as proof that such spectators are persons of high breeding. Nevertheless, among audiences there are both sophisticated and simple. For example, take the case of a young performer who, like the first petals on a flowering cherry, gives the appearance of novelty and represents the Changing Flower. Those who find only this kind of performance moving merely exhibit the appreciation of ordinary persons or rustics without any education at all. A spectator of real breeding when seeing such a performance will find what he sees attractive, but, although he will appreciate it, he will not confuse it with the true, the Changeless Flower. An ancient tree, an historic tree, or the flowers at Mount Koya, Shiga, or (in the capital) at Kiyomizu or Arashiyama[4]—if we compare our art to such things, it would be to the emotions aroused by famous and skilled players. Those who can appreciate this principle are truly persons of breeding and education. Indeed, whether with education or without, every kind of person has the ability to appreciate some of the beauty of the various flowers that

[4] All these are renowned places with beautiful natural scenery that has served as inspiration for poetry. Mount Kōya, in Wakayama Prefecture, is celebrated for the Buddhist temple complexes on the summit founded by Kūkai in the ninth century. Shiga, in present-day Shiga Prefecture, is an area of great natural beauty in the high mountains. Kiyomizudera, in Kyoto, is a Buddhist temple famous for the view from its ramparts over the city. Arashiyama, in the western suburbs of Kyoto, is well known for the beauty of various kinds of cherries and maples that grow there.

comprise the *nō*. Those with cultivation, however, as they have wide powers of observation, do not despise the Changing Flowers. An actor, too, must adopt the same attitude. He should have wide learning, so as to master all the Nine Levels of accomplishment without exception. There is a famous Zen *koan* that states the following. "The various truths of the phenomenal world are manifestations of one Essence; the one Essence only exists in various manifestations found in the phenomenal world."[5] In the same fashion, [the Changing Flowers can be seen as manifestations of the essential Changeless Flower, and so] the various levels of accomplishment can be seen as various kinds of Flowers, each with their appropriate beauties. In any case, as concerns any doubt over the differences in the kind of fascination the audience may find in the novelty of a child's performance as against that of a mature actor, the matter can be explained by the difference between the Changing Flower and the Changeless Flower.

3. QUESTION: How should the term Fascination (*omoshiroki*) be elaborated? The word is often explained by making a comparison with a flower, but that word in turn serves only as a metaphor. Yet the sensation is felt before any comparison is articulated. What constitutes the essential nature of this sensation we call Fascination?

ANSWER: In order to grasp the essential nature of the term Fascination, one must of course grasp the nature of the Flower and the deepest truths of our art. Before, I spoke of Fascination, I spoke of the Flower, and I spoke of Novelty. All three represent different names for the same conception. In fact, Peerless Charm, Flower, and Fascination, although they are in fact separate, spring from the same emotion. They too can be ranked as high, middle, and low. Peerless Charm surpasses verbal expression and lies in the pure realm that lies beyond the workings of consciousness. When this realm is

---

[5] This well-known *koan* appeared in a number of texts circulated at this period. For one version, see R.D.M. Shaw, *Blue Cliff Records*, p. 156.

given visible expression, the result is the Flower. A conscious appreciation of this beauty constitutes Fascination.

The word *omoshiroki* came about as follows: delighted by the dances of the gods at sacred Mount Kagu, the goddess Amaterasu opened the heavenly stone doors and first saw the bright faces of all the gods. Thus the word "face-fair" (*omoshiro*) came into being. Actually, however, in such a brief instant of time there would surely not have been the time necessary for the goddess to actually make such an observation. The word *omoshiroki* was thus created through a consciousness of those sensations. What word could possibly have been used to describe such sensations even before they came into consciousness?

When relating this matter to the highest levels in our own art, it can be said that this moment of Fascination represents an instant sensation that occurs before the rise of any consciousness regarding that sensation, a Feeling that Transcends Cognition. (In the *Book of Changes, hsien* in Chinese is given the meaning of a sensation before consciousness, and so the usual character [感] is written without the bottom part of the character *hsin* [心], which stands for "mind" or "consciousness.") After the goddess Amaterasu had shut the great stone door, the world and all its territories became dark. Then the light suddenly appeared. The reaction of all creatures must have been that of unreflecting joy. It resembles the instant when a vague smile without self-awareness [appeared on the face of Kāśyapa].[6] At the moment when the heavenly doors were shut and the world was plunged into darkness, the situation may be compared to that of Peerless Charm that transcends words; the sudden brightness can be compared to the Flower; and the moment of consciousness concerning that brightness might be compared to Fascination. In that instant of unconscious response before cognition, was the emotion felt not one of pure joy? And might not that appearance of a

[6] Unlike Buddha's other disciples, Kāśyapa was able to understand the Master's teaching intuitively. See D. T. Suzuki, *Essays in Zen Buddhism*, 1st Series, p. 47.

smile, without self-awareness, surpassing words, express the fact that "from the first, not a thing is"?[7] Such a mental state can also be called Peerless Charm. Such a feeling comes from having experienced the Flower of Peerless Charm. Thus it is that the very highest of the nine levels of excellence involves this Flower, which is assigned the characteristics of gold.[8] If both the chant and the dance have been fully mastered, then the exquisite appearance of the actor can astonish the heart and the senses of the spectators; and in that instant when they are moved without taking cognizance of their reactions, the Flower of Peerless Charm can be said to exist. Such a moment represents Fascination and includes within itself as well the moment of a Feeling that Transcends Cognition. All three of these expressions represent emotional states that transcend the workings of the conscious mind.

In a state that transcends consciousness, why is it that we can feel a sense of Fascination? It may indeed represent the fundamental quality that is Changeless [as in the Changeless Flower], never directly visible in any exterior manifestation. In the nine levels of artistic excellence, there are gold and silver levels, but they cannot be directly experienced in a stage performance. Such matters must be grasped on a more profound level. A smile crosses the face without cognition through the coming of a deep sense of joy. Gettan Sōkō has written as the concluding half of a couplet, "what makes one happy cannot be spoken of," expecting that those who read this line will add their own beginning.

4. QUESTION: In the various instructions given concerning the training of a *nō* performer, the term Perfect Fluency is used. Does this term mean the same as a Feeling that Transcends Cognition or the Flower of Peerless Charm?

---

[7] For a discussion of this well-known Buddhist verse, see Philip Yampolsky, tr., *The Platform Sutra of the Sixth Patriarch*, p. 94, note 17.

[8] The use of gold and silver in this context does not appear in other extant writings of Zeami, but such comparisons can be found in documents composed by Komparu Zenchiku, his son-in-law.

ANSWER: This is a matter that requires deep thought. In one sense, all three terms have similar meanings. Nevertheless, only one who has genuinely made himself one with his art can truly be said to have attained a state of Perfect Fluency. There is a Zen phrase[9] that says, "true humanity lies beyond individual rank and value." There is also the expression, "excellence without external form." Such represents a true value that transcends objective value. Such ideas represent Perfect Fluency.

As far as the *nō* is concerned, the actor must first begin to study properly, as explained first in the *Teachings on Style and the Flower* in the chapters entitled "Items Concerning the Practice of the *nō* in Relation to the Age of the Actor," "Various Items Concerning Role Playing," and "Questions and Answers," as well as in the Separate Secret Teaching, then in *The True Path to the Flower* and *A Mirror Held to the Flower*, all of which are representative documents concerning the training necessary for our art. The actor must take steps to learn the *nō* so that he can master its innermost secrets, become truly adept, find himself able to have all these skills at his disposal, and so finally attain Perfect Fluency. However, this variety of Perfect Fluency is the result of conscious practice and shows traces of the effort required to achieve it. This cannot be actually described as a Perfect Fluency that transcends the artist's consciousness.

Genuine Perfect Fluency in fact has no connection with the actor's conscious artistic intentions or with any outward manifestation of those intentions. (The mental attitude of one who has attained this state can be said to represent a Perfect Fluency that transcends his training.) When an actor has achieved a genuine level of Perfect Fluency, all that he has thoroughly learned and rehearsed is absorbed, so that any concern over

[9] The origin of this maxim cited by Zeami, in wide circulation at the time, can be found in the text of a compilation of the Chinese Ch'an master Lin-chi (died A.D. 867) entitled the *Lin-chi lu* (Jap. *Rinzairoku*) [Recorded Sayings of Lin-chi]. For a description of Lin-chi, see D. T. Suzuki, *Essays in Zen Buddhism*, 3rd Series, pp. 30-32.

good or bad no longer exists in his mind. The state when no critical concern exists can paradoxically only come about, however, as a result of the strength gained through a mastery of the performer's art. (Among the nine levels of artistic excellence, Perfect Fluency comes into being after a mastery of the middle three levels and is manifested as well in the upper three. One first begins to master the middle range, then the upper range; finally, one is able to descend to experiment with the lower three.)

It is said that "the mental state having achieved true enlightenment is like that before enlightenment began."[10] The Sung priest Tzu-te Hui said of the sixth of the Oxherding Pictures that "life, once cut off, reappears again; one life then assumes various physical forms and manifestations." And again he said, "if gold is pure, its nature will not change, even in the fire; white jade, even in the mud, will retain its real appearance."[11] Our art follows the same principles. If an artist has gone from the middle stages through the final three stages of excellence, then even if he should mix elements from the three lower stages into his performance, his Flower will be firmly established in the three highest stages. Such might be compared to gold mixed with sand, or a lotus flower in the mud: even if mixed together, one is not affected by the other. An actor who has truly reached this level can be said to have achieved Perfect Fluency. Such a person, no matter which of myriad roles he may play, will perform with complete ease, indeed even without a conscious sense of ease. His art will surpass skill, transcend intention. Truly, is such ease not that Flower of Peerless Charm that lies within that same Flower?

However, witnessing a performer who has attained the Flower of Peerless Charm and who practices his art with Perfect Fluency,

[10] This phrase is cited in the *Ching-te ch'uan-teng lu* (Jap. *Keitoku dentō roku*) [Records of the Transmission of the Lamp] compiled in A.D. 1004 by the Chinese Buddhist priest Tao-hsüan. The text was an especially important one for the Sōtō sect in Japan.

[11] For a discussion of the significance of the Oxherding Pictures and Tzu-te Hui's remarks, see D. T. Suzuki, *Manual of Zen Buddhism*, pp. 150-151.

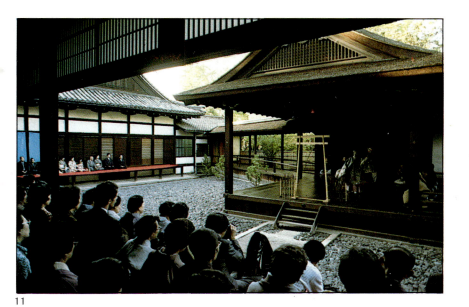

11

12

Figure 11. A performance of the play *Nonomiya (The Shrine in the Fields)*, attributed to Zeami, given on the *nō* stage of the Nishi-Honganji Temple in Kyoto. The stage, constructed about 1595, is one of the oldest remaining in Japan

Figure 12. The play *fuji (Wisteria)* attributed to Hiyoshi Sanmi staged as a torchlight performance (*takigi*) at the Kōfukujmi Temple in Nara

Figure 13. A scene from *Koi no omoni* (The Burden of Love) by Zeami. The *shite*, an old gardener, wears a mask typical of such roles

Figure 14. A scene from *Yamamba (The Mountain Hag)*, attributed to Zeami. The *shite*, "the old woman of the hills," wears a mask appropriate to the role and uses a special fan in an unusual fashion

Figure 15. (*opposite*) A scene from *Yūgao*, by Zeami, in which the *shite* portrays the elegant young woman Yūgao, an important character in Lady Murasaki's *The Tale of Genji*

Figure 16. (*above*) A scene from *Matsukaze*, by Zeami, in which two sisters, Matsukaze and Murasame, tell of their grief at losing their lover Yukihira

Three masks from the Muromachi Period, carved between 1400 and 1560 from the personal collection of the *nō* Master Sano Yoshivuki

Figure 17. A mask of the *ōbeshimi* type, used for various demon roles, usually of the Delicacy within Strength style approved by Zeami. See *Reflections* on *Art*, note 38

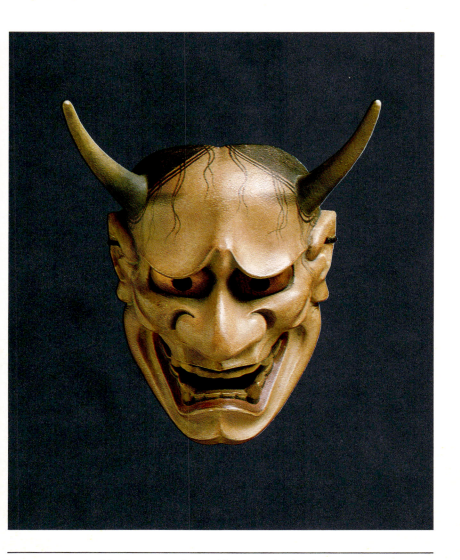

Figure 18. A mask of the *ko-omote* style, used for most roles that depict young women. The term means "small face" or "small mask"

Figure 19. A mask of the *hannya* type, used for the roles of female ghosts in such plays as *Aoi no Ue (The Lady Aoi)*. The term presumably derives from the maskmaker Hannyabō, who created the style

a young actor who may think to imitate him would be as foolish as someone who thrusts his hand in the air thinking to strike at the moon. Players in the lower and middle levels, as well as beginners, must understand this point. In terms of the nine levels of perfection, those who master the middle three can achieve an ease appropriate to their degree of mastery; and indeed, even those players who are still in the lower three levels should be able to achieve an ease appropriate to the level of development of their artistic powers. In any case, when mastering any role, an artist should be able to achieve a degree of ease consonant with his stage of development, one that his audience can experience. This is a fundamental component of the *nō*.

5. QUESTION: In all the arts, one speaks of Fulfillment in performance. Is the meaning of the term merely on the surface? Or does it harbor some profound significance? What is the real meaning of the term?

ANSWER: The term Fulfillment is made of two characters that mean "to become" (成) and "to settle in place" (就). As concerns the art of the *nō*, the word seems to explain the process by which an audience comes to feel that Fascination I spoke of before.

Fulfillment is related to the process of *jo*, *ha*, and *kyū*. This is true because there is in the composition of the word Fulfillment itself a suggestion of the process that involves a sense of completion. If this natural process toward completion is not carried out, no feelings of Fulfillment can arise. It is that instant of Fulfillment in an artistic work that gives the audience a sensation of novelty. The proper sequence of *jo*, *ha*, and *kyū* provides the sense of Fulfillment.

Thinking over the matter carefully, it may be said that all things in the universe, good and bad, large and small, with life and without, all partake of the process of *jo*, *ha*, and *kyū*. From the chirp of the birds to the buzzing of the insects, all sing according to an appointed order, and this order consists of *jo*, *ha*, and *kyū*. (Indeed, their music surpasses any question of mere skill and represents an unconscious Fulfillment.) Their singing creates a pleasing musical sensation and gives rise to feelings of a Melancholy Elegance. Still, if Fulfillment is not achieved, even if those natural sensations are pleasing, they do not create a mood of Melancholy Elegance. In the play *Takasago*, there is a chant that states how the forest in the spring is moved by the east wind, and how the insects of fall sing in the cool dew. All their music takes the form of *waka*. All the sounds of nature, from the sentient and nonsentient alike, are expressed in poetry and show the auspicious feelings of Fulfillment in accordance with the principles of *jo, ha*, and *kyū*. Grasses and trees alike are wet with rain and dew in this rhythm of *jo, ha*, and *kyū*, just as flowers and fruits appear at the proper season. The voice of the wind and the sound of the water as well follow the same design.

I have explained the principles of *jo, ha*, and *kyū* as related to the *nō* in the *Teachings on Style and the Flower* and *A Mirror Held to the Flower*.

In the case of a performance of *nō*, when the day's program has been completed, the public's expression of appreciation comes because the *jo, ha*, and *kyū* of the day have reached successful Fulfillment. Such is a truly meritorious completion, which comes about when the responses of the audience to the performance have all been brought to Fulfillment as well. Then again, within the program of plays presented, and within each piece itself, the *jo, ha*, and *kyū* must be brought to Fulfillment. Even in one dance or one section of chant, what the spectator finds of interest is related to the Fulfillment of *jo, ha*, and *kyū* within that one unit. The pattern of *jo, ha*, and *kyū* is visible even in one gesture in a dance, or in the echo of one step. As such effects surpass my ability to describe them, they should be explained in an oral teaching.

The fulfillment of *jo, ha*, and *kyū* provides the spectators with a sense of novelty, and the creation of *jo, ha*, and *kyū* by the performers brings this phenomenon about. When the audience can express its astonishment as one with a gasp, the moment of Fulfillment has come. As for the emotions produced when the *shite* first begins to sing, the process of *jo*, *ha*, and *kyū* is doubtless fulfilled when the performer brings his voice in consonance with the musical scale. Yet if, in such a moment, the chanter does not put his heart into his performance and the musical effects are not fully realized, the results will not be enjoyable. This is because the performer does not move his voice past the regular stages of *jo* and *ha* in order to allow it to flow into *kyū*. (This would be the same as constructing an image of the Buddha but never installing the eyes in the image.)[12] Under such circumstances, how can musical Fulfillment be expected? The results can hold no interest.

Without a firm grasp of these principles, the Fulfillment of the musical elements of *jo*, *ha*, and *kyū* will never materialize. As for my personal explanation of "Pitch, Breath, Voice Production," the *jo* can be said to be represented by the stage of hearing the pitch and gathering in the breath. *Ha* is represented by pushing out the breath, and *kyū* by the production of the voice itself. In all three, what gives rise through the ears to the sensation of pleasure in the senses is the Fulfillment of *jo, ha,* and *kyū*. In no matter what aspect of dramatic or musical effort, the successful response of the audience will be determined by the proper fulfillment of the process of *jo, ha,* and *kyū*.

In the *Chuang Tzu*, it is written that "the duck's legs are short, but to stretch them out would worry him; the crane's legs are long, but to cut them down would make him sad."[13] Long or short, large or small, all are equal in their endowment of the principle of *jo, ha,* and *kyū*. If this principle is firmly understood, one's own consciousness of one's art will follow the proper process to genuine fulfillment. In the same way, the actor will be able to discern clearly his strong and weak points and lessen his bad, thus becoming a peerless master in

---

[12] A reference to the traditional ceremony of enshrining a newly made Buddhist image, usually an occasion for an important festival.

[13] See Burton Watson, tr., *The Complete Works of Chuang Tzu*, Book 8, pp. 99-100.

his particular art. (An actor who has attained this stage is one who no longer needs to train or to think out his performance but can perform without artifice; his art is naturally perfected.) At this stage in an artist's career, his very soul itself will have absorbed the order of *jo, ha,* and *kyū,* and he will have made the process a natural part of himself. The sense of novelty in any performance comes from the fulfillment of the principle of *jo, ha,* and *kyū.* If a performance fails to stimulate, it is clear that such a Fulfillment has not come about.

The actor's real concern must rather be over how he can actually incorporate those principles into himself. Is it enough to suppose that, if he has in fact absorbed these deepest concepts of our art into his own personality and has achieved performances that reflect a complete freedom, he will have automatically mastered these principles? (The ability of an actor to truly grasp the *nō* will be apparent if the elements that the audience sees and hears give a sense of Fulfillment. Actors who can create this sense are gifted; those whose performances lack interest are not.)

6. QUESTION: Those who take part in the various arts all seem to have achieved their own personal artistic Sphere of Accomplishment. How can one come to understand the real significance of such an individual Sphere of Accomplishment?

ANSWER: Concerning this matter as related to the *nō,* there are many points that must be understood. In the first place, an actor who has obtained the three highest levels of the nine levels of excellence will practice a highly sophisticated style appropriate to them and so reveal his particular Sphere of Accomplishment. Such is already an indication of the fact that his art has reached the level of Highest Fruition. Those whose art remains in the middle three levels possesses a Sphere of Accomplishment appropriate to those levels. The same is true for actors whose mastery only extends to the three lower levels. Most actors, however, merely think of a Sphere of Accomplishment as something that exists in consonance with their own abilities and they do not know how to extend themselves so as to lift their art to a real sphere of excellence. Indeed, without actually playing a role oneself, it is difficult to grasp any particular actor's Sphere of Accomplishment.

Concerning the Three Roles, an actor will first consider portraying an Old Man. There is a figure in the "Illustrations for the Two Basic Arts and Three Role Types"[14] who is termed, "Relaxed Heart Looking Afar." The actor must learn to keep his soul at ease and to look off into the distance. (As the eyesight of old persons is hazy, the suggestion is that the old person looks off vaguely into the distance.) Such is the general framework for the representation appropriate for an old person. If the actor can put his body and mind alike into this mold and then perform chant and dance alike correctly, while carrying himself in an appropriate manner, he will enter into the essence of the role he is playing and so achieve the true Sphere of Accomplishment appropriate for the role of an old person.

When it comes to playing the role of a woman, a figure is included in the same set of illustrations entitled "Concentration of Mind and Relinquishing Physical Strength." An actor must concentrate his attention on producing an inner intensity and abandon any detailed stress on his physical movements (since, if the feminine spirit infuses his mind, a relaxation of physical strength will surely come about of itself). If he can carry out these principles in his own performance of the Two Arts, he will have entered the Sphere of Accomplishment as concerns a woman's role.

The illustration for the warrior role is entitled "Physical Strength, Splintered Heart." (Although a manifestation of strength is the most important element in such a role, the subtle movements of the actor's mind must be fully exploited.) Here, although the actor must make the strength of his outward movements the basis of his characterization, he must

---

[14] A separate brief treatise, not translated in the present collection, since the information it contains is largely reproduced in *The True Path to the Flower* and elsewhere. The illustrations from the treatise can be found following page l.

bear in mind the necessity for preserving the subtleties of his inner posture. If the actor can develop this ability in mind and body alike, he can when he exhibits these skills enter into the Sphere of Accomplishment of a warrior role.

Usually the role of a warrior represents one who is fond of fighting by nature,[15] so that in terms of the actor's bodily movements, he should carry a bow and arrow, move his body violently as if to fend off another's sword, and stamp about in a nimble fashion; yet beneath this strength, the performer must show concern to maintain a certain gentleness in his posture, so as to avoid pushing himself to the extremes of violence. Such a superior performance represents the Sphere of Accomplishment in a warrior's role.

However, it may well happen that an actor will not really have grasped these principles, so that, just after he plays a warrior according to the conception of "Physical Strength, Splintered Heart," he will not be able to follow the conception of "Concentration on Mind and Relinquishing Physical Strength"; he will merely assume that if he is playing a woman, all he need do is to appear beautiful. If he suddenly attempts to impersonate a woman in this fashion, however, the character will appear withered and weak. Neither the warrior nor the woman will be correctly played and both characterizations will be limp. The audience will be critical, saying "the performance shows no energy," and "it is weak"; the actor, flustered, will return to the mental attitude appropriate to a warrior's role, and the performance will become rough. Under these circumstances, how can it be said that an actor has entered into the Sphere of Accomplishment for a woman's role?

Now an actual woman living in the world has no thought at all of imitating a woman. From the beginning she was born and reared as a woman; if she is from the upper classes she has her own appropriate deportment, and if she is of the lower

[15] That is, a *shura*, originally a figure in Hindu mythology, who came to represent in Buddhist thought a kind of devil fond of fighting by nature.

classes, she too has her own style of being. As each carries
out her appropriate behavior, each, it can be said, has found
her own natural and individual Sphere of Accomplishment.
If a woman connives to make herself beautiful and expends
efforts to manifest Grace, her actions will be quite ineffective.
(In this respect, Grace is extremely difficult to grasp through
the mind.) In the same fashion, an actor, when told his performance is rough, will wither and do nothing. Then, when
criticized for the lack of any expression, he will merely become
rough again. Thus as concerns all aspects of the skill that an
actor must show (all the various Spheres of Accomplishment
that he must attain), whether his performance is strong or
weak, there will always be criticism, good and bad alike. And
indeed, since the performance by a man of a woman's role
represents the most difficult attainment of all, if the actor can
take the concept of "Concentration on Mind and Relinquishing Physical Strength" as a basis for his performance, and he
truly tries to express the body and the spirit of a woman, he
can achieve this Sphere of Accomplishment. But if he does
not take these matters to heart but merely tries to imitate the
surface appearance of a woman, he cannot attain the proper
level of attainment. A woman never imitates herself. But if
the real essence of a woman is given reality through an actor's
performance, then the Sphere of Accomplishment represented
by that woman has been portrayed. (The stage of mere imitation represents a surface copy, mere Externalization; becoming the essence of a character represents Internalization.
After attaining the level of Internalization, it may be possible
for an actor to then return and create the external aspects of
his performance as well.) These two distinctions—Internalization and Externalization—must be thoroughly understood.
The same concepts apply to the role of an old person. With
a full grasp of the concept of "Relaxed Heart Looking Afar,"
the actor becomes one with this mentality and so achieves the
Sphere of Accomplishment for this kind of role. The same
applies to any and all of the Three Roles.

As for the mad roles, they reveal the disgrace of the character and are not performed in such a way that audiences can be discriminating about them, so perhaps one might think that they need not be incorporated into the *nō*; yet in the portrayal of such roles lies the very rationale of *sarugaku* as an art. A woman, for example, has a generally modest and self-effacing bearing and therefore, in the *nō*, such a theatrical appearance is not especially striking as far as the audience is concerned; on the other hand, a mad woman dances, chants, speaks in a jesting fashion, and so adds novelty to the originally refined presentation of a female character. She scatters flowers and bestows her charms, so that there is indeed no performance potentially more striking. An actor who achieves this level of skill can be said to be an ideal performer. Such roles truly represent the Sphere of Accomplishment in terms of Fascination.

Now, in addition to the Three Role Types, there are other roles, such as demon roles. These roles too are appropriate for the art of *sarugaku*. Actually, a real demon cannot be seen in our actual world. Even though an image of a demon may appear in a picture, for example, there exists no definite model on which that picture can be based. Therefore, an actor creates a general conception, avoids presenting a character who appears merely wild, gives a certain softness to his motions, and deceives his audience into believing that they have seen a real demon. Such is the Sphere of Accomplishment as pertains to demon roles. One such appearance is called Delicacy within Strength, or, as it is sometimes referred to, "the Appearance of a Demon, the Heart of a Man." (In addition to this type of role, there is another variety of demon role called Rough Movement, which is not recognized by our school.) If an actor truly grasps the essentials involved, he will be able to perform this role in a proper fashion and so achieve the Sphere of Accomplishment for the Delicacy within Strength style of demon roles.

So it is that with any kind of performance, and with the study of the Two Arts of dance and chant as well—in all things indeed, a performer, if he strives for an art that is without artifice, can achieve a Sphere of Accomplishment appropriate to each artistic endeavor. If an actor does not achieve any proper discernment and cannot observe the proper distinctions but merely carries out his work in terms of vague approximations, it will be difficult indeed to speak of any Sphere of Accomplishment. In the end, if the actor can manifest no fundamental point of view concerning the essentials of his art, his *nō* will lose its flavor, and, as he grows older, his art will decline. This is a matter that must be kept in mind constantly.

In *The Great Learning*, it is written that "it cannot be, when the root is neglected, that what should spring from it will be well ordered."[16] Concerning the performance of various roles in the *nō*, the principle of proper roots applies exactly. If such roots are not observed, and if each role is not played in a manner wholly appropriate to it, then any genuine Internalization would seem impossible. Therefore, if the roots are not followed and the ends are not ordered, the results will merely provide an Externalization. Then again, it is said that "to go too far is as bad as not to go far enough."[17] If in playing a role there are any deficiencies in responding to the demands of the part, or, on the other hand, if there are unnecessary exaggerations, then the roots of the role cannot be properly established. If a genuine Internalization (such as is described in *The True Path to the Flower*) can truly be created by the actor, he will have no thought concerning the imitation of externals. True Role Playing represents the art of Internalization. Therefore, when an actor enters fully into the worlds that are requisite to each play he is performing, then each appropriate Sphere of Accomplishment can be said to come into existence. In Mencius, it is written that "to do something is not hard, but to do it well is very difficult indeed."[18] In a

---

[16] *The Great Learning* (*Ta hsüeh*) is one of the most influential of the early Chinese classics. For a translation of the relevant passage, see James Legge, *The Chinese Classics*, I, 359. See also *The True Path to the Flower*, p. 64.

[17] See Arthur Waley, *The Analects of Confucius*, Book XI, No. 15, p. 156.

[18] Not in Mencius. See also *The True Path to the Flower*, note 3.

well-executed copy, there seem to be no important flaws and those who observe the performance may find it easy and fluent. Such is an art in which "to do something is not difficult." But there are few actors indeed who truly can enter into the real truth of their roles and thereby gain lasting fame. They are those who prove the truth of the fact that "to do something well is very hard." It is said that "the truth and what looks like it are two different things."[19] (It is written, "Whatever merely resembles is not equal to the real thing itself. Try to mix both and you will know at once.")[20] Truly, an actor must absorb the nature of this truth into himself until he possesses it in Perfect Fluency; only in that way can he become an expert player whose fame will never fade.

This volume is a secret teaching concerning the training for our art. Komparu Zenchiku has a real understanding of the *nō*, and so I am now transmitting this to him.

1st year of Shōchō (1428), 1st day of the 6th month
Zeami

When you read these miscellaneous notes, you find dewlike gems; polish them and flowers will bloom in endless profusion.
When I was a young man, I received this collection of teachings from my teacher Zeami.

Kyōtoku 2 (1453), 8th month, eighth (?) day
Zenchiku

As I examine the flowers, the jewels collected in these notes, they are as a cloudless mirror through which one can see [to the very depths].

Komparu Hachirō

[19] See *A Mirror Held to the Flower*, p. 88.
[20] A quotation from a collection of Ch'an [Jap. Zen] Buddhist verses entitled *Pao-ching san-mei* (Jap. *Hōkyōzammai*) [Treasure Mirror Meditations] compiled by Tung-shan Liang-chieh (A.D. 807-869), one of the founders of the Ts'ao-tung sect in China (later known as the Sōtō sect in Japan).

This secret book was passed on to me down through the generations from the time of our ancestor Hata no Kōkatsu. Since the beginning, these secrets were given to the head of the house alone and it has never been permitted for other children or other descendants to make inquiries concerning these profound secrets. Unfortunately, because of the unlucky death of my older brother Ujikatsu Shichirō, my father felt that, in order to carry on the family traditions and pass them on to future generations, so that they would be bequeathed for all eternity, they should be explained and passed along to me. Therefore, I shall explain them all to you, leaving out nothing. The line of transmission must not be allowed to be interrupted.

Meireki 2 (1656), First month, 21st day
Takeda Komparu Hachiemon

to: Lord Komparu Shichiemon

The Three Elements in Composing a Play *(Sandō* or *Nōsakusho)*

There are three elements required for the composition of a *nō* play—the seed, the construction, and the composition. First one must know the seed [one's source materials] very well. Second, one must construct the various elements in a proper fashion. Third, the text itself must be well composed. One must thoroughly master the orthodox source materials to be used [selecting a central character from the classics or from legends], divide the material up into five Sequences in accordance with the principles of *jo, ha,* and *kyū,* and then finally, compose the text and add to it appropriate melodies.

1. The seed refers to the choice of a subject based on appropriate traditional sources, the actions of which are both appropriate for theatrical expression and especially effective in terms of the Two Arts of dance and chant. This is, of course, because these Two Arts form the fundamental basis of our whole art. If the subject chosen for the play concerns a character who cannot be manifested using these Two Arts, then even if the character to be portrayed is a famous person in the past or a person of prodigious gifts, no theatrical effect appropriate to the *nō* is possible. This fundamental principle must be thoroughly understood.

For example, among the various figures suitable for Role Playing in the *nō*, such characters as goddesses, sacred female deities, vestal virgins, and the like are all appropriate, as they can perform the sacred songs and dances of *kagura.* In terms of men's roles, such figures as Ariwara no Narihira, Ōtomo no Kuronushi, and Genji all are highly cultivated personages of great elegance. In terms of women's roles, Lady Ise, Ono no Komachi, Giō and Gijo, Shizuka, and Hyakuman are all famous for their artistic accomplishments in poetry or dance. All of these historical or literary characters, if chosen for the central figure in a *nō* drama, will of themselves bring an appearance of artistic elegance to the play. If the characters of priests are used, then actors can create such personalities as Jinen Koji, Kagetsu, Tōgan Koji, Seigan Koji, and other artistically accomplished persons. In addition, when characters are chosen who are unknown—man or woman, young or old—their roles must be composed in such a way that their characters can be rendered suitable for the arts of song and dance. Thus, creating a character whose very essence is involved in the art of song and dance can be termed choosing the proper seed.

There is also the category of "created *nō*" in which a new play is prepared without any specific literary source, making use of the affinities between famous places or historical sites, in order to move the audience. Such plays are difficult to compose and require the accomplishments of a highly skilled person of great talent.

2. The writer, having determined an altogether appropriate seed, must then fix the actions of that character in the play. First of all, *jo, ha,* and *kyū* must be divided up into five Sequences. The *jo* represents one Sequence, the *ha* three Sequences, and the *kyū* one final Sequence.

The first Sequence begins when the character of the *waki* appears and performs what is called the *sashigoe*, then continues on through the *shidai* to the end of the *hito-utai*. Then the *ha* section begins. The *shite* enters, and the portion of the play from the *issei* to the *hito-utai* represents the second Sequence. After this section comes an exchange of questions and answers between the *waki* and the *shite*, through the first choral passage: all of this represents the third Sequence. Then comes a musical section, the fourth Sequence, which might consist of a *kusemai* or a *tadautai*. From this point on, the play enters the *kyū* section. The final Sequence may consist of an appropriate dance or some vigorous action, performed in a brisk rhythm, such as *hayabushi* or a *kiribyōshi*. All together, five Sequences are included. However, depending on the nature of the material to be dramatized, there are occasions when six Sequences are employed. (Then too, there are circumstances when one Sequence is removed and a particular play only requires four Sequences.) Nevertheless, the basic formulization of a *nō* drama requires five Sequences.

When those five Sequences have been planned and fixed, the writer must next determine how much music is to be included in the *jo*. In the three Sequences of the *ha* as well, the use of three appropriate kinds of music must be determined, as well as the style of music appropriate for the *kyū*. In all cases, the amount of stanzas employed in the chant must be regulated. This act of assembling the whole structure is called "constructing" the play. Depending on the type or atmosphere of a particular play, the music will be composed differently for the *jo, ha,* and *kyū*. The length of a *nō* play must also be calculated, based on the number of stanzas in the chants included in the five Sequences.

3. The composition of the play involves working out a means by which appropriate words are chosen for the characters to perform, depending on their own particular natures, from the opening song on. Suitable literary material must be incorporated appropriate to the nature of the play, such as poems or songs that correspond to the varieties of emotion to be expressed—a sense of the auspicious, elegance, love, malice, sadness, and so forth.

In the *nō*, there must be a scene in which the source of the play is clearly revealed. If the artistic interest of a play centers around a famous place or an historic site, a well-known song or poem about the place should be chosen and included in the concluding section (the third Sequence) of the *ha* section. This moment is the most crucial in the entire play. In addition, one must include a quotation from a famous poetic source for the *shite* to recite. The composition of *nō* includes the proper arrangement of all these various elements.

Such are the three principles involved in writing a *nō* play—the seed, the construction, and the composition.

*Composition Concerning the Three Role Types
and Other Matters*

The Old Person, the Woman, the Soldier: these constitute the Three Role Types.

1. The Old Person. Usually such a character appears as the central figure in a *waki nō*. The aesthetic qualities of the play will involve the creation of an auspicious atmosphere. The first character to appear (the *waki*) enters and, beginning with the *shidai* up until the *hito-utai* in the first Sequence, chants seven or eight units, following a syllable count of 5-7-5, 7-5, 7-5, and so on. Normally the 7-5 count constitutes one unit, but when a *waka* is quoted, the poem should be treated as though it constitutes two units [although it consists of a 5-7-5, 7-7 syllable pattern].

The *shite* now enters and the second Sequence (the first Sequence of the *ha* section) now begins. In some plays, two *shite*, an old man and his wife, are employed. The performers will begin the *issei*, made up of units of 7-5-7 and 7-5, then present [the latter half of the *issei*, consisting of] two units of 7-5 and 7-5. Then begins the *sashigoe* section, which continues along on a pattern of 7-5, 7-5 until ten units have been completed. From the *sageuta* to the *ageuta*, about ten units will be required as well.

At this point, the performer enters the third Sequence (the second Sequence of the *ha* section). During the conversation between the *waki* and the *shite*, there should be no more than four or five exchanges. In this conversation, for example, the old man and his wife might explain [to the *waki*] some of the circumstances surrounding a matter important to the play; but in this case as well, each character should speak no more than two or three times. After this, the *ageuta* should be chanted in ensemble fashion, and from that point until the end of the chant, the series of ten syllable units may be split into two parts.

Now the fourth Sequence (the third Sequence of the *ha* section) begins. When a *kusemai* is presented, the opening section (*kuri*), sung in high voice, requires a sequence of five syllable units, the [first half of the] *sashigoe* requires five, and the concluding section [of the *sashigoe*], sung in a lower tone, requires five or six. The first half of the final *kuse* (section) requires a total of perhaps twelve or thirteen. The second half also requires about twelve or thirteen units. After this, the *waki* and the *shite* continue this exchange in a chanted dialogue, the *rongi* section, where there should be no more than two or three exchanges. The chanting should end on a light and lively note.

Here the *kyū* section begins. The *shite*, now transfigured into his "real" character, appears, often as a warrior or heavenly woman, and performs at the bridge a chant in a high-voiced mode, either a *sashigoe* or an *issei*; in the later part of that chant, he performs in ensemble fashion with the chorus in a high tone mode, both amply and at length. Finally, he should conclude in a low-voiced mode. Then two or three *rongi* should be sung, to a rapid rhythm, with the chanting at a brisk and rapid tempo. When the personage presented by the *shite* is one for whom a dance is appropriate, he should make his final exit to a *kiribyōshi*, a rapid "cutting" final rhythm. In any case, the final section must not be too lengthy. The question of length must be regulated in accordance with the number of syllable units chanted.

Such is the general pattern appropriate to a *nō* play in the *jo* category. In a *waki nō*, as the atmosphere is one appropriate to the appearance of an old person, such a role is fixed. In addition, however, there are various other sorts of *nō* plays in which old persons appear.

There are also plays of congratulationary nature in which the central characters are women, and those too should be constructed using the five Sequences as described above.

2. Women's Roles. When a woman's role is central, the play must be composed with a special emphasis on a graceful atmosphere. This type of play makes the most representative use of song and dance, the very basis of our art. Among those plays, there are some of the very highest aesthetic qualities.

For example, there are women of high court rank who appear in the plays, such as ladies-in-waiting, or such characters [in *The Tale of Genji*] as Aoi no Ue, Yūgao, and Ukifune. Their refined dignity and unusual air and appearance must be well thought out and carefully described.

The writer must carefully consider how to create an appropriately elegant musical mood and must at all cost avoid the sort of music suitable for professional women dancing performers. These characters from the court have an extremely aristocratic air about them and are beautiful; they possess Grace to the highest degree, and their music, gestures, and dance movements must be beyond compare. In sum, any insufficiency will be quite unsuitable.

Among characters that exhibit such potential seeds of artistic excellence, there are those who achieve the position of jewels within jewels. For example, an even more refined quality than the quality of aristocratic elegance I mentioned above can be found in such incidents as the curse laid upon Aoi no Ue by Lady Rokujō, the evil spirit haunting Yūgao, or the possession of Ukifune: such a seed that is full of grace yet is capable as well of providing a proper theatrical effect on the stage represents the source of an atmosphere that is rarely met with.

There is an old poem,[1]

Ume ga ka o	In the cherry blossoms
Sakura no hana ni	Is the smell of plum
Niowasete	Making the branches
Yanagi ga eda ni	Of the willow bloom.
Sakaseteshigana.	

The seeds of this level of *nō* may be even more valuable than the miracle described in the poem. And, indeed, the artists who are adept at creating such an atmosphere prove them-

[1] The poem is No. 82 in the Spring section of the *Goshūishū* (Later Collection of Gleanings), an imperial anthology completed in A.D. 1086. The author is Nakahara no Munetoki (died A.D. 1003), a courtier of the fourth rank.

selves to be actors of the highest caliber in aesthetic sensibility in terms of performance.

In addition to these, such characters as Shizuka, Giō, and Gijō represent professional entertainers (*shirabyōshi*) and so they should chant *waka* poetry, perform extended *issei*, follow the rhythms of the "eight beats,"[2] sing using the upper notes of the scale, dance [at the end of the performance] to the rapid rhythm of the drum, and exit while dancing. Therefore it is doubtless appropriate that just as the actor makes his final exit, he should create a quiet impression by using *kiribyōshi*.

In the case of characters like Hyakuman or Yamauba, these roles involve dancers of *kusemai* and so are quite easy to perform. In terms of the five Sequences, the *jo* and the *kyū* should be shortened and the *ha* given the major emphasis. The *kusemai* should be made a central focus and should occupy two Sequences with the latter rather compressed. The play should be composed with the kind of detail that will bring out the art of the specialized *kusemai* performers, and planned so that the dance is finished by the time that the *shidai* section begins.

Next come the roles of mad women. Since the element of madness is so theatrically effective, any play in this category will doubtless be enjoyable, no matter how it is composed, so long as the atmosphere is refined and the music is delicately wrought in order to match the colorful movements of the central character, who must retain some elements of Grace in performance. The costuming should be beautiful, various attractive melodies should be skillfully assembled, every striking technique employed, and true poetic coloring added.

If, therefore, the writer learns to assemble the best materials and develops an ability to distinguish the various and different characteristics that comprise noblewomen, entertainers, and mad women, he can properly apportion their lineages in ar-

---

[2] One of the basic rhythmic patterns of this music. See Harich-Schneider, *A History of Japanese Music*, pp. 380-381.

tistic terms when he writes his plays and will become known as a man who knows his art.

3. The Warrior Roles. There are also warrior roles in the *nō*. Should the source of the character central to the play be a famous Heike or Genji warrior, the play should be always composed in accord with the accounts given in *The Tale of the Heike*.[3] In this case too, the arrangement of each of the Sequences and the length of the music contained in them should be carefully planned. Then again, if the play is divided into two parts in such a way that the *shite* is transfigured and reappears in the second part, a *kusemai* should be included at the end of the second part. The *kusemai*, which is usually included in the third Sequence in the *ha* section, would thus extend into the *kyū* section as well, lengthening this part of the play. In such a case, the *ha* would contain four Sequences and the entire play six. If the play is not divided into two parts, however, it may require only four Sequences. The number will vary on the basis of each particular play. In any case, the beginning of the play must be compressed and written in as brief a fashion as possible.

As the sources for the various warrior roles will differ, there is no one means by which all such plays can be composed. In any case, the sections to be chanted should be kept as short as possible, and in the *kyū* section, the final exit should include the rapid tempos appropriate for a *shura*. Depending on the psychological character of the *shite*, it may be appropriate for him to behave as though he were playing a demon role.

The passages for the *shite* should give an atmosphere of bravery and vigor and provide for energetic physical action. When the *shite* appears transformed into a soldier in the second part of the play, a section of chant must be included in which he declares his true identity. Warrior plays must be composed with such points in mind.

[3] The *Heike monogatari* (The Tale of the Heike) is the great classic of medieval Japan that recounts the fall of the Heike clan in the disastrous civil wars around A.D. 1185. There are two translations, one by A. D. Sadler in 1928 and a second by Hiroshi Kitagawa and Bruce T. Tsuchida in 1975.

Such are the important matters concerning the composition of the Three Roles.

Nō involving itinerant entertainers in Buddhist dress. This is a style that derives from the warrior plays and possesses, within the strength appropriate to those plays, a certain delicacy. Either in the case of male entertainers, such as Jinen Koji or Kagetsu, or, in the case of women entertainers, the quality of Delicacy within Strength must be made a part of the style suitable to their respective characters. When the opening section for the *waki* is concluded, and the moment comes for the musicians to strike the drums in anticipation, the *shite* enters, dressed in the costume appropriate to an itinerant Buddhist entertainer and chants his *sashigoe* in a rich and relaxed manner. An old poem or a famous phrase—in any case, something both familiar and attractive—should be cited beginning with the *sashigoe*, mixed with ordinary spoken phrases for seven or eight units, until the point is reached where the *issei* begins. For these sorts of characters, it is especially important that, for their entrance scene, the sound of an intriguing melody should make their appearance impressive as they stand on the bridge and are viewed at a distance by the audience. This entrance must be properly prepared, the proper words chosen, and various gestures selected when the play is composed.

The chant begins with the *sashigoe* in the *jo* and should be performed in a small-scale and light fashion. The length usually adopted for a chant in the *jo* section is appropriate. As for the ensuing conversation between the *waki* and the *shite*, some argument or discussion is carried on between them, chanted in this form for four or five exchanges. Then the chant [by the *shite*], sung in a high melody, continues on for about ten units. Whatever the circumstances, the music must be applied [to the words] in a clever and cheerful manner. From the dance section through the *kusemai* section, the motions employed should be as vigorous as possible. In the *kyū* sequence, the *hayabushi* and the *otoshibushi* must be skillfully colored, so that the aesthetic qualities of the performance will be rich.

These varieties of *nō* in which the leading roles are those of itinerant players can be given conclusions that may involve, for example, a scene showing reunion of a parent and child, husband and wife, or brothers and sisters; as a finale, the play can end with such a last scene. In the case of a *nō* drama of this sort, the third section of the *ha* (the fourth Sequence) should be composd to serve as the climactic moment by the use of a rapid tempo, whereas the finale should take the form of a *rongi*; and in the case when a child is reunited with a parent, or brothers and sisters find each other again, the final scene should be constructed so as to create an atmosphere conducive to a few tears. On the whole, such plays should have roughly the same effect as those in the mad person category.

Demon plays show the quality of Delicacy within Strength. These plays derive from the warrior plays. In them, the *shite* has the appearance of a demon but the heart of a man.

The majority of these plays are constructed in two sections. The first scene, whether composed of two Sequences or three, should be written in as brief a form as possible; when the central character appears in the second scene, he should be revealed as a ghost who appears in the form of a demon.

From the bridge, the *shite* should present his *sashigoe* of four or five units in a lively fashion; when chanting the *issei*, he should walk to the edge of the stage, and, using detailed body and foot movements, press forward his words and perform in the style of *otoshibushi*. He should sing in a high-pitched mode for about ten stanzas, then perhaps continue the rapid *rongi* involving three or four exchanges. In the *kyū* or final Sequence, the actor must press forward with one rapid, rhythmical musical passage after another, using *hayabushi* or *kirufushi*. Depending on such musical effects, the actor's movements will have a colorful appeal. Such a scene must be carefully composed in terms of its visual and musical effect.

In addition to the Delicacy within Strength style of demon

roles, there is another called the Rough Movement style. Such a character has both the appearance and the character of a demon. Such a figure is the very representation of wrath itself, and represents an unorthodox type of character. This variety of role is not recognized in our traditions. Only the Delicacy within Strength variety of demon roles have a fixed form in our school that can be properly learned.

The various matters outlined above must be mastered in order to compose *nō* plays in a proper fashion.

It is possible to speak of "opening the ears and eyes" [of the audience]. During a *nō* play, such moments [of heightened consciousness on the part of the audience] occur in the *ha* and *kyū* sections.

"Opening the ears" refers to that moment when two sounds create one sensation. The play should be composed in such a way as to reveal the significance of the source material chosen, so that, just at the moment when the audience is moved by what they hear and come to understand, both the music and the words that manifest the literary expression of this truth will be harmonized together, so that both understanding and sensation will be unified, producing a moment when the entire audience will be moved, then filled with praise. "Opening the ears" refers to such a blending of verbal understanding and musical sensation into one aural source of appreciation.

On the other hand, what is called "opening the eyes" refers to the moment in a *nō* play when the deep sensations inherent in the play are suddenly experienced in one moment of profound exchange [between actor and audience]. When their "eyes are opened," the spectators receive this extraordinary impression through the aesthetic qualities related to dance and movement. This moment arises from the manifestation of the artistic and spiritual power of the actor. It may seem that such a moment may bear no relation to the drama as actually composed, but in fact this visual impression of superb skill could not come about if the actual moment for its realization had not been planned for in the play itself. The one composing the text must consider with extreme care where to place the moment when the actor's visual movements can create this effect. This moment, so crucial in the play, resembles that moment when the eyes are placed in a new statue of the Buddha; thus, this moment is referred to as "opening the eyes."

"Opening the ears" is therefore related to the writing of the play, "opening the eyes" to the skill of the actor. If one truly gifted person possesses both skills of writing and acting he will be beyond criticism.

Both "opening the ears" and "opening the eyes" come together to produce the highest level of beauty; therefore the means to bring both of these about must be carefully studied. There is a separate oral teaching concerning this matter.

Composing *nō* to be performed by child actors requires special care. When a child actor plays a subsidiary role, such as the child of another character, or a daughter, the actor's physical presence will be appropriate to the part and there should be no difficulties. But when a child actor performs the central character in a *nō*, he must not be made to appear in a fashion unsuitable for his age. It is inappropriate, for example, to make a child actor play the role of a parent or mother, who appears in grief while searching for a lost child, or to make an even younger actor play his son or daughter, so that, in a scene involving the sudden chance meeting of parents and children, two infants clutch and cling together giving the audience a sense of something vulgar through this moment of tearful sentimentality. Even when a child *nō* is well played, the fact that audiences shrink in a critical fashion from what they regard as emotionally painful is doubtless because of the existence of plays of this sort. When a child actor is the central figure in the *nō*, he should play exclusively a child or younger brother who may hunt for his parent, or mourn his separation from a younger brother. Such are the kinds of appearance suitable for an actor of this age. Even if the role he plays does not concern the relationship between parents and children, a child's skills do not permit him to play the role of an older person.

Again, caution must be taken in regard to older actors. True enough, the art of the *nō* involves nothing more than putting on a mask and adopting an appearance appropriate to the role the actor is playing; yet if the actor is simply too old, his appearance will be unsuitable and thus unconvincing to the spectators. If, for example, a young actor plays the part of an older character, there will be no difficulties. On the other hand, if an older actor plays the part of a young girl, or some young and famous warrior who is also a courtier, such as Atsumori or Kiyotsune, he will not be convincing to his audience. This point must be considered carefully. When a *nō* play is composed, it is most important to maintain a clear sense of discrimination as to what artistic effects may be suitable for a particular actor. The writer must have a real sense of the actor's important talents and know how to make use of them. For the successful composition of the play, these matters are of first importance.

Among the three general categories of *nō* described above, the following are plays that have gained success in recent years.

Yawata, Aioi, Yōrō, Oimatsu, Shiogama, and *Aridōshi* are among the plays that have old people as their central characters.

Hakozaki, Unoha, Mekurauchi, Shizuka, Matsukaze, Hyakuman, Ukifune, Higaki, Komachi are plays that have women as their main characters.

Michimori, Satsuma no kami, Sanemori, Yorimasa, Kiyotsune, Atsumori involve warrior roles.

Tango monogurui, Jinen Koji, Kōya, Ōsaka are plays concerning entertainers in Buddhist dress.

Koi no omoni, Sano no funabashi, Shii no Shōshō, Taizan Pukun are plays with demon roles in the style of Delicacy within Strength.

Along with these, there are also a number of new plays that may serve as models.

On the whole, many of the plays that have been written recently are actually based on older plays in which a few changes have been made in order to create new artistic effects. For example, the madwoman in *Saga no monogurui* is the present *Hyakuman*. *Shizuka* also exists in an older version. *Tango monogurui* is the same as the older play entitled *Fue monogurui*. *Matsukaze* used to be called *Shiokumi*. *Koi no omoni* is the former *Aya no taiko*. There are old and new versions of *Jinen Koji*. *Sano no funabashi* also exists in an earlier version. In each case, the new play is merely an adaption of the real source. Depending on the varying taste in different periods, words are slightly altered, the music is renewed, and a new Flower is created in response to changing times. In the future as well the same principle will continue to apply.

The decision as to whether a play is good or bad cannot be made by the actor himself. Whether in the capital or in the country, or even a remote region, *nō* is an art that is witnessed and widely commented upon. There is no way to escape from the criticism of the world at large. The artistry of *nō* brings about a shift in the old art in accordance with changing times; yet despite this fact, actors of great skill and high reputation are always able to manifest the artistry of Grace. Concerning this kind of artistry in former times, the name of the *dengaku* actor Itchū can be mentioned. In more recent times, I might cite the teacher of our own school, Kan'ami, or Dōami of the Hie troupe of Ōmi *sarugaku*. All these men made the Grace of dance and chant the basis of their art and were greatly skilled at performing in all of the Three Role Types. In addition, there have been actors who were highly skilled at playing warrior roles or demon roles in the style of Delicacy within Strength; yet, although they gained great renown, their reputations did not continue on in this world. Therefore, an actor who arrives at the level of manifesting the true level of Grace will possess an art that will always be effective, no matter how the taste of the times may change. A play must always be written with the basic principle of producing the seed that leads to a blooming of the Flower. To repeat again: in the past and in all ages to come, in every age, a truly gifted and

skilled player will manifest the quality of Grace. Hearing stories of the great actors of former times and observing actors
in our own day, it is clear that the reason all of these actors
are highly famed in the capital and the countryside alike lies
in the fact that they all exhibit the Flower of Grace.

My observations above are based on matters I have observed carefully in recent years and which I have thought over
deeply and summed up here. The various plays I have written
during this Ōei era (A.D. 1394-1427)[4] will continue to keep
their value in succeeding generations, I believe. Thus, take
these matters very much to heart.

This notebook has been given as a secret teaching to my
son Motoyoshi.

Ōei 30 [1423], 2nd month, 6th day.
Zeami

---

[4] Zeami refers to those plays written up until 1423. The Ōei era was to
continue until 1427.

Learning the Way (*Shūdōsho*)

Preface

Various matters concerning the training necessary for a troupe of *sarugaku* actors.

The actors who participate in any particular performance must of course work to perfect their individual skills, but there is another principle as well to which they must give the most earnest consideration. In order for them to create the impression of a truly successful and complete performance, the various skills of all the performers must be properly harmonized together. If their various accomplishments are not blended in this fashion, then no matter how skillfully they may perform on an individual basis, neither their dance nor their song will seem united and capable of creating a sense of completeness. Rather, the performers must work for the creation in themselves of a fundamental attitude of mutual concession and cooperation, in order to manifest properly their skills in dancing and singing. No one must take the attitude that he alone can succeed through his own individual skill. Using as a model for their own art the style of the actor who is the head of the troupe, the others should, on the basis of what they are directed to do, develop their own artistic accomplishments. A more detailed description follows.

The Role of the Head of the Troupe

In the course of a day's performance, the chief function of the head of the troupe, in his capacity as actor, begins with his entrance from the green room, his performance for a certain time while still on the bridge, his chanting of the *issei*, and then, upon his arrival on the stage proper, his performance of the first Sequence of the chant, beginning with the *sashi-goto*. All of this he performs alone, and all of these various stages in the performance are achieved through his own individual skill. If, because of some shortcoming in his voice, he cannot properly perform this kind of opening chant, then he cannot truly be considered an actor capable of leading a troupe. On the other hand, depending on the play that is being presented, it should pose no problems for him should he be called on to perform with another actor, in playing roles of an old couple, for example. When the actor is meant to appear alone, however, should he, because of some insufficiency in his own artistic appeal, or because he senses a lack of power in his vocal production, decide to take on the stage with him other supporting actors [who do not logically figure in the plot], then the sort of clumsy and inexperienced impression he will surely make does not accord at all with his function as the chief actor in the troupe. To repeat again, if an actor feels that, because of some insufficiency, he cannot perform an artistic task that is his alone to carry out and so chooses to rely on other actors, or on the help of the chorus to sustain his performance, his methods will be quite inappropriate to our art. Indeed, in whatever aspect of artistic endeavor, the actor who heads the troupe must be one who is recognized as superior in all things. The proof of the superiority of his skill will be clearly visible for all to see when he shows that, even if his singing voice does reveal some deficiencies, he can nevertheless find some way to command the strength to perform in a manner appropriate to the circumstances. In all things, the one who is termed "superior" and an accomplished actor is one who can carry out what may indeed seem beyond his means.

After the entrance of the chief actor, however, the various supporting players also appear. From that point onwards, the leading actor himself should attempt to blend in with the others, so that all the performers can cooperate with each other in creating an impression of unity, in order for the performance as a whole to produce successful results. Such should be the basic attitude to be taken by the actor who leads the troupe. In addition, of course, he has other responsibilities, such as fixing the pitch of the voice to be used in the *rongi* section.

Various Matters of Importance Concerning the Conduct of the Waki

He is the first performer who appears in any performance. Therefore, beginning with the congratulatory words that open the performance on the first offering of the day, he must make clear the general meaning of the play in his speech and draw the audience into the atmosphere of the drama. All of this must be accomplished through his own individual skill and invention. In particular, the congratulatory verses performed at the beginning of the first play are attended to with great care by the audience. The *waki* must therefore be most earnest in learning how to perform this section properly.

After this point in the performance, however, he must make it his principle to become part of the ensemble and so adjust himself to the rhythms established by the head of the troupe, so as to bring about a truly unified performance.

There is one important matter to which the actor who performs the *waki* roles must pay special heed. He is called a *waki* precisely because he is expected to perform in consonance with the leadership provided by the head of the troupe. Thus, even in a case when an insufficiency in the artistic leadership may occur and the head of the troupe is obliged to carry out his functions despite such deficiencies, the *waki* must follow him all the more obediently. If the *waki*, should he be a more accomplished actor than the *shite*, tries to compensate for these deficiencies in leadership by performing in a different manner, the total theatrical effect will not be unified and the performance cannot follow its regular course. A *waki* fulfills his function insofar as he follows what is good and what is bad alike. This principle represents the first step in creating unity in performance, without which no play can be successful.

The task of a *waki* is to understand this principle thoroughly and to aid the troupe in precisely this fashion.

Then too, the other actors who perform assisting roles in the troupe should practice so as to adjust themselves as well to the various changes in the rhythm of the performance as established by the head of the troupe, so that they can all be as one in creating the appropriate artistic effect. Such is the function assigned to those actors who perform these roles.

In general, no more than four or five actors should participate in a performance of *nō*. In former times, even though there were a large number of actors available, if a particular play called for only two characters, then no more than two actors would appear. On the pretext that so many actors are available, the practice of lining up large groups of them on the stage, dressed in ordinary street attire, *eboshi* and *suō*, in order for them to perform as a kind of chorus represents a practice altogether out of keeping with the art of the *nō*. Such methods are altogether unseemly. Only in recent years are such tendencies seen more and more. They cannot be condoned.

Functions Assigned to the Tsutsumi Players

Following are matters to be observed by the musicians who accompany performances on the *tsutsumi* drums. Since these musicians are to perform before the *shite* begins his chant, they should do so with all the artistry at their command up until that moment when he enters. The drummers can call out and exhaust every skill: this is the time when they can show off their own strengths. Once the singing and dancing begin, however, and the Role Playing gets underway, they can no longer indulge in musical effects for their own sake. They must plan their accompaniments in accord with the musical atmosphere created by the *shite* and make use of the Two Basic Arts that he creates as the foundation for their own performances. Such are the functions of the drummers in *sarugaku*. The same general principles apply to the use of the large *taiko* drums as well. At the beginning of a performance, it is doubtless correct to perform *ranjō*.[1]

Various Matters Pertaining to the Flute Players

Concerning flute players: they assume the extremely important task of establishing and maintaining the musical atmosphere of a particular performance, through all the stages of *jo, ha,* and *kyū*. Even before the performance by the actors begins, the players must perform quietly for a certain time in order to create for the audience an atmosphere appropriate for the beginning of the play. Then, when the dancing and the chanting commence, the players must align their music to the pitch of the voice of the *shite* and attempt to add emotional color to his vocal performance.

With regard to this matter, there is one crucial principle to be kept in mind by the flute players. As the flute is the instrument that essentially leads the pitch during a performance, it is reasonable to assume that all the musical effects of the *nō* should be governed by this instrument. Although this fact is certainly true as far as it goes, in order to make an actual performance successful, still another consideration becomes paramount. The function of the flute as used in performances of *nō* must indeed be different from that when the instrument is played in a purely musical performance. This is because, in a performance of *nō*, the pitch of the chanter's voice rises and falls slightly of its own accord from the level of pitch assigned. Therefore, if the musicians insist that it is their function to maintain the proper pitch and so proceed to play without adjusting the music [to the changes in pitch that will inevitably occur while the chanter himself is performing], the results will lack any sense of harmony. Therefore, the total musical effect of the performance will be listless and without energy. However, if the players can adjust themselves to the color of the

---

[1] *Ranjō* is a kind of free musical interlude, usually for flutes and drums. See Harich-Schneider, *A History of Japanese Music*, p. 202.

voice of the chanter so as to perform in a manner sufficiently flexible to regulate the totality of the musical effect, no disparities in the performance will be perceived by the audience, and an effective musical impression will be created. Indeed, the fact that the pitch of an actor's voice slightly rises or falls should not be seen as a serious defect on his part. In *shōmyō* and *sōga*, for example, the same slight deviations of pitch also occur. In the *nō*, all kinds of roles are performed, and the voice is used to express so many kinds of emotion—felicitation, yearning, love, pity, jealousy, wrath. Gesture and dance are involved as well. With so many vocal characteristics required of a performer, it is no wonder that without realizing it, he may slightly raise or lower his pitch. The flute players must have a real comprehension of the actor's art, play in consonance with his vocal production, and, keeping in mind the various elements necessary to such a performance, search out the appropriate pitch while they play. Then, in the pauses between dances or chant, the musicians can manage to recover the original proper pitch without calling attention to themselves, so that the spectators remain unaware of what is happening. Such is doubtless the most important function of the flute players in the theater.

The Great Flute Player Meishō

As an actor must perform all kinds of roles and in all kinds of situations, the various sorts of voice production required may result in a rising or falling of the pitch of the voice, a fact that should not in itself be seen as a shortcoming on his part.

Formerly, there was a truly gifted flute player named Meishō who performed with the Yamato troupe. The lay monk Sasaki Dōyo said of his skill that, "it is not in itself a good thing to extend the length of a *nō* performance, but when I hear Meishō play, I lose all sense of time."

On one occasion, at a performance for a religious festival, during the time when a *rongi* section was being sung by the chief actor in the troupe and a child performer, the pitch of the music had been set in the *rankei* mode.[2] However, as the child actor's voice was not fully settled, his chant rose slightly toward the pitch of the *banshiki* mode. The pitch of the chant of the head of the troupe remained, of course, in the *rankei* mode. Thus, as their chanted dialogue continued, the pair were no longer in harmony with each other, and the performance began to lose its vigor. Meishō, while playing alone in the proper *rankei* mode, slowly adjusted himself to the pitch of the child actor and colored his playing in a manner appropriate to the *banshiki* mode, while still remaining at the pitch of the *rankei* mode so as to accompany the part of the older player. As a result, no discrepancy was heard in their performances, and the presentation was a success.

As Meishō was able to play in this fashion, no one in the audience was aware of what had happened. Later, the chief actor came and praised him, saying, "your playing today was truly divine." Meishō responded, "I appreciate your gracious words, and I would only comment that it was indeed difficult for me to find the means to blend the performance of a seasoned voice with that of an immature one." That is to say, he had managed, through the coloration provided in his flute playing, to mediate between the two voices and blend them into one appropriate sound. Indeed, such a sound corresponds to the music that "bespeaks good order," and represents a voice production that can be described as "calming and delightful."[3]

So it was that, in the old days, a truly gifted musical performer, taking as his guiding principle the spirit of the head of the troupe, could bring success to a theatrical performance. Should such a person not serve as a model for our generation? In the Great Preface to the *Book of Odes*, it is written, "the music that bespeaks good order, when properly regulated, calms the heart and fills it with delight."

---

[2] *Rankei* is A# in modern musical notation. *Banshiki* is B.

[3] The two phrases are adapted from the Great Preface to the *Book of Odes* (Shih ching), Section 3. See Legge, *The Chinese Classics*, Vol. 4, *The She King*, p. 34. The phrase is quoted directly at the end of this same paragraph in Zeami's text.

Functions of the Kyōgen Actors

The functions of *kyōgen* actors: it is well known that their method of creating amusement for the audiences in the form of a comic interlude involves the use either of some impromptu materials chosen at the moment, or of some interesting incidents taken from old stories. On the other hand, when these actors take parts in an actual *nō* play, their function does not involve any need to amuse the audience. Rather, they are to explain the circumstances and the plot of the play that the audience is in the process of witnessing.

Kyōgen itself would merely be considered vulgar if its only aim were to make the audience laugh boisterously on all occasions. It is said that true gaiety lies within a delicate smile, and such impressions are always effective and moving for an audience. If a *kyōgen* actor can create such an atmosphere for his spectators and cause their gentle smiles, while still maintaining their interest, then he will have achieved the highest level of humor that shows in itself the quality of Grace. One who achieves this is truly a master of comedy. In former times, the performances of Tsuchidayū achieved this eminence.

Then again, a *kyōgen* actor who has the natural talent to stimulate in his audience feelings of winsomeness and of something attractive can truly be said to possess the divine luck of the artist. Whether in terms of words or of gestures, a *kyōgen* actor must, avoiding all vulgarity, allow his well-born audience to experience humor that is both clever and endearing. To repeat again, just because a performer's function requires him to be amusing, there should certainly be no reason for him to use vulgar words or gestures. This matter should be considered carefully.

The Order of Nō Performances

Formerly, a program of *nō* included no more than four or five plays. These days as well, as concerns performances at sacred festivals and at subscription performances, usually three *nō* plays and two *kyōgen* pieces are selected, making a total of five. Recently, however, when plays are performed at the request of the nobility, the number of plays requested has increased, so that seven, eight, even ten plays are included. Since such programs are presented by command, however, an actor is obliged to accept them.

In terms of the order of *jo, ha,* and *kyū* to be observed during the course of a day's performance, the opening *waki nō* constitutes the *jo.* The second, third, and fourth plays constitute the *ha,* during which various arts and skills appropriate to the *nō* are exploited to their fullest extent, and the fifth play brings about the final stage of *kyū.* In this fashion, the proper order of *jo, ha,* and *kyū* is observed, and the day's performance can be judged as complete. However if, unexpectedly, the number of plays to be presented is increased, the order of *jo, ha,* and *kyū* will of necessity be changed, and the arrangement of the plays may no longer be appropriate. In terms of the artists who must perform, the problem is a crucial one. Still, as the performances are given at the command of the nobility, he cannot help but follow their wishes. Therefore, in such circumstances, all the performers must take special care, so that, when moving from the level of *ha* to that of *kyū,* they allow a certain leniency, and, using their skills to the utmost, engender ever richer means of expression, so that, as concerns the aesthetic qualities of their performance still greater reserves of skill seem to lie behind their accomplishments. The artistic skill of truly seasoned performers is doubtless manifested under just such trying circumstances. Thus, with those matters well in mind, the succession of plays that conform to the order of *jo, ha,* and *kyū* can either be extended or other alterations made.

Preparations for a day's performance of the *nō* should be carried out in this manner.

The 3rd day of the 3rd month of the 2nd year of Eikyō (1430), written on behalf of the actors in the Kanze troupe.

An Account of Zeami's Reflections on Art (*Sarugaku dangi*)

Notes taken down by Hata No Motoyoshi

Preface

The way of Sarugaku   Although the way of *sarugaku* is chiefly involved with Role Playing, it should be said that since the origins of *sarugaku* derive from *kagura*, the real fundamentals of our art lie in the Two Basic Arts of dance and chant. When it comes to defining the basis for the dance in *sarugaku*, as far as our own traditions are concerned the dance in *Okina* should undoubtedly be cited. The basis of the chant is surely the *kagura* song in *Okina*, as well. It was said in ancient times that "it is poetry that moves the heart."[1] This maxim applies to all kinds of poetry and to the chant of the *nō* as well. If an actor has not truly mastered these Two Basic Arts, how can he be called a truly accomplished performer?

In *The Three Elements in Composing a Play*, it is written that "an actor who has truly reached the level of highest fruition has made the Grace of dance and chant the basis of his art, and has mastered the Three Role Types. In the ages that have passed, and in the ages to come, there have been various arts in which actors have become proficient, yet the performers who have truly earned undying fame are those who have never strayed from the path of creating a true Flowering of Grace. Those artists who have created warrior or

---

[1] A citation from the Great Preface to *The Book of Odes* (Shih ching). See Legge, *The Chinese Classics*, IV, 34, for another translation.

demon roles may have achieved temporary renown, but their reputations have not continued on."[2]

Then again, it is written in the *Teachings on Style and the Flower* that the arts of the Yamato and the Ōmi school of *sarugaku* and *dengaku* differ. A truly gifted player, however, whatever the style involved, should possess the requisite skills to perform it. An ordinary actor, on the other hand, who can only learn his own style without coming to know the others, will merely dislike them. Although there are many styles and models, the fascination of the Flower is common to all— Yamato and Ōmi *sarugaku* and *dengaku* alike.[3]

Then again it is written that, particularly in our art, the greatest happiness for a troupe is to possess the love and respect of its widely varied public; and thus, depending on the time and place, such happiness consists of performing in such a way that even untrained spectators will be pleased.[4] [For this reason, the actor needs to know every style of performance.]

An actor must therefore proceed through the various stages of his training in the proper order. In general, it is not necessary for him to learn to play demon roles as such during his career. Once the Two Basic Arts and Three Role Types have been mastered, and the actor has gained extensive experience in his art, it will then be time to perform roles that carry a slight flavor of a demon's vigor. Even after the age when an actor thinks to secure his reputation [at about the age of thirty-four or thirty-five], he should not take on roles of this sort.

Itchū   Itchū (in *dengaku*), Kiyotsugu (Buddhist name Kan'ami), Inuō (Buddhist name Dōami), and Kiami: these four are the ancestors of our art.

---

[2] See pp. 160-161. Motoyoshi's text does not agree in every particular with the original citation.

[3] See pp. 38-39. Motoyoshi has again given a reduced version of the citation.

[4] See p. 39. Again, the citation is adapted.

Of Itchū, Kan'ami said that "he was the model for my own art." Dōami was also Itchū's disciple. Zeami himself never witnessed a performance by Itchū, but from the accounts left by such men as the lay monk Sasaki Dōyo or Nan'ami, the extent of his abilities can be surmised. He was, of course, a rather light and witty artist. This is because he came from *dengaku nō*.

In *dengaku*, generally speaking, movement and chant are always separated. Thus, in the sections devoted to the chant, the actors merely line up on stage to perform their chorus in a simple fashion. Then, with a sudden change, drums are beaten, "ya! tei, tei!" and various tricks such as somersaults are inserted at the end of a performance as part of a regular routine. Ashikaga Yoshimitsu was supposed to have said, "Kōshōshi (Matsuyasha) is a bad actor, but then he is typical of [the gimmickry of] *dengaku*."

Kiami Kiami is the father of the chant. It is said that he modeled his performances on those of Ushikuma of the Hie troupe. Kiami performed a style of *nō* in which music was paramount. Later, however, Shizuya sometimes performed in his stead. Among the five orders of excellence [that lie beyond an ordinary level of success] the art of Kiami fits perfectly that of the voice. In terms of the nine levels, he belonged to the second highest, the Art of the Flower of Profundity. As it is so difficult to define the level of Peerless Charm, it can only be surmised that he was gifted with this highest quality, since he had already risen to one of the upper three levels.

[Zeami said that] "When I was twenty, I heard that there was to be a performance of the '*nō* for the bestowing of clothing'[5] at the Hōon-in [of the Kōfukuji Temple] in Nara, and I went to see it, wondering what sort of music I might hear. Kiami appeared as an old man, wearing a hempen wig but no mask, and performed his chant 'Long ago, in the cap-

[5] Performances given in thanks for clothing bestowed on the actors by the temple authorities.

ital, I cut a dashing figure, but now . . .'[6] in a straightforward and artless manner; yet thinking over the effect he produced, I later realized how fascinating a performance he had given."

In a performance of the *nō* play *Sumiyaki*, Kiami wore a wig of hemp that he folded back on his head, and wore the same kind of mask that Dōami wears these days, tinted in a single shade. He wore a *mizugoromo* over a *kosode* woven of raw and polished silk, bound with a cord, and appeared using a cane and with a bundle of firewood bound on his back. Stopping midway on the bridge, he gave a cough and began to sing. "The old man of the mountain, is his load a light one? Does he hurry home? Does he hurry along because of the cold from the storm? Does he hurry away because he can cut his wood from the same forest on the mountain where he lives? . . ." Then he began his *issei*, "From the tips of the trees on the mountains, one piled upon another. . . ." He was truly a brilliant performer. His appearance was that of a vessel of bronze [simple and dignified].

From the time of these performances of the *nō* for the bestowing of clothing given in Nara, it was said that Kiami began to lose his voice. Thus he did not perform a chant to its conclusion. He would have Shizuya sing and then merely add certain phrases. For example, in the line "the wind blowing on the windswept shore" [from an unidentified text], he had Shizuya sing the entire phrase and he only chanted the phrase that followed. Yet in his musical gifts, heaven-sent as they were, he was exceptionally talented, even among the great actors of the days gone by.

Zōami   As for Zōami (who followed Kiami), and is performing at the present time, both his acting performances and his musical skills surely reach the level of the Flower of Tranquillity. His performances are in perfect harmony with his music, his music with his performance. On one occasion at

---

[6] The work from which these lines are taken has not been identified. There is a poem with a similar title by the Chinese T'ang poet Po Chü-i cited in the *Wakanrōeishū*, which may have served as the basis for this entertainment.

the Tōboku-in [of the Kōfukuji Temple] at Nara, during the performance of a *tachiai* dance, he turned from east to west, then ceased his movements, completing them with just a slight motion of his fan. Being moved to tears, Zeami said to himself, "there is no spectator here watching who appreciates this moment, and our art is in decline." Still, Zōami's movement of such high artistic fruition did manage to attract the ears and eyes of some of his audience. A number of spectators remarked that "the *tachiai* of Dōami is somehow different from that of the others." In the *nō* play *Shakuhachi*, as each note was played, he performed his chant in a straightforward, artless fashion and finished abruptly. His was an art of profundity with utmost simplicity.

Zōami's skills are by no means limited to those of *dengaku*. He is proficient in every style. Nevertheless, his particular method of chanting in chorus and his performance in *Sumiyaki* carrying wood on his back are typical of the style of *dengaku*.

Dōami (Inuō) The performances of Dōami were always in the upper three levels and never fell even as far as the top of the middle three levels, to say nothing of the middle or lower levels of our art. Only his chanting was doubtless lower, on the highest rank of the middle level.

In the play *Aoi no Ue*, he rode on a bullock cart wearing a robe lined in willow-colored cloth with a skirt so long that it concealed his feet. A maidservant, played by Iwamatsu, clung to the shaft of the cart. On the bridge he began his *issei*. "Riding on the three vehicles of the law others may escape the burning house. Mine is but a cart in ruins like Yūgao's house; I know not how to flee my passion," and then moving the cart forward, he continued on, in a full voice. "Like an ox-drawn cart this weary world rolls endlessly on the wheels of retribution. . . ."[7] In this *shidai*, he sang the last syllable of the word "cart" in a high-pitched and beautiful fashion, and,

---

[7] This translation is taken from *Japanese Noh Drama* II (Tokyo, 1959), 93.

as he finished, he stamped his foot to the rhythm of the music. Later in the play, when he appeared as the spirit of Lady Rokujō, at the moment when the *yamabushi* priest[8]—played by Toyo—prayed to the ghost, he looked back at the priest, holding the sleeves of his costume in such a way as to hide his face, truly a moment of theatrical effectiveness beyond any description.

Then again, when performing the "dance of the angel,"[9] he would dance as though he were a soaring bird that had given itself to the wind. Handing over to the *waki* a sutra written in gold dust, he was already dancing as he drew his hand back from the sutra. In the first half of the dance, he raised his fan to his left, an unusual but striking movement in itself; at the end, when he chanted the words "what, what to do . . ." he moved his fan to the left and made a powerful gesture, as though drawing a large circle in the air. Zeami wondered why he performed such a peculiar dance. At first the form seemed somehow incorrect, but Zeami soon realized that Dōami had reached the level of Highest Fruition and that his motions were altogether appropriate. The other [actors in his troupe, however], finding his eccentricities successful, try to imitate them in a superficial manner [so that their art] resembles an *obi* come untied, which they do not know how to fasten and so bring their art under control.

Then again, in the *sarugaku* play *Nembutsu*, Dōami wore robes woven of raw and polished silk, loosely gathered in front, and over them, a silk garment dyed black. He covered his head thoroughly with a hood made from a long piece of cloth. Thus even his appearance was fascinating. As though calling from the green room, he appeared chanting ceaselessly from the midst of the crowd, "Praise to Amida Buddha." Then, proceeding along, he rang a hand gong and gave out

[8] A kind of itinerant Buddhist priest, often living in the mountains, who sometimes served as an exorcist.

[9] A specialty of Dōami, the importance of which is also mentioned by Zeami in "The Flower of Returning." See "Kyakuraika," tr. by Mark J. Nearman, *Monumenta Nipponica* 35, No. 2 (Summer 1980), pp. 186-190.

cries of lament. Casually striking the gong two or three times, and ignoring the musical rhythm those sounds established, he assumed an attitude of prayer, putting his two hands together in the old-fashioned pious manner. At the end of every phrase he kept repeating the prayer "Praise to Amida Buddha," which he spoke with fervor, as though it were an expression that never left his lips, and he moved back and forth in a composed fashion. "I can still see him before me even now," Zeami said.

In the *sarugaku* called *Morikata*, at the moment when Dōami was seated and reading the Buddhist scriptures, his wife and mother both appeared on the scene; when they said, "how is this?" he gazed for a long time at his mother, then turned and looked down with displeasure at his wife. This affecting expression of anxiety gained him high praise at the time. In the *sarugaku* on the theme of "the child who is not our child," on the lines, "ah, he hurried away!" he was also highly praised for the expressiveness he showed with his eyes.

In general, the art of the Ōmi *sarugaku* players does not aim at the kind of theatrical effect that can cause an audience to start with amazement; rather, their basic principles call for the creation of a quiet appearance, rich in atmosphere. At the very end of a play, for example, the whole cast merely stands singing on the stage before making a rapid final exit. Dōami alone, as his art was based on such a simple style, achieved the level of Highest Fruition, and as his performances were truly effective, these days all the members of the Ōmi troupe attempt to imitate him, although they are not equal to the task. Their chanting and stage movements are merely sluggish and slow. Such is the situation wtih this company.

Among the *waki*, Toyo was a straight and earnest player, who always worked to perform in a manner appropriate to the situation. Iwamatsu was a *waki* who always followed the *shite* perfectly. On occasion, Ushikuma also performed as the chief *waki* in a performance in which more than one supporting actor appeared.

Kan'ami Our ancestor Kan'ami earned an enormous reputation for his performance in such plays as *Shizuka ga mai* or *Saga no dainembutsu no onna monogurui*, and his appearance in performance was on the level of Peerless Charm. All of this is mentioned in the *Teachings on Style and the Flower*. In the highest reaches of his art and in the top rank of the middle level as well, Kan'ami played difficult parts in an easy manner. And he was the only one who was able to descend as far as the lower levels with the intention of mingling with the dust by performing in a popular style for the sake of the ordinary public.

In plays such as *Sumiyoshi no sengū*, he wore an *akujō* mask,[10] with a *tateboshi*, and held on to a cane with a T-shaped handle. As the play began, he appeared on the bridge and began to speak with great vigor. In the *rongi* section, when he spoke the line, "It is this old man's error to divine that you are Ki no Aritsune's daughter!" the kind of control he showed in tightening and slackening the rhythm has never been equaled. He had a large manly build, yet when he portrayed a woman he looked frail and slender. In plays like *Jinen Koji*, he wore the wig of a mendicant Buddhist priest, and when he stood on the raised sermon platform, he looked to be twenty-two or twenty-three years old. When he began his speech "this Buddhist teaching for a lifetime," the marvelous way in which he varied his chanting as he progressed caused Lord Ashikaga Yoshimitsu to turn to Zeami and say jokingly, "You are up to all kinds of tricks, but you have never achieved anything like that!" so moved was he by the force of Kan'ami's performance. Indeed, in every role that Kan'ami played, each time he aligned the music [so that the chant and the dance moved together], he showed a skill worthy of the gods themselves.

Then, when it came to the fierce demon roles, such as in

10 The style of mask used for a mysterious or frightening old man, often a god or ghost. Literally, a "wicked old man" mask.

plays such as *Tōru no Otodo*, when he became a demon and persecuted the Minister, he performed in a serene and magnanimous manner, so that his movement of Delicacy within Strength was moving yet revealed an interior gentleness. In the *nō* play *Kusakari*, after the line "This horse is starving and now must die," he used a quotation from the Chinese and added such phrases as "my horse runs no more, runs no more;"[11] then when he began the chant just before the end of the play, "here is the grass pillow I must endure," he moved his eyes in a most expressive way and made a quick exit. Even a player descended from heaven itself could not have achieved such a level of art.

At this time, *waki* roles were performed by Junisaburō and Sukekurō. Jūnirokurō, who was a young man at the time, performed lesser parts. Ōtsuchi served as *kyōgen*.

This is what I have heard and written down in outline concerning the four ancestors of our art. Examining the synthesis of all their art that Zeami has created, it can be seen that his art is based on that of his father Kan'ami and that he has added nothing particular of his own.

Zeami One quiet evening, after listening to a passage from *Kinuta*, my father Zeami said to me, "In the generations to come, there will be no one able to catch the real flavor of a serene play like this. I cannot summon up the energy to write it down." When it comes to plays composed on such a peerless level, beyond any "flavor," then in the ordinary sense of the word there is nothing to "savor." Even if one wished to write down this quality, there would be no words with which to express it. If an actor has really attained these supreme heights, he will be able to understand it within himself, I have heard. Thus I myself can write no more concerning the matter. In any case, it can only be said that when plays such as *Ukifune*

[11] The quotation is adapted from the famous song of the contender Hsiang Yü, at the time of the founding of the Han Dynasty in China. See Burton Watson, tr., *Records of the Grand Historian of China*, I, 70, for the full text of the song.

and *Matsukaze* are well performed by an actor equal to their demands, he will be proven a peerless performer.

Commenting on Zeami's *nō*, Zōami said, "when he spoke a phrase such as 'how auspicious! The light that shines, protecting the rulers of countless generations, falls richly under the heavens' [from *Hōjōgawa*], he does so with the fullness and richness of Inuō himself. From the beginning to the end of *Aridōshi* he performs in the style of Kiami. His control at every crucial point makes his dancing resemble the art of Kan'ami."

In *Aridōshi*, there are such phrases as, ". . . thinking of Aridōshi of the stars—what a fascinating poem!" and "the six roads come together in one crossroads, and six colors can be seen," or "somehow, at the temples and shrines, the sound of the bell in the depth of night, and the very light of the lamp itself," and "there is no light, and the voices of the shrine maidens can no longer be heard." All of these are chanted by Zeami in the style of Kiami. In a phrase such as "the god instructs the young priests," Zeami uses Kiami's precise style of articulation. In the phrase, *"miyamori hitori mo"* ("one of the shrine guards"), Zeami contracted the syllable *hi* to give it a special emphasis when he chanted. Zeami's method of performing a phrase in *Matsukaze*, "pillars of pine, fence of bamboo, how cold the night seems!" was also like that of Kiami.

On the other hand, Zeami performed the chant at the beginning of *Ukai* incorporating the style used by his father. Chanting lightly with the lips was Kan'ami's special achievement. The entire play, from beginning to end, involves chanting on the level of Perfect Freedom. Only from the line, "What an interesting appearance," should the lines be chanted with the chorus.

Then too, Zeami performed the demon role in this play in the same fashion that Kan'ami performed in *Tōru no Otodo*. It is said that the way of playing this particular role was that used by Uma no Shirō, and that Kan'ami modeled his own performance on that of the earlier actor. Uma no Shirō played his part in a surprisingly nimble and expansive fashion. Zeami was not able to see Mitsutarō's famous performance in the demon roles. According to the accounts of older persons, however, Mitsutarō usually performed the role of the spirit of a dead man in a subtle and self-composed manner. Kan'ami himself composed a *nō* called *Tōrō* in which he took the part of the *waki* and had Zeami, [still a child], perform the demon's role; Kan'ami said that Zeami's style when he appeared transfigured into the spirit of the dead hero had "the appearance of Mitsutarō." It was in this play *Tōrō* that my father Zeami first performed a demon role.

1. Fixed Procedures

One must know the fixed procedures in the *nō*. In *tachiai*, for example, no matter how many performers participate, they must all perform exactly in the same fashion. The very meaning of the term *tachiai* ["performing together"] explains the principle involved. Now, in the midst of such an ensemble performance, there may be some scenes in which the central actor will move himself in a more vigorous fashion. In *Torōkyō* for example, the actor performs in just such a fashion at the spot, "together with Torōkyo." In some performances, there are three moments involving this kind of vigorous action. On the last of the three, the actor spreads his fan, brings it to the right, spreads out his hands, and calling out "ya, ya!" moves forward with high steps, gathers in his sleeves with his hands, and then, with a powerful gesture to the left and right, furls them out. Such is one fixed procedure. It has been in use for many generations. There is also a moment of vigorous action in the *jo* section of a *kusemai* [which is generally danced in a slow tempo]. At the moment in that section when the syllables of the verse are emphasized and elongated, vigorous action is employed in just such an assiduous fashion.

Generally speaking, in *kusemai* the fixed procedures require that the *jo* be danced in an appropriately slow and gentle fashion, then the rapid sections in a correspondingly spirited fashion, so that this pattern of alteration is maintained. For example, in *Utaura*, at the line "I hear that even those sword-like trees have all melted away; here, the fiery hell of breaking stones," the actor must crouch down intently and move with small steps. Then he continues along, alternating moments of tension and repose. Finally, at the line "The pulling fire burns the soles of the feet," since he will have exhausted his fixed gestures by this time, the actor, as a temporary expedient, can step back or turn sharply [even when such a movement has no relevance] while waiting for the phrase that follows, "starving, swallowing balls of iron." At that point he may now bring his fan to the left and, with it still open, use a strong gesture and circle the stage, both appropriate fixed gestures. Although there is a proper method that calls for fixed movements at certain times, an actor, thinking to add something that he finds of interest, may choose to perform his own turning movement, even though properly fixed gestures are still available to him—a foolish thing altogether.

When performing indoors, it is crucial to grasp the principle of *jo, ha,* and *kyū.* If an actor begins to chant in an atmosphere of *jo* that matches the mood of his audience, he must begin his dance in an atmosphere of *jo* as well. When the atmosphere of the audience is at the level of *kyū,* however, he must begin at that level. On such an occasion, should the actor still insist on using the level of *jo,* as usual for an introduction, the results will inevitably be unsatisfactory. When a banquet is well advanced, or a performance of *nō* is suddenly requested as part of a larger entertainment, then for the same reasons, the performance must be designed to suit the pleasure of the nobility.

Then again, when two performers are called out at once, if the adult performs after the child actor has finished, he must be careful not to duplicate the same atmosphere. If he is not careful, he will appear extremely childish. Rather, he should use the child's dance as the *jo* for his own performance, make the very end of the *ha* the basis for what he will do, carry out with circumpsection a dance appropriate to the level of *kyū,* and then retire.

Then there is a repeated gesture of Zōami called "letting go the fan," in which he used to drop his fan, take hold of the bottom portions of his sleeves, then pick it up. Dōami as well witnessed this gesture in performance. This technique is not part of our tradition, however. Thus it cannot really be called a fixed procedure. (There is a separate teaching concerning this matter.)

As for the fixed procedure called "giving back the knee," an actor turns quickly on one knee. This trick must be only used within the prescribed limits and not outside of them. For example, when the actor picks up a *kakko* drum in *Tango monogurui*, as the drum is normally on the ground, the actor can go down on his knees to pick it up, then turn his body. Such an example shows an appropriate use of this technique.

2. Artistic Effects

Everything depends on a proper elegance of atmosphere in performance [rather than on any specific skill or contrivance]. Even in a theatrical endeavor that seems to have no special atmosphere about it, the spectators can find this simplicity fascinating because of the special mood it creates. As long as the atmosphere is appropriate, the performance will show no shortcomings. As long as beauty is created, what may be missing in terms of technique from the performance will not cause any difficulties. On the other hand, if a performance is technically complex but without elegance, it will seem all the worse.

Making sidelong glances while dancing can create a successful theatrical atmosphere. Looking to the left is not often recommended; the actor should rather look to the right. Appropriate movements must be made as well in accordance with the 5-7, 5-7 patterns in the chant.

In the *nō* play *Matsukaze*, if, at the line "please pray for our remains" the actor should draw close [to the *waki*, who takes the part of a priest], his movement will merely be dull [as it will end before the chant itself is finished]. If, on the other hand, the actor maintains himself, without moving, almost to the end of that line, and then approaches at the words, "I take my leave" and moves back at the word "return," a fascinating artistic effect can be created. At the words, "only the wind in the pines remains" [which, repeated twice, form the conclusion of the play], should the actor merely withdraw while still pronouncing the final verb "remains," the effect will not be enjoyable; rather, he must wait until the final syllable. Especially on such an occasion as this, if the significance of the text and the movements of the actor do not coincide, the effect will not be satisfying.

In the *nō* play *Obasute*, at the line, "I feel ashamed to see the moon," there exists a moment when the acting can be so effective that it may truly be said, that without effort "gold can be picked up in the middle of the road." In the *nō* in general, the principle of suggesting a larger view through the imagination serves as the basis for our art, and so a play of this sort should be performed expansively so as to create a wealth of overtones. However, it is painful to see an actor who speaks the line "I feel ashamed to see the moon" and then hides his face with his open fan while speaking to the actor facing him, without looking at the moon, all the while stooping and crouching in a realistic manner. Rather, at the words "see the moon," the actor should lift up his open fan high, so as to reveal the fact that his shame concerning the moon forms the basis of his gesture. Then, while glancing at the other actor, he can perform with a slight suggestion of emotion [revealing his embarrassment toward human beings as well]. In this way the actor can give rise to a striking artistic effect.

In the *nō* play *Kōya*, the line, "At some point, indeed, those who come seeking" must be chanted in a light and rapid manner. If such a section [in which excitement is revealed] is performed in any heavy fashion, the artistic effect will be insipid. In the *nō* play *Tango monogurui* there exists a similar situation at the line, "If I could only see the sea of Yosa without this burden on my mind," the chanting should be performed in a calm manner, and the artistic effects created by the actor should serve to support the music. The *shite* need do nothing to make this section finish more quickly. Rather, the music itself should be performed in such a way as to make the richest artistic effect possible. In the *nō* play *Ukon no baba* at the line, "Is it necessary to wait for the moon, visible at daybreak?" the passage should be sung as rapidly as seems appropriate. On the other hand, pressing forward too rapidly will not be effective.

In the *nō* play *Koi no omoni*, at the line "The smoke of love is divided into two streams," the artistic effect requires the use of a gentle rhythm, employed in the quietest fashion. This play must seem a mixture of two artistic effects, as though delicately colored cherry blossoms were mingled together with willow leaves moving in the breeze. In a play like *Funabashi*, the atmosphere is rather that of an old and manly pine bending in the wind.

[Both of these plays are in the demon category.] However, since no one has ever seen an actual demon in this world, the essentials for the actor's performance lie in the creation of an interesting general atmosphere rather than in any specific details. Generally, compared to plays in this category, the performance of *nō* that involves human characters can be said to be all the more difficult and important.

3. Role Playing in the Nō

Whatever the role to be played, a performance must be based on proper motivation [growing out of the subject and meaning of the text to be presented]. Only after these matters are fully understood can effective movement and atmosphere in a performance become possible.

In terms of the audience, there are times when the spectators will watch a play in a state of great tension and excitement. Then again, there are times when they will observe a play with interest, but in a distant and easygoing fashion. If an actor observes that the entire audience seems to wait breathlessly, thinking that the play is coming to an end in a dramatic fashion, he should surprise them and finish his performance gently. If, on the other hand, the spectators merely seem to be enjoying the performance in a detached way, the actor must then pull himself up and end the performance in a sharp and firm manner. A performance will always be exciting to his audience if the actor ends by creating an emotional atmosphere different from that already held by the audience. So it might be said that a successful actor has the ability to beguile the hearts of his audience. It is all the more important that this tactic itself is kept a secret, so that those who watch the play do not anticipate the means by which the actor accomplishes his results.

As concerns the matter of "beguiling" an audience, it has been often said recently [as a criticism] that "such deceptions are gradually becoming apparent." Remarks of this kind merely show the dull wits of those who make them. Those spectators have merely been deceived by the charm of a child actor and so become disillusioned when he grows up and performs less well. True tactics in captivating an audience, on the other hand, require the performance of a really superior actor who, while aware that he may be performing in an unorthodox manner can, as he grows older (as did Zeami, after he took holy orders at age sixty), perform a dance in an interior space in a sophisticated style. Such is the real meaning of "beguiling an audience." The whole matter of "deceptions becoming apparent" is an unrelated matter altogether, and those who speak slightingly in this way reveal themselves as spectators of poor discernment.

In the nō play *Ukifune*, the line "This Ukifune knows no place of shelter" represents a crucial point in the whole drama. The actor should therefore perform this section with the greatest interior concentration, with the feeling in himself that it would take him a day or two to exhaust all the emotions that lie in that moment.

In the nō play *Tsunemori*, the heavy thoughts of the mother represent the paramount emotions that are to be portrayed.

However, actors often play the role in too shallow a manner. While Tsunemori chants, the mother should keep her head lowered in anguish, then raise it to perform her own lament in an appropriate fashion. In general, the suitable appearance for a woman in a role of this type requires her to keep looking down, while occasionally raising her head just a little.

Concerning the *nō* play *Sumidagawa*, Zeami said "the play would be all the more fascinating without employing a real infant actor hidden inside the mound. In this play, after all, no living child appears. It is rather a ghost. The basis of the performance should be grounded on this fact." My brother Motomasa, who wrote the play, replied, "this kind of performance would be very difficult, and I do not think I could bring it off myself." Zeami replied, "in matters of this sort, one must actually try both ways of performance in order to see which method will be more successful. Without doing so, there is no way to determine what is good and what is bad."

The *nō* play *Shii no shōshō* is complex [and made up of many elements of Role Playing]. Dōami said that he could not perform it properly. It is said that he remarked that even to bring one aspect of the play to life would require a musical accompaniment in the Yamato style [which provides a strong rhythmical base]. Yet the moment when the lines "waiting for the moon, waiting for the moon, I am . . ." are spoken will succeed splendidly when properly prepared and performed.

In the *nō* play *Kōya*, the *shite* shows his madness at the phrase "this writing becomes my keepsake of you; how vague to me your whereabouts. The cuckoo. . . ." If the actor feigns madness for too long a period and still performs the *issei* "how tempted" in the same manner, he will not be effective. The phrase "the cuckoo" should form the basis of the actor's intent, so that the audience will retain the feelings already engendered. Then the performer can give rise again to this atmosphere in his gestures as he moves into the *issei*, "how tempted. . . ."

In the *nō* play *Tango monogurui*, at the phrase "what the flowers speak," a particular pattern of foot rhythm is employed in which sounds are made with the feet that color the movement of the music that is chanted. Using the phrase "what the flowers speak" as the emotional basis of the scene, the performer continues [with his chant] while beginning to produce this stamping sound in such a way that no one can tell just when it begins. Nowadays, however, young performers tend to rely on the musical rhythm instead as a basis for this moment, and so begin stamping only when their line is finished. The results are peculiar. In *Shii no shōshō*, in the same way, at the phrase "a rain of tears?" one single stamp of the feet should be added. If the timing is established too quickly, or too slowly, the effect will be spoiled. In *Sano no funabashi*, at the phrase "evening after evening," the same stamping should be employed. The proper use of such rhythms is crucially important. As for the rhythm to be employed at the phrase "the willows are green, the flowers scarlet" in *Yamamba*, the basic technique of two rhythmic steps is used on the word "flower [*hana*]." On the last syllable *ri* of *midori* [green], an additional step is included as well, thus increasing the allure of the artistic effect. Such are the sort of special techniques to be employed.

In the case of demon roles, the methods used in our troupe are different from those of other schools. Even though the basic rhythm employed may be the same, others beat out the rhythm in a stiff and hard manner, while we are more supple. Such is a special characteristic of the Delicacy within Strength type of demon roles [as performed in our school]. There are many other aspects of rhythm that the actor must experience for himself.

On the famous occasion when a subscription *nō* was presented [in 1349] in the Kamo riverbed in Kyoto, on that occasion when the specially built reviewing stand collapsed, Itchū of the Honza troupe and Hanayasha of the Shinza troupe, as well as others, in groups of four, performed, eight altogether, in the "*tachiai* of love." At the phrase "if the end of resentment should ever pass by," when it came time to stop their voices, Itchū's throat tightened and he coughed; he took a firmer grip on his fan and wiped away the perspiration in order to pull himself together. Hanayasha, however, [became nervous] and stopped his chant abruptly and so found himself laughed at by the audience. Those who witnessed the performance said that Itchū had brought shame on Hanayasha.

Then too, on one occasion Enami and Zeami presented a *tachiai* before Ashikaga Yoshimitsu. During their performance of *Okina*, at the words "how gently!" Zeami quietly stopped dancing, but Enami continued on, and so he was laughed at by the audience. At the time, some of those who saw the performance said, "look how Zeami brought shame on Enami by the trick he played." Yet the essential quality involved reveals the kind of mental attitude of readiness and quick-wittedness appropriate for a highly trained actor. There was no idea in either case of wanting to bring any harm to another performer.

When an actor holds himself while on the bridge, just at that moment before he steps onto the stage proper, he should wait until he senses an expectation in the audience that he is about to dance. He must not simply begin. If he begins to dance too soon, while still on the bridge, his sequence will finish too soon and so create an awkward situation for him. Zōami sometimes danced on the bridge but never earned much success with the technique.

In the *nō*, there are certain performers whose gestures do not give an impression of Fulfillment. For example, as concerns the matter of weeping, some actors pull their sleeves away too quickly after putting them in front of their eyes. Or again, they may appear to wipe only one eye with their sleeves.

In the matter of the so-called "curving return," [in which an actor rapidly turns on his heel using his left leg as the axis of his movement], the performer must return to his original position using his hips and knees. This action should be like that of a taut bow quickly released. The return motion must happen in an instant. When the actor returns his body to its original position, he must leave no trace in the perceptions of the audience of his appearance from behind. The trick is to begin to return at full height and end in a crouch.

When it is time to finish a dance, the open end of the fan should be used as though it were covering the end of the sleeve, and the actor should cease his movement quietly and cleanly.

In addition, there is a kind of performance referred to as "dancing unseen." "Seeing the dance" occurs when the performer, while moving, looks directly at the tips of his fingers when his arms are extended. [In the case of "dancing unseen," however] the dancer, [should he lift high his right hand in a gesture], will slightly incline the nape of his neck, so that his neck and right shoulder remain as far apart as practical while he lifts up his hand [without looking at it].

When an actor opens his hands quickly, he should finish the gesture by closing them in a slow and heavy fashion; when he extends his hands gravely, however, he should then finish by withdrawing them quickly. If an actor moves his body more quickly than usual, then he must complete his movement in a solemn manner. If, on the other hand, he is moving more slowly than usual, in a quiet fashion, then he must cease his movements in a quick and nimble fashion. (I heard of this matter while still a child and so I may not have remembered properly every detail.)

"Counterfeit *nō*" represents a performance in which an actor strives for a kind of success beyond his own artistic means. The phrase does not necessarily refer to a performer's imitation of the work of any specific superior actor.

When the performance of a dance seems to take far too long, the dancer is not effective. Those who have waited with anticipation but lose interest as the performance goes along will merely find the experience tedious.

When performing informally indoors, an actor while on the stage may sometimes make a gesture of adjusting his clothing before he stands. This gesture shows his courtesy; if he merely bolts up and begins, his appearance will suggest a lack of concern for the niceties of the situation. If the actor arranges his clothing mechanically, however, without a sense of the occasion, he will stand out in an unseemly fashion.

4. "Ah!" as a Level of Art

The level of art that causes a spectator to merely say "ah!" in expressing his wonderment lies even below the beginnings of the true way of our art. This is nothing more than the reaction of a country bumpkin, up to the capital for the first time, who expresses his amazement when he sees the great Tōji temple. The highest level of skill may be termed Fascination. A master is one who has truly mastered every aspect of his art. When an artist has surpassed this stage, he can truly be called skillful. Still higher than the art of the skillful lies that art which represents Fascination. This highest level of true effectiveness can never be imitated, just as a beginner cannot imitate the elegant calligraphy of a master written in the flowing style. Rather, he must begin by learning the simple block style; and after success gained over the years, he will come to the point where he can use his brush in whatever style he prefers.

In the *nō*, the term Placidity refers to a sensation of comfort, one kind of manifestation of the Flower. Even if an actor has achieved the Flower, he may not necessarily come to make an impression of Placidity. To accuse an actor of failing to possess this Placidity is to be too meticulous in one's criticism.[12]

5. Matters Concerning the Voice

On occasion, an actor [caught up in the excitement of his performance] will add the interjection *ya!* [into the text], and there are those who try consciously to imitate this effect. If such a sound is inserted by design, however, it will not seem

---

[12] Literally, "to blow off hail to find scars." The reference is to an early Chinese text, the *Han Fei Tzu*, Chapter XIV. See W. K. Liao, tr., *The Complete Works of Han Fei Tzu*, I, 278, for the entire passage.

genuine. Recently, in the *nō* play *Yawata hōjōe*, when [the actor added such a sound to] the line "autumn has come, *ya!*" the spectators were especially excited and praised the performance highly. Thus, a *ya* can be added quite unconsciously on an appropriate occasion.

On the other hand, there are those who interject *yara yara* into their lines in a performance. This is done through a spirit of calculation to excite the audience. When such a trick is visible, however, it serves as a sure sign that the true skills of the performer have begun to fail him. These days, there are a number of declining performers who have been heard using such expressions.

6. The Chant

Concerning the chant: the chant forms the very basis of the *nō*. The way of the chant is crucial to our art. Those artists who have reached the highest levels of accomplishment in this art must learn the five-note scales and the four voiced accents, as well as the mutual musical systems of *ritsu* and *ryo*. The system of the "relation of the five notes" is no doubt too difficult to be fully mastered just by learning the rules, yet a *nō* performer must take cognizance of these principles and try to understand them as best he can.[13] An artist must know the basic distinctions involved in choosing the appropriate voice and manner in order to create a sense of felicity, as opposed to what is needed in order to create a sense of melancholy and sadness.

Concerning the proper way to proceed in practicing, an actor must first of all come to a firm understanding of the real nature of his vocal instrument, in order to determine the appropriate way to proceed. Only then will he be able to follow the proper path.

The most straightforward style is that of the congratulatory

---

[13] Zeami's explanation of these various terms is confusing, and scholars have not agreed on the significance of the relationship, if any, of the "five notes" to the *ryo* and *ritsu* scales.

mode. If an artist masters this mode and uses it as a foundation, he can go on to learn the modes of Grace, love, and grief or lamentation; and as he masters these various modes, he can learn in turn the distinctions concerning the way to perform them in both an adorned and an unadorned fashion and so finally reach the final, highest stage of Perfect Freedom. An actor must avoid a preference for one kind of music and a corresponding antipathy for the others; if he can manage to avoid this error, he will truly be able to absorb the whole body of the *nō* into himself. Finally, it must always be remembered that a beautiful and fluid sound represents the ideal in musical production.

Next, it is important to keep in mind the distinctions between *kusemai* and *kouta*. [In the beginning], *sarugaku* made use of only *kouta* [which stresses melody], whereas *kusemai* [which stresses the rhythm] represented something altogether different. From the time that Kan'ami performed in *Shirahige*, however, both styles came into use. However, the *kusemai* style we now employ is not the original, which consists of a monotonous use of rising and falling musical scales. Elements of *kouta* have been added to soften that stiff pattern. Thus, those sections calling for *kusemai* should be performed with its original characteristics, and the actor must keep in mind that there are a number of styles in which to perform *kouta* as well. Then too, an actor must understand that Ōmi *sarugaku* and *dengaku* have their own specific features when he composes a play and plans the melodies. Only when, to the highest degree, the play and the music alike can meet in achieving the same emotional effect will the wonderful Flower of myriad virtues open, and the highest levels of our art be attained.

7. The Congratulatory Chant

In a congratulatory chant, it is best to use the *ryo* style of chant [which involves strong and straightforward vocal production]. An actor requires a deep understanding of this principle. Indeed it is true that each audience creates its own unique emotional atmosphere. The actor must investigate beforehand to determine what musical effect may be suitable for any particular occasion. If he is truly able to anticipate this atmosphere and make himself one with it, the result may well match that gained from one or two days of rehearsal. When the performance begins, he must put himself in a state of calm, listen to the pitch [established by the accompanying instruments], and then begin his chant.

The congratulatory chant is by nature simple and straightforward and does not depend on a striking melody. If one were to place this art in the Nine Levels, such a chant would fall into the realm of the Art of the True Flower. It is Kiami who first began [to chant with an emphasis on effective melody], yet such melodies are not appropriate for *waki nō* or congratulatory pieces. Such melodies are doubtless more appropriate in plays where a female role is central. Various matters concerning music are treated in detail elsewhere, so no more has been added here.

When performing indoors, it is customary to chant one particular *issei* to begin. These days, however, the practice is looked on as somewhat old-fashioned and so is not widely employed. The *issei* usually chanted began, "Is it the large stone that remains? Fine pebbles. . . ."[14]

When chanting at a high pitch, the term "stretching" is used; when the chant flows, the term "lengthening" is used. [In matters of rhythm] the modes referred to as "waiting" and "holding" are largely identical. An "undulating" style of chant should be performed in ten sections, broken down into six units of six and four.

There are two categories of pitch, First [high] and Second [low]. [However, they are sometimes confused in the musical notation.] For example, when a singer performs covering four sets of scales, the third set, usually referred to as the First Pitch, is in this instance referred to as the Second. Banqueting

---

[14] The source of this text is unknown.

songs and the like provide one example of this usage. Various rules concerning these matters can be found in separate teachings.

The term "perfect music" should not be thought of as merely applying to the congratulatory chant. After an artist has reached the level of Perfect Freedom, then he can of course make the distinctions necessary in chanting the various modes—grace, love, grief—and all of these should partake of the qualities of "perfect music." Among these, the mode of love is the most difficult to perform. Unorthodoxy beyond Accomplishment itself represents the highest attainment of all. Music that partakes of this quality should not be used in a group performance. Even if all the artists involved are highly gifted, such music cannot be effective when the performers sing together.

Since ancient times the *tachiai* called *Torōkyō* has come down to us. As with *Okina*, the text we have of *Torōkyō* is difficult to understand; yet no one should think that for that reason they should simply make changes.

8. Kusemai

There is a basic distinction to be observed between the styles of *kusemai* and *kouta*. Since *kusemai* is performed while the actor is dancing, rhythm serves as its essential element. Besides, in a performance of chant for *kusemai*, the performer must be careful to make a clear distinction between the parts to be performed with a broad and strong vocal production and those requiring performance in a restrained and attenuated fashion. The chant normally used in the *nō* has melody as its central element [as in the *kouta*]. The music must be composed with the expectation that the performer will blend both styles as appropriate when shading the melodies that he performs.

In the *nō* play *Shigehira*, at the line "Here, at the hill of Nara, is the Island of Defilement," the melody used should not employ the mode of *kusemai*. A melody for *kouta* is suitable. When *kusemai* is involved, the actor should slur over the details by altering the accents. Once, in the *kusemai* called *Saikoku kudari*, at the line "The moon that reveals the leaves of the reeds, the light of the moon hidden in the clear pond of Kōya," an actor tried to sing the word "hidden" in an extended fashion [in order to articulate the syllables]. Nan'ami, hearing this, said that "for a *kusemai* melody, the accent must be rather slurred and altered," and since that time such has become the practice in peforming these kinds of melodies. In the *kusemai* sections of *Yoroboshi*, true *kusemai* music was employed in creating the scene.

The *kusemai* begins with a *shidai* and finishes with a *shidai*. The whole occupies the space of two sequences. In the latter sequence [before the return of the *shidai*], the pace should be increased. For example, the actor, performing in the First [high-pitched] mode, chants such phrases as "since such is such, something is so and so . . ." for a space of two, certainly no more than three stanzas, all sung in the same musical style. Then he finishes with another musical phrase, "so it is, so it is. . . ." It will not be effective for him, however, to merely repeat his use of the high-pitched mode for this final phrase.

At the end of the latter sequence, when the moment preceding the use of the high-pitched mode arrives, a "rising melody" should be employed. One example of this occurs at the line [in *Yura no minato*] "How quickly I am tempted. I, as though severing the roots of the floating grasses. . . ." Other examples are the lines [in *Hyakuman*] "How grateful, to appear at this temple," or [in the *Jigoku no kusemai*] the lines "Once, choking on flames of heat, scorching heat, once. . . ." These examples do not always employ what might be strictly called a "rising melody"; still, as the music used does involve a series of rising phrases, it can be regarded as such. All of the music can be viewed as a means to soften and mitigate [the nature of the music ordinarily employed] for the *kusemai*.

The *kusemai* called *Saikoku kudari* was once performed by those who were expert in that form, using their own special skills. On that occasion, they did shift the accents at the phrase "hidden, in the clear . . ." in their performances. This piece is a truly effective *kusemai*. One particularly striking spot occurs at the line "Owls cry in the tops of the pine and cinnamon trees." Kan'ami was very gifted at attaching melodies to those lines. He used the style of Otozuru.[15] Nan'ami was also greatly skilled at adding melodies to such texts. Kiami did not really dance *kusemai*, but actually made use of the mode of *kouta*.

In the *kusemai* called *Tōgoku kudari* there is a section greatly praised by audiences that begins "This is the Palace of Eternal Youth only in name; rather, it seems a place of punishment"; indeed, from the line "Praise to the Buddha, to the God of Mishima," the piece is of the highest interest. Nan'ami added the melodies to the text. Kan'ami added the melodies for *Tōgoku kudari*. The texts for both were written by Tamarin. This Tamarin managed to offend the Shōgun Ashikaga Yoshimitsu and so was banished to the eastern provinces, where, after a certain time, he composed this work. When Zeami was still a young actor [using the child name of Fujiwaka], he performed the work for Yoshimitsu, who had Tamarin recalled from exile, so that he might serve again at the Shōgun's court. Tamarin composed *Saikoku kudari* after this incident.

Other well-known *kusemai* are *Yura no minato, Hyaku-man,* and *Yamamba.*

9. Musical Effects

More than anything else, the choice of an appropriate musical mood is important for the chant. In the old days, no importance was given to the choice of style in the Yamato *sarugaku,* so that many misplaced accents on the words could be heard during the chant. If the flow of melody is properly emphasized, however, such changes of accent can remain hidden. For example, in the line [from the play by Kiami entitled *Ominaeshi*]

---

[15] A celebrated female dancer who performed in Nara. According to Zeami, his father learned to perform *kusemai* in her style.

"In this fleeting, useless world of dreams, we too have been left behind; thus this once I may be spiteful . . ." contained a number of such misplaced accents, but it was performed in the proper musical mood and so any faults were hidden. Nan'ami was considered the finest chanter in Japan because of this play, for which Kiami provided the melodies.

In the lines [from an unidentified play] "Ah, ah, how evanescent . . . but for this the Buddha would never have attained eminence in this world. For us, so unlucky, is this not our good fortune?" as chanted by Dōami, the performance was filled with misplaced accents, yet because the musical effect he chose was so appropriate, he was also praised as "the greatest performer in Japan." He was indeed a fine performer all his days.

When the musical atmosphere has reached a level of Perfect Freedom, its true Magnitude will be revealed to the ears of the listener. When Kiami performed the lines [from *Atsuta*, now called *Gendayū*] "As the old man answers, we are Tenazuchi and Ashinazuchi. The girl is Princess Inada," or "The Father, the aged Tenazuchi, now appears as the god Gendayū, who has taken an oath to protect those who travel on the Eastern Sea Road," he performed his chant in a strong and majestic fashion, without any fear of making errors. He truly gave the impression of possessing Magnitude.

When Nan'ami performed the final sections of plays, in which those phrases such as "what is happening?" are recapitulated, he had a specialty of dropping the pitch of his voice in a moving manner. In *Eguchi* [of Kan'ami] he included a line from *The Tale of the Heike*, "I have become a woman of pleasure through retribution from another life, painful to think upon." [In the *Hatsusei Rokudai* of Zeami], at the phrase "Praying to Kannon for his protection against the sword of the enemy," the melody, the words, and the rhythm were altogether in consonance.

Among the various musical modes, that concerning love is the most affecting of all. The word "melodic structure" [*fushi*] has also the meaning of "knot" [*fushi*] [as in the grain of wood], however, and just as these are to be found in nature in the bamboo, such flaws also appear in music as well. The overall musical mood, rather than the melodic structure alone, must form the real basis for a performance. For example, techniques such as suddenly cutting off a chant, then letting it trail away, or concentrating on a portion of the chant before extending it are used for the purpose of enhancing the musical mood. There are some examples of poetic inversion made for the creation of musical mood suggested in *The Analects*.

10. Alterations of Accent in Independent Words and in Particles

In terms of the chant, these two kinds of accent changes exist. For example, in singing the phrase "of something" [*nani no*], an accent given to the syllable *no* is a "particle" alteration. When an independent word itself is involved, then a "word" alteration comes about. Both independent words and particles form the vocabulary of a text; when it comes to assigning accents, however, it is crucial for the performer to make the proper distinctions between them.

[According to a criticism by Kiami, in *Yura no minato*], at the phrase "in the pines, the wind—Otowa mountain," the particles *ni wa* employed at the words "in the pines the wind" [*matsu ni wa kaze*] represents this kind of accent change. Yet in Kiami's own work as well, a phrase like "the rough wind" [*nokaze*] in the line "caught up in the wild wind of autumn" carries the same accent change, in this case an alteration on an independent word. Actually, of course, an effective change of particle accent can be quite successful; but if the device is employed to no truly effective purpose, alterations had best not be employed. The situation is similar to that in the art of poetry. If a poem is effective, it will not suffer from the illness of repeated words.

In the phrase [citing the name of the poetess Ono no Komachi] "*Ono no Komachi wa*," the particle *wa* is particularly conspicuous to the ear. It should be sounded lightly, then thrown away. In the phrase "If only some lodgings might be lent," the effect will be lost if the voice drops at the end of the verb. Sometimes that method can be effective, but not in this instance. In this particular case, the voice should only be dropped at the voicing of the final particles.

In the congratulatory chant for the summer,[16] at the phrase "the nation, carrying on" [*uketsugu kuni*], no musical emphasis should be placed on the syllable *tsugu*. It should be spoken in a simple, straightforward manner. In the phrase [from a play, no longer performed, entitled *Shigehira*] "In the forest of Mikasa" [*Mikasa no mori no*], the particle *no* should be performed in a flat, even manner; but in the phrase "earnestly to Buddha" [*ichinen midabutsu*] the syllable *nen* may sound too stiff if it is pronounced in a straightforward manner. Thus the performer should ride with the musical rhythm when pronouncing that syllable. On such an occasion, the melody determines the means of performance.

In the phrase [from an unknown play] "When the divine wind . . . first began to rise" [*kamikaze ya . . . hajimete tatematsuri*], the syllables *tate* should be given no special emphasis in the chant but should be performed in a simple manner. In the phrase "Blessings after so long" [*megumi hisashi*] [from the play entitled *Unoha*], the syllables *hisa* should be given no alteration in accent. In the phrase "Each spring, to offer you congratulations" [*harugoto ni kimi o iwaite*] [from the play, no longer performed, entitled *Yukiyama*], the syllables *iwaite* should not be sung in a high-pitched, emphatic fashion. In the phrase "Tempted by the evening breeze" [*yūbe no kaze ni sasowarete*] [from the play *Eguchi*], the voice can be dropped on the syllable *be*. In the phrase "not an old man" [*rōō imada*] [from a *kusemai* entitled *Shirahige*], the syllables *imada* should be pronounced simply, without any musical emphasis.

In the phrase [from *Eguchi*] "truly all mankind wanders in the Realm of the Six Defilements" [*ge ni ya mina hito wa*

---

[16] Evidently one of a series of ancient chants performed to welcome the changing seasons.

rokujin no kyō ni mayoi], at the syllables *mina hito wa ro-kujin*, the actor should pronounce the particle *wa* quickly and lightly, so as to be able to carry on smoothly through the rest of the phrase. The chanting of the syllables *rokujin* should not begin at a low pitch.

In the phrase [from *Suma Genji*] "He is called Genji the Shining One," the syllable *to* [*hikaru Genji to nao yobaru*] should be sung in the *ritsu* mode with an upward thrust and not performed with the same thrust as in the preceding syllables. Nan'ami said he always found this phrase of great interest. In the phrase "Mistaken for a yellow rose" [in the play *Hibariyama*], no accents should be used. Kiami, who was a master in musical performance, occasionally did use such accents. Yet his methods should not be imitated. At the line [from the same play] "I am Kinmitsu" [*Kinmitsu to mōsu mono nari*], the syllables *mono nari* should be spoken in a light, throwaway manner.

11. Rhythm

In terms of establishing the proper spacing of the rhythm to a text, it can be measured out just as [in architectural space] pillars are spaced at regular intervals of one, two, and three to serve as supports. Thus during a specified interval of chanting, if a phrase has too few syllables, they must be stretched out; on the contrary, if there are too many, they must be compressed to fit. Various details on these matters are discussed in a separate teaching. [What follows here are some specific examples.]

In the play *Motomezuka*, there occurs the phrase "We pluck spring greens in Little Field at Ikuta, a sight so charming we delay the traveler who stops to watch. Such foolishness, all these questions!"[17] When the play is presented, it is not effective to perform the latter half of this phrase in the same

[17] This translation is taken from Keene, ed., *Twenty Plays of the Nō Theatre*, p. 42.

manner as the first. There should be a definite break at the words "such foolishness" [*yoshi na ya*] before continuing on. Thus the phrase will be properly compressed to suit the rhythm.

In the phrase [from *Fujisan*] "truly this fisher-girl seems to have no heart, yet this spot is interesting," the beginning of the word "interesting" [*omoshiroi*] should be extended, and the latter part [*omoshiroi*] contracted. In another phrase [from the same play] "It has been said [by the poets] in ages past that this mountain knows no time," the word "mountain" [*yama*] should be compressed. Those kinds of adjustments must be made, whatever the text concerned. If any detail of a musical rhythm is treated negligently, the entire chant will appear listless and dull.

[In *Hanagatami*] at the line "How frightening!" [*osoroshi ya*], actors have recently tended to extend the words spoken in a straightforward manner, which is unfortunate. Rather, from this point on, the musical mood [rather than the words themselves] should serve as the basis for performance, and the chanting should be aligned closely to the rhythm. On the other hand, [in the same play] at the words "Even if it is said that my companion is mad," the melody should not be followed in too literal a fashion. At the words "it is said" [*iwaresase*], a sharp break should be made at the syllables *sase*.

In *Sumidagawa*, there is a phrase "Flowers piled up of human grief, following along the sound of the storms of mutability." At the word "mutability" [*mujō*], even if the effect seems already extended, lengthening the chant at that point is appropriate. A rich and full emotional atmosphere is most important. In the word *mujō* itself, the syllable *mu* should be chanted voicelessly, and the syllable *jō* pronounced sharply and clearly. [In the play *Matsugasaki*] the line "The depths of the desolate valley" should be performed in an expansive fashion. In *Yawata*, at the line "Seven days, seven nights," or at the line in *Fushimi*, "Long live the hundred kings!" [Zeami] always compressed the syllables to fit the rhythm.

In chanting, there is a method by which the final particle at the end of the preceding phrase is attached to the beginning of the following phrase. For example, in *Shōkun*, there is a phrase "The painted eyebrows of this beautiful Shōkun have about them the scent of green, as though spring had come, the threads of the willow. . . ." When the final particle *no* is pronounced, a sharp cut should be made at the preceding word "willow" [*yanagi*], and the particle *no* connected to the phrase that follows, "thoughts in confusion."

In the *nō* play *Ukai*, the line "The true moon seems already to have appeared" [once caused difficult problems with rhythm]. When the play was presented at the riding grounds in the palace of the present Shōgun [Ashikaga Yoshinori], the chorus performed this section quickly and so was not able to harmonize with the performance of the leading actor. From the word "moon" onward, the chorus should carry the chant along precisely on the rhythm. When arriving at the phrase "really appeared," the actor should hold his moving foot in the air for a moment, then step in a deliberate fashion. In such a case, the rhythm should be firmly maintained by the chorus. On this occasion, the performance was not successful because, since the chorus consisted of actors from different troupes, they were not in natural accord with each other.

When considering the crucial importance of rhythm, one might think for example of moving around some heavy object. Those who are moving that object bind their spirits together as they push, while shouting in rhythm. Such is the importance that rhythm should play.

12. Various Matters Concerning the Chant

It is written as well in the *Fūgyokushū*[18] that "to truly grasp the deep and true principles of the chant, one must first master the fundamentals of exhalation and inhalation, train the voice, learn to color the melodies, and thus arrive at immovable heights of an art founded on a mastery of the breath."

[18] A short treatise by Zeami on *nō* music. See *Notes on the Treatises* under "the specialized treatises on music" for details.

The artist known as Inō no Zen'emon was a disciple of Ken and was an expert in *sōga*; yet although he was highly gifted, he was not chosen as one of his master's favorites. What then were his faults, you might ask? My father heard the following from another of the disciples. There is a particular piece that contains the phrase "In the province of Tsu" [*Tsu no kuni no*]. It was said that Inō had the habit of singing as though he were taking a breath between the *no* after *Tsu* and the *no* after *kuni*. The artist is at fault if the audience ever hears him taking a breath. Even a sound that is almost inaudible can be heard by a discerning audience. Inō took a breath as well between *ni* and *no* in the phrase *kuni no*. Thus his faults become all too evident. Because he never mastered points such as these, he never joined in the group of favored disciples.

In everything, a thorough knowledge of the principle of *jo, ha,* and *kyū* is paramount. Even in terms of the individual syllables themselves, even one syllable can be said to provide an exhibition of this relationship. For example, when a person, in answering, pronounces the syllable *o* ["yes"] too suddenly, the working of these principles cannot be observed. Generally speaking, the moment of silence before the person speaks should constitute the *jo*, the word *o* itself constitutes the *ha*, and the moment after the actor's voice stops constitutes the *kyū*. If such a proper construction is not followed, the voice will not carry properly.

To use a naturally broad and strong voice as the basis for a performance requiring a restrained and attenuated voice is doubtless a simple matter, but what of the performance of music meant for a broad and strong voice when an actor who has an innately restrained and attenuated voice is assigned to perform? Concerning this matter, [Zeami] explained that in the case of a performance of music appropriate for a broad voice, the artist using a restrained voice must chant using a suitably low pitch. When a voice technique is changed in the course of a chant from restrained to broad, or broad to restrained, the performer must make skillful use of this natural shift [rather than stressing the melody] in order to bring that alteration about. To give another kind of example, sometimes the pronunciation used in the eastern provinces [which shows a heavy accent] turns out to provide the proper pronunciation [for the chant].

It is also possible to chant mixing the two styles of *ryō* [broad] and *ritsu* [restrained] at once [in order to bring about that change]. For example, in the *nō* play *Tango monogurui*, there occurs the line "Ah! thinking that if only I might see him, I have searched the spot where he died, yet all I saw was bubbles floating on the water. . . ." The phrase "bubbles floating on the water" should be performed with a restrained voice; thus, to continue on with the use of a broad voice as in the previous section would not be effective.

When it comes to chanting with the beauty of pure melody as the object, there is often a danger that the chant cannot be brought to a perfectly sharp conclusion. In the case of when a clear stopping point is to be created when chanting in a restrained voice, the artist would do best to arrive at the level of *kyū*. If such is not the case, the chant will merely conclude with one *ha* followed by another [without the proper sense of an ending]. A truly beautiful chant surmounts the rhythmical beat, giving a rich and full effect. Those actors who find this technique effective and indulge themselves in it only end by dragging out the rhythm when they perform. Just as a floating waterfowl moves energetically [out of sight] under the water, a gifted performer will chant smoothly and beautifully while taking full cognizance of the rhythm in just the same way. Those who merely imitate the surface smoothness cannot achieve success. For example, when listening to a gifted performer, it can be clear that, when chanting a phrase like "it is said that . . ." [*to ka ya*], he will put a rich emphasis on the syllable *to*. The inexperienced performer, however, feeling envious, will mistakenly try to imitate the effect merely by lengthening the phrase to *tō ka ya*.

In the *nō* play *Tsunemori*, the story should be related in a fashion quite different from that appropriate to a Benkei.[19] The atmosphere of the play is one in which a woman tearfully asks questions, so that the atmosphere should be quiet and pathetic; nevertheless, some gallant feelings [appropriate to Atsumori] must be conveyed to the audience as well. In the play *Furu*, at the line "In the fields of Furu, the sacred cryptomeria trees of Miwa have long been sung of; how fascinating to find this reminder of them," the earlier part of the line should be given the greater emphasis and the latter part sung in a light and easy fashion.

In *Hanjo*, the lines "Indeed, even the moonlight that comes into my bed chamber has been absent from my pillow for a time, and again I have come to sleep alone" reveals the basic musical character of the play. In particular, the final phrase is especially striking. Of course there are such moments in many plays, but this particular *kusemai* is crucial and must be performed with the utmost care and seriousness. In the phrase "To speak of the sky there [*sonata no sora yo to*]," the syllable *yo* should be chanted in a naive fashion, and with a rapid, upward thrust. In the phrase "A message from the one who waits for me [*waga matsu hito yori no otozure*]," the *o* sound [in the word *otozure*] should remain unvoiced. The same principle holds true of the syllable *mo* in the phrase "Thinking that it is fine [*yoshi ya omoeba*]." When the performer reaches the phrase "The room of Hanjo," these words should be given neither too much nor too little emotional emphasis.

In the play *Ukon no baba*, at the phrase "a flower cart" [*hanaguruma*], the syllable *ma* can be extended in the chant, as that syllable is the crucial one. In *Matsukaze*, in the phrase "the house of the fisher-girls on a road passing by separated from the village," the words "house of the fisher-girls" should

[19] Benkei is the faithful priest who accompanies the young and heroic Minamoto general Yoshitsune (A.D. 1159-1189). In the *nō* and elsewhere in Japanese literary texts, Benkei is usually portrayed as having a violent and boisterous personality.

be emphasized, and the words "road passing by" chanted lightly. In the play *Shigehira*, at the line "the devil has struck, how frightening!" the words "has struck" should be given a powerful emphasis, and the syllable *o* in the word "frightening" [*osoro*] should be held back when the actor delivers his line. If the phrase "has struck," on the other hand, is delivered in a natural way, then the syllable *so* in *osoro* can be delivered with intense feeling, and so can be chanted with a considerable thrust. In the opening chant in the play *Nishikigi*, "regrettably, asking" [*kuyashiki tanomi*], the syllable *ki* should be sung simply and without emphasis. When beginners try to imitate these performance practices of superior actors without fully understanding them and so mistake careful singing for physical stress, they merely drag out the musical line. In the *kusemai* in the play *Tsuchiguruma*, there is one syllable that stands out crudely when the text is heard. Great care must be taken with difficulties such as these.

In *Hatsusei Rokudai*, at the words "what indeed, my favorite child, the seed . . ." [*nani o ka tane to omoiko no*], the actor must employ the device of a "voice pause" to give the words their full impressiveness. This device is also referred to these days as "psychological rhythm." In this particular example, the pause should be inserted after the syllables *omo*, and then the syllable *i* should be given special emphasis. This section is one that should quiet the spirit; the least distraction will destroy the artistic effect.

In *Tsutsumi no take*, at the words "is heaven itself intoxicated by the flowers in full bloom?" [*ten hana ni eri ya*], the chanter should make a break at the syllable *ri* before chanting the syllable *ya*. In *Hakozaki*, at the phrase "this pine that serves as a sign—how grateful . . ." [*shirushi no matsu nare ya arigata ki no*] serves as a celebrated moment in which to employ the "principle of sliding syllables" [That is, *ya—a*, to be sounded in consonance with each other]. [In the *kusemai* called *Saikoku no kudari*] in the phrase "help with the difficulty of the windblown waves," the singer should change the color of his voice from broad to restrained then back to broad.

[In *Unoha*] in the phrase "whatever, in Michinoku province" [*ika nareba Michinoku ni wa*], the syllable *wa*, if slurred and drawn out, sounds ugly. This *wa* should be pronounced with a short intake of breath. The same principle applies [to the syllable *ya*] in another phrase from the same text, "ah, the reed cutters" [*ashigari ya*]. In the old chant text *Kōya*, at the line "it is useless to wait for spring and fall, our parting," the syllable *ru* in *haru* ["spring"] should be performed in a high-pitched tone, with intensity.

Such a phrase as that in *Tsunemori*, "what is it that has come out, grief in the light of the full moon" provides an opportunity for music that lies beyond melody, and the utmost taste and skill should be used in performance. In this particular case, the elegance of the whole should be stressed, and this particular line performed in a light manner. The preceding phrase as well, "even our bond . . ." should be performed in the same fashion, so as to give a naive and artless flavor to the chant.

In *Matsukaze*, at the line "the moon above is one; below it has two, no three reflections which shine in the flood tide tonight,"[20] a "voice pause" should be inserted when moving to the phrase "flood tide," in order to emphasize the effect of the word play. If the pause itself becomes obvious, the effect will be spoiled; rather, the actor should be aware of the pause within himself. In *Sakuragawa*, a phrase such as "it may be said to be cloudy" should be chanted in a very smooth manner. Phrases such as "the old root, there from the beginning, yet remains" or "geese alighting on the level sand" should be delivered in the same fashion. Kiami said that such phrases should be chanted "with the root of the tongue [in order to avoid its articulating movements]."

When the syllables of a text are sharply articulated when chanted in strict accord with the rhythm, the effect will be unpleasant. Rather, they should be articulated with the breath

---

[20] This translation is taken from Keene, ed., *Twenty Plays of the Nō Theatre*, p. 25.

alone. The method chosen will depend on the circumstances, of course.

On occasions when a number of performers come together to chant in the presence of the nobility, the quality of the performance is of the greatest importance. [For example] at the home of a certain nobleman, [the *renga* teacher] Fujiju performed some *shirabyōshi* music, and his lengthy performance created a certain emotional atmosphere. Making use of this, Zeami then began to chant "the wind in the pines as well in quiet," thereby earning the praise of all. An actor should make the performance of the one who precedes him serve as the *jo* for his own chant, so that when that earlier performance—a short chant or whatever—has finished, he can immediately come forth with his own chant and alter the general artistic effect while still remaining in consonance with the general emotional atmosphere that has already been established. For that reason, the performer must pay special attention to the mood of the final words chanted by the player who comes before him. At a banquet in the home of a certain nobleman, Zeami was summoned; "Zeami, Zeami, come and sing for us," they cried, and when he had performed on command, as he had done so often before, he was complimented as follows: "As Zeami is always inwardly alert and prepared to perform, there is no reason for him to feel nervous or uneasy."

On the occasion of the Gion Festival,[21] it was said that one particular performance might be given before the Shōgun himself; as the actors were making their private preparations, Kiami arrived. During the discussion, he suggested that, if only *sarugaku* artists were to be included, they should, after the opening congratulatory words, chant an entire number beginning with the opening section of the *jo*. If, on the other

---

[21] The Gion Festival, associated with the Gion Shrine in Kyoto, was first held in the seventh month of A.D. 876 and is still carried on as an annual observance today. Originally a Shintō purification right against pestilence, the festival soon developed into one of the most colorful events in the yearly ceremonies held in the capital.

hand, should special *kusemai* performers be summoned to dance and the *sarugaku* players were to be added as well, then once past the opening congratulatory words, the performers should begin the piece to be chanted at the final section, such as at the line "the Emperor for fifty generations" [from *Fushimi*].

13. The Art of the Chant

Levels of excellence: in the *Fugyokushū*, it is written that "music that seems to transcend artfulness, since all technique has been absorbed within it, is on the highest level. Music that gives the sensation of artfulness, as it has not transcended such technique, remains on the second level." It is written there as well that "the artist who wishes to achieve this highest level of artistry must master every musical element, beginning with the four tones, the two scales (*ryo* and *ritsu*), know the means to move from one phrase to the next in a musical fashion, and possess as well the ability to move smoothly from one word to the next. Then, when he has reached a level of True Ease, he must bury all such concerns so that when his performance is heard, although there may be nothing extraordinary in the music itself, the effect of the whole will be peerless nonetheless."

There is another kind of artfulness, of course, that exists through a lack of learning. It is altogether different from what is mentioned here and is a source of disappointment to the audience.

In the chant, the Highest Fruition consists of a performance that is fluid and beautiful in sound. True music itself has no form and cannot be grasped of itself. When an artist, musically speaking, has reached the level of True Ease, this true music seems to issue forth of its own accord in a performance of a melody. It is like a shadow. If an actor finds this true music effective and tries to imitate it directly, however, the results will be despicable.

In *Matsukaze* there is an extremely effective melodic passage at the phrase "as the waves come and go, the cranes stand in the reeds, the winds sounding together from all four directions, and we must pass a cold night." Interesting as this passage is, however, it must be placed in the second category. The phrase "the four winds sounding together" must be performed in a compressed fashion. Vocally, there is something stiff about this passage. A performer would do well to begin at a high pitch and gradually lower the sound. Such was the technique used by Kiami. Kiami's melody is doubtless still performed by chanters in this play even today. It was Hosokawa Man-gen,[22] the governor general, at whose wishes the fashion of performing the chant was reversed, so that at the words "on a cold night" the performer began with a low pitch that rose at the end. The change was probably made at the Inari *nō* performances. The *rongi* [used in *Matsukaze*] is actually taken from the play *Tōei*.

In performance, some chanters have particular habits in performance, such as singing through the nose. Actually, such peculiarities are striking [and need not be suppressed].

There is also a style of performance in which music is not involved that is referred to as "only words." The phrase "using a blank voice" is also used to describe this phenomenon. There are no actors now who can manage this technique perfectly. It represents the highest level of artistry. This is not a technique that can be learned by rote. Even a great artist such as Kiami, in a passage such as that in *Ashikari*, "if you appreciate the reeds that grow in Naniwa, how happy indeed I feel" could only approximate the style. The technique involves an attempt to truly become the person the actor is attempting to imitate. Any distractions must be set aside. In *Sanemori* a line such as "I would tell my name, if I had one," involves this technique, and from the beginning, many have tried unsuccessfully to master a proper style. The use [by Zeami] of this technique in pronouncing the words "I would" [*seme*], however, won

---

[22] Hosokawa Mangen (A.D. 1378-1426) was a member of the Hosokawa family, one of the three most powerful clans active during the period. He was celebrated for his interest in the arts.

wide favor. Hosokawa Mangen himself said, "Zeami is talented in every way, of course, but in this particular skill he stands alone."

14. Composing the Nō, 1

The writer must first come to a full comprehension of the special characteristics inherent in his chief character. There will be certain means of expression appropriate to such a character, and in order to create that person, the author must have a deep knowledge of the *nō*. This most important matter of all was described in *The Three Elements in Composing a Play*. Models for the creation of new plays are also contained there.

The beginner must first learn to write an opening congratulatory piece that creates a bright, refreshing atmosphere. *Yumiyawata* provides a good example. It is a play that demands no showy display of skill yet quickly creates a strong and robust atmosphere. The play was written as a congratulatory piece for the beginning of the reign of the Shōgun Ashikaga Yoshimochi [in A.D. 1395],[23] and requires no knowledge of any special secrets in its performance. On the other hand, in *Hōjōgawa*, during the scene when the fish are to be released from the bucket, [Zeami, the author] did create a moment when some of his special skills as a performer were required. To a lesser extent, *Takasago* also shows some addition of these elements.

Aside from the congratulatory pieces, there are also other plays composed in a simple and serene style, such as *Izutsu* and *Michimori*. Plays such as *Sanemori* and *Yamamba*, on the other hand, have moments that deviate from this. Once Zeami had a wish to perform the play *Michimori* at a shrine on a festive occasion, but, at the wishes of his superiors, he per-

[23] Some scholars believe that the Shōgun mentioned here is Yoshimochi, which would make the date of the performance 1395. Others identify him as Yoshinori, which would make the date 1428.

formed instead *Sanemori* and *Yamamba* before the Shōgun, Ashikaga Yoshimochi [thus missing a good opportunity].

In terms of the levels of excellence, *Izutsu* can be said to be on the highest level, that of the Flower of Peerless Charm. *Matsukaze* doubtless reaches the level of the Flower of Profundity. *Aridōshi* doubtless achieves the level of the Flower of Tranquillity. *Michimori, Tadanori,* and *Yashima* are all three effective plays that involve *shura* as protagonists. Among them, however, *Tadanori* surely achieves a place in the upper three levels. The two plays *Saigyōzakura* and *Akoya no matsu* resemble each other in many ways [dealing, as they do, with characters who are old men]. Thinking that, in the times to come, there would be no one who could write plays of this character, Zeami therefore wished to leave them as his testament.

The play *Ishikawa no jorō* is generally performed as one of the "ten plays,"[24] and was considered one that was suitable for Montomasa after he reached his middle years. In this regard, it may be said that as regards a play such as *Chikata* as well, an actor can only feel the part deeply after he is older. In *Ishikawa*, the costume used for the opening scene should disguise the actor so that he looks unkempt and poor. Still, if the play is performed in the summer, the actor might wear a single-layered embroidered robe. Or again, a lightly colored *mizugoromo* might be suitable as well. If the play is performed by the Ōmi troupe, the actor might well wear a white hood with long tails. Indeed, if our troupe should perform the piece, it would serve as quite a novelty. Unfortunately, however, the second part of the play tends to give a rather insipid, weak feeling. It helps if the woman [presumably the *shite*] should have a scene in which she actually speaks out. In any case, Motomasa's wishes should be respected in these matters. From the line "if the end of resentment should ever pass by," the chant can be performed in a fluent fashion in the style of

[24] The significance of this term and the titles of the ten plays included have not been determined.

dengaku as performed in the style of the Shinza troupe and, sung in this fashion, the passage should present no particular problems.

The second half of the *nō* play *Saigyōzakura* has a particularly lonely and solitary flavor. It demands an older style of elegant performance. Zeami said as well that there would be a few in later generations who could understand a similar play such as *Kinuta*, a sad thought for him. He also set down the "ten plays" as a legacy [for the next generation], so that they might serve as guides. Thus these works can serve our troupe as models both for text and for music.

Originally the *nō* play *Sotoba Komachi* was an extremely long play. From the line "who is that who passes by?" the actor chants at great length. Later in the play, Komachi, because the god of Tamatsujima [the deity of poetry] is enshrined nearby, makes an offering to that spirit, at which point a raven, representing the deity of the shrine, appears. An actor in the Hie troupe was so skillful at performing this role that he was given the name "Master Raven." These days, however, the entire scene has been eliminated. The play *Michimori* too had far too long a text, which was cut by Zeami in order to improve it. In the original version of *Tango monogurui*, a husband and his wife [who lost their child] appear on the stage in a distracted manner. One day, in the greenroom, just before the performance, Zeami suddenly realized that the role might better be performed by the father alone, and from that moment on, the play became a success. So it is that the *nō* should show itself capable of capturing the attitudes of each succeeding generation. (For example, the *nō* play *Kasama* is doubtless no longer suitable.)[25] Old methods of performance cannot be maintained merely for their own sake.

Zeami wrote in *The Three Elements in Composing a Play* that the plays he composed during the Ōei era might still retain their value in the generations to come. Still, even in the case

[25] Perhaps a reference to the play *Yasuinu*, no longer performed. As the plot dealt with a rebellion against an ancestor of the family of the Ashikaga Shōguns, the play was doubtless withdrawn out of deference.

of those particular plays, the performers, while always maintaining their allegiance to the spirit of those works, must color their presentations to the tastes of their period.

15. Composing the Nō, 2

In composing the *nō*, it is not enough to use the principle of *jo*, *ha*, and *kyū*; merely to apply these concepts mechanically to the structure of a text will produce bad results. A *nō* play must be composed in such a way that the atmosphere of the performance itself moves through these three stages. The atmosphere of the *jo* must be truly "broken" by the *ha* [as the term literally suggests]. If these three stages are considered merely in terms of the written text, the words may sound attractive to read, but they may not create a proper atmosphere in a stage performance. No objections can arise, however, if a proper consonance is established between the written word and the effect of the performance itself. For example, just as in such phrases [from *Tamamizu*] as "to face Tamamizu," or "facing to the east, then to the west" [from an unidentified play], the writer must compose his text in such a way that the actor can create a suitable effect in performance.

In the course of composition, a writer may get caught up in the desire to give the words a poetic bloom of their own, so that the text becomes too long. Many such attempts must be set aside for the proper composition of a play. Considered from this point of view, the chant in *Susano-o* is well composed. In the play, there are such phrases as "in the age of the gods, there were such divinities as Amaterasu Ōmikami; in the age of men, there were such heroes as Yamato Takeru no Mikoto, who attacked foreign lands." The writer might have been expected to compose something concerning the subjugation of the eastern provinces, but he avoided this and, at the end of the *kusemai* inserted the phrase "I am the Prince with Eight Swords," thus reversing the normal order by inserting a phrase that should well draw applause from his audience. If, on the other hand, a writer merely composes the play following the order of the original narrative, his text will be too long and quite unsatisfactory. This matter deserves careful consideration.

In the *nō* play *Furu*, when the priest begins his exchange with the woman who is washing cloth, it would be necessary, if the order of the story were to be strictly followed, for the actor to chant the history of the sacred sword of Furu.[26] However, to chant instead the line "the first deep snow falls [*furu*] on the high bridge at Furu" helps give the audience a larger, more profound sense of the imaginative landscape being created, the essential effect of any *nō*. Indeed, the need for the use of such legends on ancient sites in terms of artistic material to construct a play is related to the matter of creating this "larger view" in the minds of the audience. Then again, if the history of a place is to be the subject of a chant that can provide the basis for effective theatrical gestures, then the chant must begin with the legend itself. In fact, the opening section of the *kusemai* of this play too, the phrase "now indeed, what is called Furu, . . ." and the recounting of the legend of the sacred sword give an impression of strength to the chant. On the other hand, when the phrase "the first deep snow" is chanted, the word *furu* ["fall"] appears [both as verb and noun at the same moment] creating an effect [of euphony] so appropriate to the *nō*. In *Sanemori*, after the scene in which Sanemori dyes his beard, the action should, if the order were to be strictly followed, lead to a battle scene; however, by speaking the lines that begin "then again, Sanemori" [another element of the story is introduced], so that the fighting can occur at the very end of the play, thus observing the rhythm of *jo, ha,* and *kyū.*

In general, a play written in two parts, in which the *shite* leaves the stage and then returns, is relatively easy to compose. A *nō* that is played straight through must be written so that there is sufficient variation for the audience. The point is a

[26] The sword, the chief treasure of the Isonokami Shrine near Kyoto, was supposed to have been presented to the Emperor Jimmu by the goddess Amaterasu.

vital one. If such variation is not provided, the play will languish and seem ineffective. In the case of *Matsukaze*, for example, the play appears to have such a break, even though it follows straight through. When the line "I no longer feel the pain" is finished, the movement and the music come to a brief pause. Such effects must be carefully studied.

On one occasion, when Motomasa planned to compose a play concerning the battle of the Genji clan at Yashima,[27] he thought to write the text in such a way as to give the audience a broad and poetic vision of the scene; Zeami found fault with the idea, however, saying that the emotions of those who go to fight in a battle are very different indeed from those who wish to stroll through the beautiful scenery.

In the *nō* play *Moriya*, at the line "cut off Moriya's head," the gesture should be performed in consonance with the music of the chant at that moment. If Seiami, the author of the play, were to be born again, he would not recognize the way [in which the play is now performed]. Moriya should be beheaded during the exchange with Hata no Kōkatsu. In the course of their argument, the words "cut off his head!" should be spoken, just as the play comes to an abrupt end.

Often in the *nō*, when the *kusemai* is finished, a chanted *rongi* is employed; yet depending on the occasion, it may be effective to use a *rongi* that begins with spoken lines. In the case when a *shite* appears as the manifestation of a god, this technique is particularly appropriate. If the play has Yoshino for its setting, the time should be set in the spring [because of the cherry blossoms]; if at Tatsuta, it should be set in the fall [because of the colored leaves]; Mt. Fuji is a particularly appropriate setting for the summer.

A [final] *kiribyōshi* can be used when a powerful dance with strong movements is required [as in the case of the appearance of gods, demons, and the like]. Both writers and performers should take note of this. It seems that these days those who

[27] Yashima, a large island near the modern city of Takamatsu in Shikoku, was the site of a celebrated battle between the Heike and Genji warriors in the 1185 civil wars.

compose *nō* plays tend to insert such effects in an inappropriate part of their compositions.

In the congratulatory opening words for a day's performances of *nō*, such lines as "then you, Prince, on whom the fortunes of war have smiled" are often improvised. The insertion of such phrases as "then you, Prince" makes the speech too lengthy. With such a phrase as "in this age when all under Heaven is at peace," it is clear that a ruler is being referred to. To lengthen such a speech unnecessarily is to spoil its effect. Of course, the usefulness of this principle depends on the circumstances. A play like *Matsukaze* is a complex one, but one has no sense of its being too long. [In the composition of a play] every aspect that comprises the totality must be carefully considered, and the proper balance should be struck between the various elements. In rearranging the various elements [in the original story or legend] for the purpose of the dramatization, the transitions should not be made too suddenly. A writer must understand the overtones that words can possess. The text should be as compact as possible, yet clear and easy to understand.

16. Composing the Nō, 3

When composing music for a play, if the author thinks to alter the melody after every unit [of a 7-5 syllable count] and concentrates on this aspect of his task, rather than concerning himself with the overall effect of the music, he cannot achieve the proper results. Rather, he should plan to create the same effect for [at least] two units and then bring a sudden change into the melody being employed. The device of using the same music during two units in order to bring about a sudden novelty in the chant is truly an effective one.

The actual words to be performed must be composed on the basis of an understanding of the nature of the various characters who appear on the stage. For example, in the play *Hatsuse*, when the woman's line was spoken, "well then, to speak of Chōkokuzan in Washū," Lord Ashikaga Yoshimitsu himself criticized the composition of the text, saying that phrase such as "Chōkokuzan" ["Mount Chōkoku," which uses so many Chinese characters and sounds so stiff] was inappropriate for a woman to deliver. Thus for a play that involves a woman character, lines such as "the temple at Hatsuse in Yamato" that sound appropriately graceful should be composed.

It is important never to repeat verbal devices within a single play. If, for example, the syllable *furu* serves a double function in the phrase "the field of Furu where the year grows old" [*toshi o furu/toshi o furu no*], then such a phrase as "the rain falling on Furu field" [*ame no furu no/ame no furu*] must be avoided at all cost. In a play in which Ariwara no Narihira appears, for example, if the syllable *nari* serves a double function in such a phrase as "for Narihira, the past has become . . ." [*mukashi ni nari/mukashi ni Narihira*], then a repetition in the same play of a similar usage, such as "what might happen, Narihira . . ." [*nani ni nari/nani ni Narihira*] is equally bad. Such usages, in fact, should be employed only once at the moment when the musical and literary elements in the play are most strongly blended. [There is an extreme example of such usage] in the play *Ukai*, where the syllable *na* serves a double function three times: "how useless amidst the waves" [*kai mo na/kai mo nami na ni*], "no one to bring aid! at the bottom of the waves" [*tasukuru hito mo na (ki)/tasukuru hito mo nami no soko*], and "that heart, again, in the Natsu river" [*sono kokoro sara ni na (ki)/sono kokoro sara ni natsukawa*]. At the least, the first line should be changed to read, "the pitiful cormorant fisher, rowing his boat" [*kai no naki mi no obune kogu*] and all the rest eliminated.

In the *nō* play *Matsugasaki*, the phrase "the pine has blossomed" [*matsu ga sakikeri*], [since it relies on a play on words with the geographical location named in the title] represents just such a crucial spot in the text. Therefore, in order for the audience to truly grasp the significance of the phrase, proper emphasis should be given to phrases in the preceding *rongi* that hint at this moment, such as "indeed, as for the flower of Tokiwa," so that by composing a series of phrases of this sort, effective results may be assured. If such an atmosphere is not established, then when it comes to the composition of the climactic moment of the play, the author's carelessness in constructing the section will cause the audience to miss the significance of the crucial phrase, and the effect will be unsuccessful. In the *nō* play *Yashima*, there is the crucial phrase "ah, the usual sadness of this world" [*yoshi tsune no ukiyo*], [which is a play on words with the name of the protagonist Yoshitsune]; it is therefore important to have the audience hear the phrases that precede it, such as "indeed if one speaks of that name, our name is what?" Thus, when the phrase *yoshi tsune no* is spoken, the audience will be able to pick up the phrase and find the effect enjoyable.

In the case of the *nō*, it is wise to choose familiar phrases from the classics, old poetry, and *waka* [for incorporation into the text of the play]. If the phrase chosen is too complex, the audience will not be able to comprehend it quickly enough. Such difficult phrases are more appropriately enjoyable when read.

In composing the *nō*, a careful distinction must always be maintained by the writer between the sounds *ha* and *wa*. When a distinction between the two cannot be determined by the ear, the actor must take care to slightly pucker his lips so as to produce the appropriate sound.

In particular, the author must be careful of appropriate verbal accents when fitting music to his text [so that the meaning of the words will be clear]. Then again [in terms of the musical scales], if the previous phrase is at the pitch of *shō*, then the following phrase should move higher to the pitch of *kaku*.[28] Such are the various matters that must be considered when composing a *nō* play.

Zeami has written the following plays: *Yawata, Aioi* [now called *Takasago*], *Yōrō, Oimatsu, Shiogama* [now called *Tōru*],

---

[28] For a discussion of these traditional musical scales, see William P. Malm, *Japanese Music*, pp. 66-67.

Aridōshi, Hakozaki, Unoha, Mekurauchi, Matsukaze, Hyaku-man, Higaki no onna [now called *Higaki*], *Satsuma no kami* [now called *Tadanori*], *Sanemori, Yorimasa, Kiyotsune, Atsu-mori, Kōya* [now called *Kōya monogurui*], *Ōsaka, Koi no omoni, Sano no funabashi* [now called *Funabashi*], *Taisan-moku* [now called *Taisan Pukun*].

Kan'ami has written the following plays: *Sotoba Komachi, Jinen Koji,* and *Kayoi Komachi*.

Seiami has written the following: *Shizuka, Michimori,* and *Tango monogurui*.

The play *Ukifune* was written by an amateur, Yoko-o Motohisa. Zeami set it to music.

These are the texts that should serve as models for the composition of new plays. They are listed in *The Three Elements in Composing a Play*, but the names of their authors have been entered here as well.

Such plays as *Ukai* and *Kashiwazaki* were written by Enami no Saemongōrō. However, both plays have sections that are badly written, and as [Zeami] rewrote and improved these texts, they can be considered as his. When *Kashiwazaki* is performed these days, the *kusemai* from *Tsuchiguruma* [by Zeami] is included. In the case of *Kayoi Komachi*, the basis for the present composition was written by the preaching monks at Mt. Hiei, and that version was performed by the troupe of Komparu Gon no kami [for a festival] at Tōno-mine.[29] Later, the text was revised [by Kan'ami]. In the case of *Sano no funabashi*, the play began as a *dengaku* piece. Zeami rewrote it. Such old plays existed even before they were performed by *dengaku* troupes; indeed they have been in existence for a considerable time. Details are written in *The Three Elements in Composing a Play*. As this treatise was composed in Ōei 30 [1423], there are a number of plays written after that time that can also serve as models.

[29] *Sarugaku* performances were presented during yearly readings of the *Vimalakīrti sutra* in the tenth month at the Danzan shrine, near the base of Mt. Tōnomine to the south of Nara. The shrine, first erected in A.D. 701, is dedicated to Kamatari, founder of the powerful Fujiwara family.

17. Subscription Nō: Stage Arrangements and the Performance of Okina

In the case of preparing the stands for a performance of Subscription *nō*, the total circumference should consist of sixty-two or sixty-three sections [of five feet], [or a total circumference of about 315 feet].[30] One side of each section should measure about five *shaku* [five feet]. It is true that, recently, stands containing more than seventy sections [about 350 feet] have sometimes been constructed, in order to accommodate a larger number of spectators. Kiami, who performed in *dengaku*, constructed stands that had no more than fifty-four sections [with a circumference of about 270 feet]. As his voice had diminished in power, he wanted these arrangements so that his audience could still hear his chanting. Such performances as those held at Tadasugawara and Reizeigawara[31] can serve as models, and plans for performances can be made accordingly. (These matters I learned from my father Zeami when I was a child. Some details should doubtless be carefully investigated.)

The stands should be tightly arranged, so that, since they are placed close together, the voices of the performers will be well confined and the quiet beauties of the performance can be properly realized. The bridge should be constructed so that its highest point is at the curtained entrance to the greenroom and it slopes down toward the stage. If the bridge is arched in any fashion, the effect will be unsatisfactory. The spot where the bridge reaches the stage proper should be at one side between the pillars that hold up the roof over [the rear of the] stage. The stage itself should be exactly in the middle, extending neither to the right or left, nor too far to the front or the rear, but perfectly centered in terms of the surrounding

[30] This passage is difficult to interpret with accuracy, as the exact length of a *ken* (間), here translated as "section," is not precisely known. Modern scholars estimate the distance at about five feet, which would make the circumference somewhere between 270 and 350 feet.

[31] An area in the northern outskirts of Kyoto where the Kamo and the Takano rivers meet.

seats. In all instances, the voices of the actors are best heard from the front when projected. Those sitting to one side may of course have difficulty in hearing the voices of the performers that come from the back so that the chanting must be planned with these concerns in mind. Before the performance, the stage and the bridge must be thoroughly examined so that any nails can be removed and other dangerous spots repaired. The seating area for the chorus should be arranged by spreading straw mats on the ground, at a level slightly lower than the stage. The spot where the *waki* perform can be prepared by spreading a fine carpet.

The proper costume that is appropriate for the role of Okina is fully described in a separate teaching. In any case, the costume should not be gaudy. The performer should suggest a calm and serene atmosphere when he appears. Costumes sewn with gold thread have seldom been seen in this role. The color should be one of the "pure colors" [red, yellow, white, blue, and black, as opposed to colors blended from them]. The role of the person who carries the box for Okina's mask is one highly appreciated by the audience. The performer should be chosen from among a large group of handsome young men, and a youth is most suitable. He should wear an *eboshi* and a *hitatare* and be altogether appropriately dressed when he appears. When Okina makes his ceremonial bow, he steps to the spot where the bridge touches the stage, grasps his fan, and performs the gesture, then walks onto the stage and sits in his proper place. At this time the role of Tsuyu Harai[32] was danced by Tsuchidayū. He was a highly skillful player, and I heard that he even performed among the *waki* performers. This dance has sometimes been performed twice running, surely a foolish countrified practice.

In the old days, the role of Okina was performed, according to the proper order, by the eldest actor in the troupe. At a performance of *sarugaku* at Imagumo, however [in 1374] the

[32] Tsuyu Harai is another name for the role of Senzai in the play *Okina*, the most ancient of the *nō* dramas still in the repertory. In the play, Senzai's dance precedes that of Okina.

Shōgun Yoshimitsu was to see the art for the first time. When the subject came up as to who should dance, only the leader of the troupe, Kan'ami Kiyotsugu, seemed the appropriate choice. Such was the advice given by Nan'ami, and therefore Kiyotsugu appeared in the role. This is how the practice began, and it has become a fundamental principle for the Yamato *sarugaku* troupe. These days, even in performances of *sarugaku* held in the capital or before the Shōgun, the *Shiki samban*[33] is not always performed. Indeed, at the moment, other than for a few performances held at shrines, these dances are not presented.

In the capital, the phrase "how broad indeed" [sung during Senzai's dance in *Okina*] is performed by the chorus. When the dance is finished, and the actor playing Okina removes his mask, he should only give it to the appropriate player, who serves as a prompter and who should then place the mask in its proper box. Under no circumstances should the mask be given to a drummer or to any other of the musicians. Only the young actor designated as the box carrier should receive it. When Okina leaves the stage, he should doubtless have the box carrier exit with him. (A number of details concerning these points will require close investigation.) The box, of course, should be retired at the conclusion of the *Shiki samban* performances. When the actor portraying Okina has finished his dance, he should remove his mask, straighten his costume, bow facing the audience, and then exit. (Various questions can be raised concerning the details related to these various points. I have written down here merely matters that I myself have observed.)

The role of Sambasō [in *Okina*], which is danced by a *kyōgen* actor, must never be played in such a way as to create a comic effect. The sort of performances staged in recent years that make people laugh are absolutely out of place.

There are a number of important related matters. First,

---

[33] The *Shiki samban* represents a group of dances, originally of a religious nature, that eventually developed into *Okina*.

those who are lined up together to serve as a chorus must sing in perfect unison. Second, the actor must take care that if his costume is in disarray, he adjust it properly. Performers from other troupes should never be mixed into the company, and every effort must be made to keep in mind the fundamental nature [of these sacred pieces].

The portions of the text that are to be performed by the chorus are more or less fixed. If there are any doubts in the matter, the actors themselves should be consulted. Errors are likely to occur at those moments when the chant begins and just as it concludes. Any raggedness in the chanting will be harmful. Various rules and precedents should be carefully studied and those points in the chant [that may cause difficulties] should be given every attention. There are a number of points that those performing in the role of Sambasō need to understand, and so one should ask about those matters and write them down. What I have written here only concerns what I myself have observed.

When a performance is given in the presence of the Shōgun, the *tsutsumi* and *taiko* should not be brought out and left on stage ahead of time. The instruments should be carried on by the musicians in a fashion that does not attract attention, I have been told.

The actor who carries the box for the Okina mask should of course be young, but the choice of a person who appears too childlike should be avoided. This is because of the fact that he must carry the heavy box; [if he is too young] his efforts may appear dangerous to the audience. In making exits and entrances, it is absolutely forbidden for an actor to look back over his shoulder. This matter must be strictly observed.

18. Costumes and Properties

Various matters concerning the management of the personnel of the troupe have been fixed and recorded elsewhere and thus need not be repeated here.

In addition, the proper arrangement of costumes and properties in a performance is of importance. In a *waki nō*, the costume used for the role of a Minister of State, for example, should be a *suikan*, with both upper and lower sections made of silk. The *tsure* who accompany the minister should wear an *ōkuchi* style of formal pleated skirt. On one occasion, when Ushidayū began to chant the opening congratulatory phrases at a performance, he faced the drummer, squatted down, blew his nose, made the musician in charge stop the playing, aligned his voice with the final sounds, and then began to perform.

The pattern of performance for this opening section divides the spoken sections in two. The first lines are spoken, then a section of chant [the *shidai*] is inserted, then finally another spoken section is performed. The chant proper can thus begin as soon as this section has finished. Both *waki* and *kyōgen* actors must perform precisely according to the written text of the play. If, through their ignorance, they deviate from tradition and perform according to their own ideas, the results will be unfortunate.

When the *shite* comes back in the second part of the play and appears again on the bridge, he continues on through his performance of a *sashigoe* or *issei*. At this juncture, the function of the *waki* [as leader] is crucial. If the two do not pass the chant back and forth from one to the other in a suitable fashion, the fault will lie with the *waki*.

When the opening play has finished, the second play on the program might well include two priests in the *waki* category. The third play, however, should have only one.

In a *nō* play with a woman as the chief character, the actor should wear a *kosode* with skirts sufficiently long to hide his feet. His undergarments of refined silk should be fully wrapped around him as well. They should be closed, and nothing should be seen of his body below the neck. The actor must always remember that the undergarments are for his body, and his own skin is not to be seen by the audience. A wide hair sash in an actor's wig is already ugly enough, and the use of any red material looks unspeakably vulgar. Then too, one must take care that the end of the sash is not out of place and odd in appearance. When a *kariginu* is worn, one must not wear a sash in a sloppy fashion, thinking that since it is worn under [the outer garments] the audience will not actually see it.

In the *nō*, it must be remembered, the particular coloration provided [for the costuming and properties] helps create the special artistic elegance of each play. In *Aridōshi*, for example, the entrance of the *shite* with an umbrella and a flaming torch provides the most striking moment in the play. To substitute a fan would ruin the effect. In the play *Hanagatami*, the flower basket itself should be handled with the greatest of care. In *Tsunemori*, the boat should be made of blue silk cloth in order to give a slight sense of elegant decor. In the play *Sumidagawa*, since the first portion of the play is altogether too colorless, the traveler [played by the *tsure*] may in this particular case be dressed in *ōkuchi*-style robes. At the beginning of *Ukai*, the sight of an actor who appears without a mask and wearing a bamboo hat could only be appropriate for some kind of country performance. The appropriate costuming must always depend on the circumstances.

It would be eccentric indeed to maintain the idea that there need never be any change in the arrangement of costumes, even though their appearance has become all too familiar, and that one must continue on with things just as they always were. Recently there have been too many plays in which the black wigs worn are too bushy and obvious. Depending on the play involved, they should be adorned to some extent in order to vary the artistic effect. Actors of short stature who play *waki* roles of ministers and the like often bend and twist their folded-over *oboshi* hats when they wear them, which looks altogether unsightly. Tall actors as well must take care [concerning their headgear].

Recently, Iwatō of the Ōmi troupe, in a performance of Subscription *nō* performed in the capital, took the oars [used with a boat in the play] and wrapped them in some sort of silk or cotton cloth which he then bound on with some kind of sash. Some connoisseurs in the audience who saw this went home without having been given any artistic stimulation worthy of the *nō*. Great care must be taken over matters of this sort. Dōami himself [on the other hand], in the play *Shiba-bune*, carved two thick oars, and, playing the role of the boatman, rowed with them, a most artistic effect.

Recently, at a performance given before the Shōgun Yoshinori, On'ami, when performing in *Miidera*, placed the bell to his right, since the stage faced the south [rather than the north, which was usual]. Thus he struck the bell from his left [turning his body from left to right, which was in error]. No matter what the occasion, the bell should be set up and struck to the left of the actor.

Then again, in *Sakagami*, the fact that the Princess Sakagami is deranged makes her appearance [both as a princess and as a madwoman] of crucial importance to the artistic success of the play. Thus, when [Zeami] had the *mizugoromo* [used for the costume] colored with those special considerations in mind, he obtained great praise from his audiences at the time. From then on, however, this sort of costume has become quite fashionable, so that such robes are worn even by such characters [as the fisher-girl] in *Shiokumi*, creating a most inappropriate effect. The proper costuming depends on the nature of each particular play. In a *nō* such as *Kōya Shōnin*, for example, the use of a hood made of thin silk woven through with metallic threads is somehow inappropriate. Rather, a hood without any embroidery, such as a priest might wear, should be used, one suitable for an old person that is subdued in appearance. The costume itself should be dyed in some shade of dark grey. When Dōami performed in the *Nembutsu saru-gaku*, he wore a robe of silk and a long hood pulled well down over his head, creating a fine artistic effect.

One should not send a child into a performance when his presence is not required by the text. The Shōgun Ashikaga Yoshimitsu disliked the practice very much. However, when the play requires a child's voice and a young actor must appear, he should be made to wear an *ōkuchi* robe and he should be accompanied by other actors. Performers who sing as a group should never wear *eboshi*. Otherwise, they may be confused with members of the chorus. Details on such matters are written elsewhere.

Above all, the *nō* creates an illusion, so that the audience becomes absorbed in the characters they see on the stage. For this reason, the greenroom must always be kept tightly closed, so that no occasion can occur when the spectators can see inside. An actor, for example, may appear as a beautiful woman on the stage, yet naked in the dressing room, dirty with perspiration; there will be precious little atmosphere left, and any illusion will be difficult to create.

When it came to chanting indoors [before a noble audience], [Zeami] would sit, holding a fan in his right hand, and, to balance it, in his left hand a *shakuhachi* [a bamboo flute, to be used for determining his pitch]. He put the mouth of the *shakuhachi* into the sleeve of his robe, then pressed the sleeve closed with his finger. [Zeami] also performed the chant kneeling before a noble audience. Concerning such matters, it is important to ask as many detailed questions as possible. [Even small details are important. For example], even a flintstone bag carried by an actor should be made of gold brocade. Such things give color to a dance performed indoors.

19. Masks

The forehead of a mask should not be too high. Recently actors have thought it a shame to whittle down their masks and so have left them as they were, which seems odd. When wearing something on the head, be it an *eboshi* or a crown, the headgear normally comes down to the middle of the forehead. Thus [if the forehead is too high], the headgear falls back and looks like a kind of inverted comma,[34] creating an unpleasant effect. If a wig is worn, the forehead itself is actually not seen. Yet if the forehead is too high, it can still be discerned behind the fluttering hair of the wig, an unsightly

---

[34] Literally, a *tomoe*, a comma-shaped design derived from a figure drawn on the leather shields worn on the wrist by archers. The shape is a common one in traditional Japanese design.

affair. Thus it would be best to cut off the upper part of the masks that are too high in the forehead.

20. Flutes and Famous Kyōgen Players

There are a number of matters set down in *Learning the Way* that do not have to be repeated in any detail here. Concerning flute playing, however, there is the incident of the old man and the child which involved Kan'ami and Zeami. The play being performed was *Shōshō*, in which, when Naritsune and Yasuyori return to the capital, they sing together the poem "As I Remember."[35]

[At this time], among *kyōgen* players, Tsuchidayū the First and Kiku of the Shinza troupe were truly superlative performers. Kiku was exceptional. For example, in the play *Hatsuwaka*, a child [named Hatsuwaka] has been disinherited by his father; hearing that his father is engaged in battle, however, the young man goes himself to fight in Yuigahama, where he is severely wounded [and kept as a prisoner]. When his father [who was also captured] was asked, "who is that prisoner there?" he replied, "how frightening!" Then he came close, revealing that the prisoner was indeed Hatsuwaka, his son. Kiku [who played Hatsuwaka] had pondered the situation carefully in order to perform this moment when, limp with sadness, he thinks how to inform his father of all that had happened to him since they were parted. He earned great praise on that occasion. *Kyōgen* actors should take note of moments such as these which provide them with such admirable opportunities.

Tsuchidayū the Second was signaled out for his skill by the

---

[35] The story of the play is drawn from a famous incident involving the exile of Naritsune, Yasuyori, and the priest Shunkan, in connection with the 1185 civil wars. The poem cited reads in full, "Moss has grown between the wooden shingles of the eaves of my old home; the moonlight no longer shines in as I remember." For the incident, see Kitagawa and Tsuchida, tr., *The Tale of the Heike*, Book III, Chapter 4, "Naritsune's Return to the Capital," pp. 180-184, from which this translation is taken.

Shōgun Ashikaga Yoshimitsu himself. An actor who performs *kyōgen* must assume such traits during his activities in everyday life. If the actor merely adopts this kind of deportment when performing on the stage, the spectators will find it difficult to lose themselves in the truth of his performance. Once when Tsuchidayū the Second was near the Shōgun's northern villa [in the suburbs of Kyoto] he passed by a high government official at Takahashi. Realizing that the passerby was Tsuchi, the official hid his face behind his fan and walked on. Tsuchi came close to the official in order to sneak a look at him, then put up his fan as well to hide his own face and walked on. This kind of attitude reveals the soul of a truly gifted player.

Such is the artistry of those who have truly gained eminence in the eyes of the world.

21. Artistry in Country Performances

Concerning performances in the countryside: Komparu Gon no kami and Kongō Gon no kami never earned high success. The Shōgun did not attend their subscription performances in the capital. Komparu himself, in his subscription performances in Kyoto, was not a success, abandoned his series after two days, and retired to the countryside. Kongo, too, when performing in a *nō* competition at Nara, was asked to stop and leave after only two performances. Still, the fact that these two accomplished as much as they did in an age when the standards of *sarugaku* were so high meant exceptional good luck for them. These days, when the standards of our art have fallen, even those who do not perform the *nō* with any dexterity can on occasion push themselves forward. Yet such success does not represent true accomplishment.

Kongō himself was an actor whose art had weight and breadth. Yet there was somehow too massive a quality about his work, so that his performances sometimes seemed overblown.

Komparu was not able to dance such things as *kusemai*. He performed various aspects of his art in an incorrect manner. For example [in the play *Kashiwazaki*] he performed the lines "tapping with the fan; calling the water of the cascade" as though he were about to dance; then he suddenly continued on with the line "ah, my child Kojirō" and quickly left the stage; as the meaning of this was altogether unclear, he was much criticized by spectators at the time. Then again, when he performed the line "at Inoue, where the paulownia trees are in flower" [from the same play], he held the bamboo hat he wore to his chest and looked up [to match the word 'up' (*ue*) with the similar sound in the word *Inouye*] in an exaggerated manner. He was the kind of player who consciously sought out effects of this sort. He was criticized for this even by the Kongō family. In dancing performances held indoors, as well, he would leap and turn noisily, then bring his knees together to stop, a feat of agility. "How can such insolent behavior be thought suitable in a place such as this?" was the criticism given this sort of performance by a person in Lord Akamatsu's family.[36]

[In the *nō* play *Ama*] at the line "ah, thinking with longing for the fisher maiden, your noble tears flowed," the music sung to the words "noble tears" was Komparu's own. It is not necessary to continue on in detail. [Suffice it to say that] in the same play, for an artistic effect at the line "cutting below the breast, concealing the gem" he wore a black wig, dressed in light robes, and moved with light, mincing steps. All of this was quite unsuitable for a woman's role.

Kongō played any and all sorts of parts. He was particularly known for roles of old men. Yet he performed the *rongi* sections in a somewhat aimless fashion. In the play *Unrin-in*, at the line "Mototsune's unusual appearance, Narihira," he entered brandishing a torch and sat down, firm and immobile. His appearance ceded nothing even to the grandeur of the Great South Gate of the Kōfukuji Temple at Nara, in front of which the performance was held. His dancing was in the

---

[36] The Akamatsu family served as advisors to the Ashikaga court. The person who made this criticism is not identified.

style of Bettō of the Ōmi troupe. He danced in an ample and nimble style, with a great concentration of strength.

I learned about the art of these two men privately [from my father Zeami], but I have written about them openly here in order to show the strong and weak points of the troupes that perform both in the capital and in the country. I do not propose to discuss these matters in any further detail here. Yet it can be said, for example, that these artists performed such tricks as knee stamping and quick turns on the knee [which are forbidden in our troupe] even at indoor performances at the capital.

Among *kyōgen* performers, there was an actor named Yoshihitoue. [Although he was well known in the country], he was never brought to perform in the capital because of the shallowness of his art. Those in the capital who knew little of the nature of his performances said "perhaps it is because Tsuchidayū was afraid of being overwhelmed by him." In fact, however, Yoshihitoue was not at all talented, in spite of his far-reaching yet empty fame. Indeed, he was scoffed at by those from his own province. If one has a real grasp of the differences between performances in the country and in the capital, then the significance of this matter will be clear.

Yojirō and Yotsu were two *kyōgen* players of high accomplishment. Roami too was a highly gifted player.

Then again, the leader of the Jūniza troupe [Gorō Yasu-tsugu] was a player who performed in the lower three levels yet whose skill sometimes enabled him to rise spontaneously to the Art of the True Flower. On the advice of Zeami, he came to play his devil roles in the "refining movement" style. In the first year of Shōchō [1428], he was called to perform before the Shōgun Ashikaga Yoshinori; on this occasion, when the performances went very well, he sent the following letter to Zeami:

> I have not had the pleasure of seeing you for some time. I have been missing you profoundly. Recently, thinking how much I would like to spend some time with you, in order

to talk over in detail a number of matters, I came to call on you twice, but as you were out on both occasions, I was not able to see you, which is a great pity. In fact, I was recently summoned [to perform] here in the capital. This year, as I am such an old man [of seventy-six], I felt it would be better to decline. Although I explained those circumstances, I was unable to oppose the shōgun's wishes and so made my appearance and performed in a number of plays. The fact that the shōgun and the others found nothing to complain of in the performances represents the greatest honor that an old man can receive. Now, concerning this matter, there is something that I would like to say. The fact that I could be treated in such a manner, without criticism, is due altogether to your advice. In years past, I have needed the guidance from you concerning my own art that you so generously gave me, especially when you were so kind to me on the occasion of the performances at Kitayama.[37] I can never forget what you have done for me, and until this day I have attempted to perform in the spirit of the guidance you gave me. Nevertheless, if I had followed the spirit of your instructions yet performed in plays unsuitable to me, I would not have received the welcome reception that I did. Because you wrote for me plays suitable to my abilities, I was able to perform them successfully. These plays have been staged by other actors as well. But as these plays were not written for them, their performances were not effective. Indeed, if a play is not suitable for an actor, he has no means to show off his own abilities. Thus what I have accomplished is entirely due to you. Thinking how much I wanted to tell you what was in my heart, I came to visit you twice but was truly saddened to find that you were away. I have always lacked the ability to write, even using the syllabary. Thus I have had this letter composed for me, as I was not able to write it down myself. The words them-

---

[37] Presumably a reference to performances held at the villa of Ashikaga Yoshimitsu, which was located in this area.

selves doubtless do not match my emotions. Although I would like to come again to speak to you, I must now take my leave. It is not possible for me to remain long in the capital, and I am planning to return to the country this evening. Thus I want to send this letter to you. Should you yourself happen to travel to the country, I hope that we might meet and talk over many things. I wait for an occasion to see you with the greatest pleasure.

With deference,

Sincerely yours,
Yasutsugu
4th day of the 8th month

Then, in the margin, the following was written in addition:

How difficult indeed it is to write of such things in a letter. How I wish to meet you and talk to you. What I have received from you will last me all my life and will never be forgotten by my family even in the generations to come. Again and again I want to thank you.
To: Zeami

In this letter, the emotions of one who truly revered the way [of *nō*] stand revealed.

Dōami, on the nineteenth day of each month, the memorial day of Kan'ami, always arranged for two priests to carry out a service for him, as he had helped Dōami rise to a position of eminence. On the occasion of the Imagumano performances, the Shōgun himself began the custom of observing *sarugaku* presentations. This was in Zeami's twelfth year.

22. Masks

Concerning masks: Nikko made the best Okina masks, and Miroku was also highly skilled at carving them. The mask used by our own troupe was carved by Midaroku. The mask was discovered in Iga when our troupe was founded there at Obata.

Among the Ōmi mask makers, Shakuzuru, who was also an actor, was particularly skillful at carving demon masks. Recently, there has been a fine mask maker named Echiuchi. He is attached to the Zazen-in [a subsidiary temple of Enryakuji] on Mt. Hiei. He is particularly good at carving women's masks.

Among mask carvers in Echizen, there are a number of skillful men, including Ishiō Hyōe, Tatsuemon, and then, ranking after them, Yasha, Bunzō, then Koushi, and finally Tokuwaka. The masks made by the first two can be used by anyone without reservation. As for the masks made by Yasha and the others, however, the efficacy of the results in performance will depend on the actor who wears them. The masks worn by the head of the Kongō troupe were those actually made by Bunzō himself. The mask of the old man used by our troupe was carved by Tatsuemon. The mask of the laughing old man that won praise when used in the play *Koi no omoni* was carved by Yasha. The mask worn in the second half of *Oimatsu* was made by Koushi.

The mask carvers of Echi made various masks and presented them as gifts to the players of Ōmi *sarugaku*; then, saying that they wished to give some as well to "the famous actor of the Yamato troupe," they presented some masks to Zeami through the good offices of Iwatō dayū, including the woman's mask, as well as the mask of an old man with a thin face now in the possession of Hoshō dayū. This mask was painted and worn from time to time for performances of *Yorimasa*. As for the men's masks, those that are highly valued in recent times are made by Chigusa. Excellent young men's masks are made by Tatsuzaemon.

[In the category of demon masks], the *tobide* mask used by the Deai troupe, and the *tenjin*, *ōbeshimi*, and *kobeshimi* masks[38]

---

[38] The *tobide* mask, literally a "protruding" mask (referring to the eyeballs) is used for god figures. The term *beshimi* supposedly derives from the verb

that belong to our family were all carved by Shakuzuru. Other troupes refer to the *ōbeshimi* as the "Yamato beshimi." This is the particular mask to which they refer. The *ōbeshimi* and *tenjin* masks were the first used by Kan'ami and were then passed on to successive generations. The *tobide* masks were carved to depict the legendary portrait of [the ghost of] Sugawara no Michizane, who spit out the pomegranate seeds that turned into burning flames.[39] The mask got its name of *tenjin* because of its use in the play of that name. Once someone borrowed the mask, but because they had a peculiar dream concerning it, they returned it. At that point the mask was retired from use and highly revered, but on the basis of a second dream it was restored to use and is still worn today. The *kobeshimi* mask was the first that Zeami wore. There is no need for any actor in the present generation to wear it. The mask was used for the first presentation of *Ukai*. When another sort of mask is used in playing *Ukai*, a more emotional atmosphere is created. Thus, a mask should be chosen with the particular artistry in mind of the actor who wears it. Our troupe possesses an excellent mask of a somewhat older woman carved by Echi. Zeami wore the mask in various performances involving women characters. (In addition to these, there are many other masks of high craftsmanship.)

23. Various Sarugaku Troupes

The Yamato *sarugaku* descends in a direct line from Hata no Kōkatsu. The Ōmi *sarugaku* descends from the line of Ki no kami [who was an offspring of Kōkatsu]. Thus they belong

---

beshimu, meaning to press the lips together in anger. *Ōbeshimi* (literally, "large *beshimi*") masks are used for the roles of demons called *tengu* and often show a slightly comical quality. *Kobeshimi* (literally "little *beshimi*") masks are fiercer and are used for more malicious beings. The meaning of the *tenjin* mask (literally, "god in heaven") is a reference to the spirit of Sugawara Michizane, as explained in the text.

[39] The dramatization of this incident occurs in the play *Raiden*. An earlier version was called *Tenjin*.

to the Ki clan. (Various investigations need to be made about the periods concerned.)

As concerns Yamato *sarugaku*, the troupe at Takeda [the Emman-i], the Deai troupe [which later died out], and the troupe at Tobi [the Hōshō troupe] are related through marriage. Down through the generations, the Takeda troupe has been in possession of the mask that came from Kōkatsu. The origins of the Deai troupe are found in the Yamada *sarugaku*. [The beginnings of the Yamada *sarugaku* are as follows.] In the province of Iga, in a place called Hattori, a child named Suginoki from a family of the Taira clan became the adopted son of a person named Naka who lived in Ōta. This adopted son was the father to a child born to a common-law wife in the capital. This child in turn was brought up as a foster son by a person named Minodayū, who lived in Yamada. The foster son was father to three children. The eldest [who took the name of Yamada] became the foster son of Hōshōdayū and carried on his line. The second child was named Sōichi. The third was named Kanze [and later was named Kan'ami]. Thus these three men all descend from Minodayū of Yamada. The oldest son [who had taken the name of Yamada] died at an early age, [but the second son carried on his father's line and became the head of the Deai troupe].

The origins of the Kongō troupe go back to the time when two men named Matsu and Take came from Kamakura. They had no family name. (Concerning these matters, a number of inquiries must be made concerning various details.)

Among the Ōmi *sarugaku* troupes, the Mimaji troupe is the one that has been in existence for a considerable time. [As for the origins of the Yamashina troupe], a warrior of low rank, who lived at a place called Yamashina, married a daughter of the leader of the Mimaji troupe. He himself had a great desire to become proficient in *sarugaku*. He secluded himself in order to pray to the deity Yamashina myōjin [of the Kasuga Shrine at Nara]—who is doubtless enshrined as Kasuga myōjin—for a sign as to whether or not he should enter the profession of *sarugaku*. At that moment, a crow dropped something from above the main shrine building. Looking at the object, he found it was a mask of Okina. Finding this the sign he sought, he became a *sarugaku* performer. Later in his career, he set up one son to work in Yamashina, his second son in Shimosaka, and his youngest son at Hie. This is how these three troupes began. However, the Yamashina troupe remains the head of all three groups. At the *sarugaku* performances at the Hie shrine, which are now held from the first through the seventh day of the New Year, only the Yamashina troupe performs *Okina*. The Okina mask used on these occasions [is that dropped by the crow]. These *sarugaku* performances at the New Year came about because of the occasion when the head of the Yamashina troupe went with his wife to pray on the last day of the twelfth month, since their three-year-old child had suddenly died. They prayed to the deity that if the child lived they and all their descendants would perform *sarugaku* on the first day of the New Year at the shrine. Indeed the child revived, and the performances are the direct result of that prayer. [As for the Shimozaka troupe], at the time of the generation of the grandfather of the present Iwatō dayū, the name "Shimozaka" was abandoned and he [like his younger brother] took the name of Hie. This action was evidently taken at the orders of the priests [of Enryakuji on Mt. Hiei], which was a great pity. [The groups above represent the Northern Troupes of Ōmi *sarugaku*.] The Mimaji troupe, the Ōmori troupe, and the Sakaudo troupe represent the southern troupes of the Ōmi *sarugaku*.

As for the Tango *sarugaku*, the head of the troupe was named Shuku. When he performed before the Retired Emperor Kameyama [A.D. 1249-1305], he was assigned the designation of *chōja* [elder]. Thus he became the official head of all the families of the Shinza, the Honza, and the troupe at the Hōjō temple. No actor could expect an honor greater than this. Uma no Shirō [Shirō of the Horse] of the Enami troupe of Kawachi was granted the use of a crest in the image of a horse by, I believe, Lord Kaji-i [a member of the emperor's family who served as a monk at Sanzen-in Temple to the north of Kyoto]. (Investigations should be made to be sure that it was actually he.)

The character *dō* (道) in Dōami's name was given to him by Ashikaga Yoshimitsu himself, and was taken from the Shōgun's Buddhist name Dōgi [altogether an extraordinary honor]. Zeami himself [had been called both Seami and Zeami]. The Shōgun remarked, however, that when the character *se* (世) is included in the compound Kanze (觀 世) [our family name] the sound is produced as *ze*. This, he said, should serve as a model. Just about this time, Kade no kōji, of the Headquarters of the Imperial Guard [resigned as supervisor and] was appointed as Inspector of Military Maneuvers in Hyōgo. In the record of participants, the words "previous supervisor" [*sen kanrei*] [using the pronunciation *sen* as a mark of honor] were used. Since that time, he was always referred to as "the previous supervisor." In just the same way, Zeami's name was fixed in accordance with a decision of the Shōgun, which was a great honor for him. In the case of Kiami, the character *ki* [turtle] was borrowed from his old name Kameyasha, where it had been pronounced "kame." Eventually, however, his name "Kiami" usually came to be written with another character pronounced *ki* [meaning "joy"]. In the case of Kan'ami, [he had taken that name while in Buddhist orders, but] he returned to the secular world and retained his Buddhist name until he died, as a layman.

24. Zeami and Divine Revelations

In Ōei 9 [1412] (as memories are inexact, the precise year will have to be ascertained), in the eleventh month, the Master of the Tachibana Storehouse,[40] which is located at the road by the Hōshō Temple near the Inari Shrine in Kyoto fell gravely ill from a wound and was on the point of death. A woman at the shop suddenly became possessed by the spirit of the Inari Shrine. The spirit spoke through the woman, saying that

[40] Probably a moneylending establishment of some kind.

if the Kanze troupe would give a *nō* performance, the master would recuperate. Zeami therefore performed before the Inari Shrine. The woman who was possessed spoke as follows. "It would be well to perform ten plays. The first three will be watched by the goddess Amaterasu, the second three by the god of Kasuga, the next three by the god of Yahata, and the last by me, the god of Inari." Accordingly, ten plays were performed. When Zeami went to pay his respects to the Tachibana family, they called from inside the house, "Zeami is coming!" asked him in, then presented him with a quantity of red silk. The material is still in the possession of our family.

Then again, on the nineteenth day of the eleventh month of Ōe 29 (1422), the daughter of a carpenter living near the Shōkoku Temple, who thatched roofs with cypress bark for a living, fell gravely ill. At this time, there was a mysterious revelation at the Kitano Shrine,[41] indicating that the poem that begins "if the east wind blows this way"[42] should be used as the basis for the composition of a series of new poems to be written, using each of its thirty-one syllables as the first syllable of each new poem, and that each series should be dedicated to the god. (Such verses are called "dedicated poems," *susume-uta*.) "Kanze" was to mark the best ones at a ceremony to take place before the shrine. Many people were asked to prepare poems as soon as possible, and through various connections, Zeami was asked if he would indeed participate in choosing the best poems. As there was no way to refuse, Zeami underwent a ceremonial washing and performed the task. At this time, Zeami had already taken holy orders, so

[41] The Kitano Shrine, in the northwest corner of Kyoto, is dedicated to the spirit of Sugawara Michizane.

[42] The *waka* cited is a famous one by Sugawara Michizane. Burton Watson has translated it as follows:

Kochi fukaba	When east winds blow,
Nioi okose yo	send out your fragrance,
Ume no hana	plum flowers—
Aruji nashi ni te	though masterless,
Haru na wasure so.	do not forget the spring!

See Burton Watson, tr., *Japanese Literature in Chinese*, I, 129.

he did not know if the revelation concerned him or his son Motomasa, now head of the Kanze troupe, but he learned that in the revelation he himself had been singled out.

On another occasion, when Zeami still went by his childhood name of Fujiwaka, a group of priests at Tōnomine in Yamato possessed a treasure handed down for many generations, a sample of the calligraphy of the deified Sugawara no Michizane. Michizane's Buddhist name was written in his own hand. After receiving two revelations from the god Michizane himself, the priest gave this treasure to Zeami. It is still in the possession of our family. The calligraphy is written with gold dust.

All of these stories may sound somehow overexaggerated, but they have been written down as proof that the way of the *nō* has been favored by the gods. Since the ancient days, when it is said that Hata no Ujiyasu received a special benediction from Ryōzō gongen of Hatsuse,[43] there has never been any such mysterious incident, as far as this writer knows.

25. Dengaku

It is said that *dengaku* began when Sakanoue no Ryōa Hoshi, a warrior-priest at Enryakuji on Mt. Hiei, secluded himself in the Eastern Pagoda at the temple; [in his revelation] he saw a man wearing a flat straw hat, in a red costume, riding on the end of a pole and swinging a sword about. When he told his dream [to the authorities] at the Shōren-in Temple, he was told that he should study the theatrical arts. As a result, both he and, in all, a group of thirty warrior-priests began to learn [the art of *dengaku*]. It is said that this is how the tradition began.

Then again, according to another account, when the Spirit of Mt. Hiei made a ceremonial procession down the eastern slope of the mountain, a certain person who used to accompany the deity (this information must be checked) began the

---

[43] A god associated with the Hase Temple near Nara.

tradition of *dengaku*, which continued on through his descendants. Thus it is that, even now, at Shintō ceremonies held [at the Hiei Shrine], three *dengaku* players wear a dark mask representing an old man and participate in the processions.

Before the time of Itchū, Tōren and Kōren were famous actors in *dengaku* tradition. Both belonged to the Honza [main] troupe [in the capital]. Hanayasha and Fujiyasha belonged to the Shinza [new] troupe [located in Nara].

26. Matsubayashi

At the present time, there is no proper group constituted to carry on the traditions of *matsubayashi*.[44] The sorts of activities carried on at the time of the Gion festival might be expected to serve as a model, but in the first month of the second year of Eikyō [1430], at a performance of *matsubayashi* held at the Shōgun's mansion, it was learned that no group now exists that can carry on this practice. Zeami was asked something about the matter and replied that the first section of the chant should be performed using words of congratulation, something appropriate such as "the wind in the pines has ended, and the clouds too have all gone; Inari mountain, Inari mountain, a gorgeous robe of blossoms adorns our Emperor's reign and blesses the spring. . . ." Present performances, Zeami indicated, are a little too drawn-out.

27. Nō by Torchlight

In the beginning, the dates for the ceremonial performances of torchlight *nō* in Nara were never fixed. Indeed, they were sometimes held during the summer. As our *sarugaku* troupe

---

[44] Literally, "pine *hayashi*," a form of New Year's entertainment when Buddhist begging minstrels (called *shōmonjin*), nobles, and ordinary citizens alike dressed in elaborate costumes called at various homes in the city, singing and dancing to celebrate the new year. Pine branches are used for decoration at this season. For a general description of the music of *hayashi* ensembles, see the various entries in Malm, *Japanese Music*.

was not free to participate at that time, Kan'ami was summoned and examined concerning the reasons. He explained
the circumstances in detail. Hearing this, the authorities replied, "of course, how inconvenient for the troupe to wait [in
Nara, rather than going out to do their usual performances
in the countryside]," and so the date for the performances
was fixed for the second month. Kan'ami then promised that,
if the performances could be given at that time, his troupe
then and in the generations to come would never fail to participate. For this reason, members of the troupe should be
careful in the future never to absent themselves.

28. Performances of the Nō at Kōfukuji in the First Year of Eikyō [1429]

In the third month of the first year of Eikyō, torchlight ceremonial performances of *nō* were carried out. On the fifth
day of the month, the Komparu and Kanze troupes were asked
by the priests of the Ichijō-in [who were in charge of the
festivities] to perform in competition. On this occasion, lots
were drawn to see who would perform the opening play. The
Kanze troupe won, and Motomasa performed *Hōjōgawa*. The
year before, the temple authorities had asked that lots be
drawn for the order of performances. When the priests of the
Daijō-in [had been put in charge of the proceedings, however],
each troupe performed by itself, and no difficulties arose over
the performance of the opening play.

29. The Decorum Appropriate for Actors

These days, when *sarugaku* actors appear in public, they have
their retainers equip themselves with swords, a practice that
is altogether unsuitable. Indeed, Shu-amidabutsu [an important retainer of Ashikaga Yoshimitsu] severely rebuked Dōami
when he had his retainers wear battle swords in a bold manner.
If swords need be taken they had best be enclosed in attractive
sheaths. And, on occasions when swords and the like are

required, retainers should doubtless be provided with ceremonial weapons that have short blades. In the old days, there
were no examples whatsoever of this kind of behavior. As
this is so, then what can be said about the Ōmi *sarugaku*
players and the like, who behave in a fashion quite below
their station, and who, both in Ōmi and elsewhere, carry on
as though they were priestly warriors from Mt. Hiei? There
is no reason to act in such a fashion. One must have a sense
of one's own social position and behave accordingly. Usually
one should dress as simply as possible. An actor should always
reflect on his proper station.

Although a properly respectful attitude is to be assumed
when performing in connection with religious ceremonies, when
such a performance involves the nobility, the actors, of course,
must suit the pleasure of their patrons. On occasion, however,
such attitudes of respect fail to manifest themselves in an
actor's outward appearance, resulting in what appears to be
a discourtesy. In a performance before Lord Hosokawa,[45]
when a particular actor in a certain troupe made his greetings,
the lord responded that "this is the rudest person I have ever
seen!" Proper attitudes and etiquette toward others is of the
utmost importance. For example, should an actor appear at
a gathering where the nobility is appreciative of the performance of another troupe, he must take careful note of the atmosphere, so that, for example, when he leaves his seat, he
can do so quickly and without causing any commotion. Any
hesitation in such matters will be most unfortunate. For example, on an occasion when Dōami held his performance of
subscription *nō*, Iwao [of the Ōmi troupe] got up with a large
group of his followers during the performance and moved to
the Shōgun's seat to greet him. Iwao was severely criticized
for creating such a disturbance. It was said that Zeami, on
the other hand, "came quietly by himself and proved to be
indeed a great artist." This behavior earned him great praise.

[45] Hosokawa Yoriyuki (A.D. 1329-1392) aided Ashikaga Yoshimitsu for a
time as deputy shōgun; later the two had a number of personal difficulties.
Yoriyuki had a considerable reputation as a *waka* poet.

If one were to weigh the art of the *nō* in terms of [the Confucian concepts of] virtue and pleasure, ours must be considered an art of pleasure. It should therefore render the hearts of its spectators gentle and mild. Now if a man is not one who is wise in the ways of the emotions of this world, he will be unprepared to adapt his feelings to changing circumstances. For example, among those highly revered by the Shōgun Ashikaga Yoshimitsu was Lady Takahashi (a beauty from Higashi no Tōin); she understood everything concerning human feelings, knew the will of her lord, and indeed finished her own life without suffering any adversity. She could follow her lord's moods: even when serving *sake*, she gave it to him when she knew that she should and withheld it when she felt that she should. Thus, by continually understanding such concerns, she became truly successful. I have recorded here these episodes as they are discussed in the world. In this regard, Zeami was particularly adept at understanding the feelings of others, I have been told, and as a result, he was always highly praised.

30. The Question of Successors

No matter how gifted with talent a famous actor may be, if he does not by means of constant practice come to consolidate the highest reaches of his art, there can be no question of his successors carrying on that tradition. He may become a great actor himself [but he will produce no followers]. This is why, among the most gifted actors, there are few whose traditions will be carried on to the next generation. It is most important that [according to the system of the nine levels] the middle three levels, then the upper three, and finally the lower three be studied in the proper order, so that an actor who follows this path will in the future come to be a superior performer. Most actors, however, begin their study at the lower three levels, so that [nothing further is accomplished], and the line of proper succession is broken. Great discretion must be shown over such matters.

31. Performances at Shintō Shrines

There are those who, on the pretext of traveling about in various regions to perform, neglect the various sacred presentations [to which they should be committed], either arriving too late for the performances, for example, or omitting their appearances at the Kasuga Shrine festival. Those with such attitudes cannot hope to achieve a proper career. Even if [secular performances] should temporarily bring them a greater income, in the end they will be punished by the gods. Rather, sacred performances should be made the basis of an actor's art; between them, in order to assist in his livelihood, he may travel in the provinces to perform.

On occasions when *Okina* is performed by request as a sacred offering, there are those who perform it in an indifferent manner. They dance in a perfunctory manner and receive a hundred *mon* from each of those present. If the crowd of contributors is too small, the actor makes a sour face. What can be done with performers of this description? One who possesses such attitudes cannot finish well. It can be said that in the life to come, he will surely fall into hell.

Additional Matters: Rules of the Kanze House

Kan'ami forbade the following: licentiousness, gambling, heavy drinking, the raising of nightingales.[46]

Rules fixed by the Kanze troupe:

1. Money allotted for a celebration when a new person becomes head of the troupe: 10,000 *mon*.

Money allotted for a celebration when a child is installed who will later become head of the troupe: 3,000 *mon*.

Money allotted for a celebration when a performer is given the rank of *tayū* [Master]; if of the lower grade: 2,000 *mon*; if of the higher grade, whatever seems appropriate to the occasion.

---

[46] For the purposes of holding singing contests, presumably for gambling.

2. Rules by which stipends are divided for the four nō performances held in connection with the Eight Lectures at Tōnomine:

The troupe receives as a stipend one [box of food and drink] for a performance to be given every other day [since usually two troupes perform on alternate days]. As for the food and drink bestowed during the course of the Four Lectures, the head of the troupe also receives [a box] every other day.

From the monk's headquarters, the head of the troupe will receive such things as one basket of fruits or foodstuffs in a quantity that would fill a tray table [at a Buddhist altar], or dyestuffs, or cloth. If the piles of decorative ceremonial cakes and the like are made available during the Four Lectures [on those occasions when the actors participate], the head of the troupe is to receive one of the three items provided by the three priests involved. The second of the three is to be received by the assistant. If a third is available it should be divided for distribution down to the lowest rank of those holding the title of *tayū*. In the case when funds equal to the value of a horse are granted, the head of the troupe should receive a thousand *mon*. Every two days the head of the troupe should receive *sake* of a good grade bottled in large jugs. Of these, one should be divided among the assistants.

3. Rules Concerning the Distribution of Income among Members of the Troupe:

The head of the troupe should receive three portions. The person directly behind him in responsibility should receive two portions. The *tayū* of the third rank should each receive one and a half portions. Then, one portion should be divided in three and given to the *tayū* of the fourth, fifth, and sixth rank. Then, the oldest member of the junior troupe should receive a portion of one-half. The person second in responsibility after him should receive a third of one portion. In addition, the various items bestowed on the troupe, such as those items given during the Eight Lectures, should be divided in the same proportions.

4. Rules Concerning Funds Donated for the Wakamiya festival[47] or the torchlight *nō*:

In the case of the torchlight *nō*, four hundred *mon* should be received by each senior actor. If the actors do not participate in the religious observances at the *tō kondō* and *nanendō*,[48] they will be given only a jug of *sake* instead of their proper fee. If they fail to participate as well in the performances of *sarugaku* that follow at the Kasuga Shrine, they will receive no payment whatsoever.

The members of the junior troupe will receive two hundred *mon*.

Those who cannot appear because of illness will be permitted their absence. Those in mourning will also be excused.

5. The Wakamiya festival:

Those who do not participate in the procession will be fined 100 *mon* for negligence. Drummers will be fined fifty *mon*.

6. Performances at Tōnomine:

Actors from all troupes must participate, including not only those from Yamato but the troupes from Iga, Yamashiro, Ōmi, Izumi, Kawachi, Ki, and Tsu as well. Those who do not appear when summoned will be cast out of their troupes forever. Those from troupes in other provinces, however, will be exempted.

7. Participating in the Work of the Troupe:

The troupe will participate during the entire length of the torchlight *nō* festival [which usually lasts seven days]. In the case of the Nara and the Tōnomine festivals, usually four days are involved. When it comes to proper seating for such occasions, the older members of the troupe should be given

[47] The Wakamiya festival was an important celebration held at the Kasuga-Wakamiya Shrine building of the Kasuga Shrine complex in Nara. In Zeami's time, the festival was held during the eleventh month, and *sarugaku* actors normally participated.

[48] Two of the most important buildings in the temple complex of the Kōfukuji in Nara. They are among the important ancient architectural structures remaining in Japan.

seating according to their rank, even if they arrive later than the rest of the troupe. If actors are of the same age, they should draw lots [to determine who should have the preferred seating]. Excepting for those three occasions, however, they should be seated in the order in which they enter.

8. Entrance Fees to Join the Troupe:
From the total amount, the head of the troupe should receive a thousand *mon*. A thousand *mon* is required to enter the junior troupe, and the amount should be divided equally between the head of the troupe and the oldest member of the junior troupe.

9. If a parent fails to participate in a scheduled performance, his son, even if he appears, will not receive a fee. On the matter of age: even on an occasion when a father does perform, if the child is over ten years of age, he [will be treated as an adult, and so] will not be paid unless he performs.

10. In the case of the funds needed to purchase *sake* when the troupe is assembled, the head of the troupe is liable for a thousand *mon*. In the case of *sake* needed for the Wakamiya festival, the head of the troupe is also liable for the same amount.

Matters such as the entrance fees for joining the troupe have not been recorded in detail, perhaps because the change in the assignments of the assistants [whose duty it is to make note of such matters]. Such details must be sought and carefully written down.

Postscript:
I do believe that, in the thirty-odd items listed above, I have recorded what I heard without error, but of course, there may be some mistakes, for all I know. In any case, I have written down in all sincerity the various things that my father said. After glancing at what I have written here, please consign the manuscript to the flames.

Has it been ordained by my father's pledge to his art that

he has gone on working for seventy years, even until his old age?

> The dew on the oak [of my mother's affection]
> touches me deeply;
> yet how painful to leave behind
> the benevolence of the world should I abandon it.

> To abandon affection
> and enter the way of enlightenment
> is the true way
> to repay kindness.

> I believe that the road I must take
> will protect the future life of my dear parents:
> thus you must permit me to take that path.

The 11th day of the 11th month of Eikyō 2 [1430]
I have written this to leave a sign to my father of my own determination.

Motoyoshi

Item: A certain Tokuju of the Enami temple of Kawachi was particularly talented in performing the lion dance. The dance was miraculously colorful. When Zōami was still a child actor, he performed such dances before the Shōgun Ashikaga Yoshimitsu, and they were quite effective.

Item: As a medicine for the voice, Zeami used a powder called *shōkisan*.[49] He particularly disliked preparations involving bean paste or oil. Just before going on the stage during a performance, he would drink water heated until it bubbled, saying that it was good to "burn the throat." He used both methods. Also, in a greenroom [just before a performance], the use of a thin gruel was particularly effective.

Item: The arrangement of the *Shiki samban* dances was the

---

[49] A medicinal powder popular at the time. It was evidently looked on as a kind of cure-all for various ailments.

same as that used for the Wakamiya festival. As an allowance, each troupe was given twenty or thirty thousand *mon*. In accordance with what had been written down in advance, the troupe was provided with high-quality food. Such foodstuffs were not given to those who were not part of the troupe. White Shintō robes were also worn, as at the Wakamiya festival. The decorations were also duplicated. On the day chosen for the postponement, rain fell and so the stage was removed.[50]

The following items rightly belong in a collection of verbatim notes but as they take so few pages to write, I have added these items here, since there are still blank spaces of paper left.

Item: There is no set form for the performance art of picking up a fan that has been dropped. If the fan is held in front and then dropped, it can be picked up on the next occasion when the hand is extended. If the fan is dropped when the hand is drawn in close to the body, it can be picked up when this gesture is next repeated.

Item: In the chant, major words written mainly in Chinese characters should be sung in a full and precise manner, while those particles written in the phonetic syllabary may be performed by either expanding or contracting them, depending on the appropriate circumstances.

Item: [In the chant], the *kyū* tone is employed when expelling the breath, while the *shō* tone is employed during the intake of breath. Expelling the breath represents "earth"; taking in the breath represents "heaven." The *ritsu* scale can be said to represent "heaven," while the *ryo* scale represents "earth." Thus [as heaven should precede], the term *ritsuryo* is used, not *ryoritsu*. However, mankind lives on the earth, and thus should use the mode of the "earth," *ryo*, when chanting words of congratulation. Should *ritsu*, or the scale of "heaven," be used therefore when chanting on a mournful occasion? Actually, from a logical point of view, heaven is

---

[50] This section is difficult to interpret. The dates and details of the performances mentioned have not been identified.

the basis of the universe [and the earth is subordinate to it]; therefore, the scale of "heaven," *ritsu*, should be considered as the sound of joy. As for *kyū* and *shō*, various musical moods can be created, depending on whether the scale is rising or falling. These various methods are central to our art.

Item: Kan'ami never danced the role of a celestial goddess. However, because he said that it was proper for Zeami to dance such roles, my father began to perform them in Yamato.

Item: The great founders of our art, and Zōami as well, showed various faults.

Itchū, for example, walked in a somewhat pigeon-toed fashion.

Kiami was quite skillful in chanting, but surprisingly enough, when he began singing in a broad vocal style, he would end in that mode as well [rather than with an attenuated voice, as is proper]. In the *kusemai* called *Seisuiji*, there is a section of *kouta*, "obeying the storm, the various pine brances play of themselves the harp. . . ." He performed the opening phrase, "obeying the storm . . ." in a voice that pushed the rhythm forward, in the *kaku* mode, appropriate for *kusemai*. From the phrase "pine branches" onward, however, he used a voice appropriate to *kouta*. [In the same *kusemai*], the phrase "Gyōei flew away to the east" was also performed in the *kouta* style. Thus in actuality he never truly performed in a true *kusemai* manner. Kiami was a man without education. For example, hearing the phrase "receiving your exalted affection [*mikokoro o ete wa*], he misheard it, and asked, "what is this business about according to your will? [*mikokoro ni oite wa*]," thus showing that he had confused *o ete* with *oite*. Dōami was critical of the fact that [in the *nō* play *Unrin-in*] Kiami spoke the line "I am a man named Kinmitsu" with a peculiar accent. Kiami himself remarked that in the phrase "the sound of the wind in the pines in Otowayama [*matsu ni wa kaze no Otowayama*]" [from the *kusemai* called *Yura no minato*], the syllables *matsu ni wa kaze* involved difficulties of pronunciation; but in a work of his own composition, Kiami made the same error of pronunciation on the word "wind" [*kaze*] in the phrase "led away by winds in the fields in autumn [*aki no nokaze ni sasowarete*]" [from an unidentified play]. If an accent is well used, of course, it can be effective. Nevertheless, in the old days, not much care was taken in polishing the words.

Zōami himself said he wished to correct the errors of [his predecessor] Kiami. However Zōami himself, for example, in an opening congratulatory piece, allowed his voice to drop on the words "peace and tranquillity" in the phrase "may your long-lived administration, never growing old, bring to our times peace and tranquillity." Such a means of chanting is quite unsuitable for this sort of contratulatory passage. It is often said that Zōami's chanting on such occasions was always most effective, but this success is related to his skill in a more melancholy category of chant. The effect of a congratulatory chant does not depend on an effective melody.

Then too, in the dance, Zōami tended to make exaggerated gestures with his sleeves, which was in poor taste. Occasionally he would begin his dance while still on the bridge, which did not please his public. An actor should rather pause on the bridge, so that he can increase the expectations of his audience. Otherwise, he will have exhausted his appropriate gestures [by the time he continues his dance on the stage].

It seems to me that the *kusemai* called *Tōgoku kudari* is actually not really effective. The same devices are repeated too often. The author, Nan'ami, was a highly skillful composer of melodies, but there are too many of them that begin at a high pitch and then rise still higher; people at the time said that this sort of chant was only appropriate for women's roles.

The *tachiai* called *Yumiya* is a most peculiar piece. The opening words of the chant are "bow of mulberry wood, arrows of mugwort," and the obligatory congratulatory opening is therefore bypassed. It is said that for various reasons it must be performed in this way; yet the author must have been someone with a superficial knowledge indeed of the kind of melodies appropriate for the *tachiai*.

[From the point of view of those of us who perform in the *nō*,] there are certain means of applying melodies when *The Tale of the Heike* is performed that are difficult to accept. For example, the phrase "it seems that this horse is sad to part with its master"[51] is sung at the highest musical pitch employed in this sort of chant, which is not effective. Such a passage should rather be spoken. Places in the text that make use of figures of speech should be sung at a high pitch. It is wrong as well to sing a passage [such as the one from the section "The Imperial Visit to Ohara,"][52] "the time was about the twentieth day of the Fourth Month" in a high pitch. Why is this? Even when pressed by others, I can find no words to explain my reasons. Those associates of mine who understand the art of the chant, however, will nod in agreement.

Concerning questions of pitch, the terms *kamimujō* and *shimomujō* are used, but it is said that these terms merely represent additions to the basic five tones.[53]

Zeami said that in terms of his level of artistic accomplishment, there was one area in which he was inferior to his father, but that no one knew what his failing was. When I asked him, he replied, "because my feet move nimbly, I have [shown a tendency to perform certain roles calling for such dexterity. This tendency on my part] can be seen as a shortcoming."

[51] A passage from Book IX of *The Tale of the Heike*. See the Kitagawa/Tsuchida translation, p. 565.

[52] *Ibid.*, p. 769.

[53] According to Harich-Schneider, these two auxiliary tones represent C# (*kamimujō*) and F# (*shimomujō*). See *A History of Japanese Music*, p. 255.

Glossaries

1. ENGLISH-JAPANESE GLOSSARY

What follows is a list of technical and aesthetic terms used in the treatises for which the translators have attempted to establish a working English analogue.

Appeal (*kasa*) (嵩). Literally, "weight, loftiness, dignity," a combination of force and clarity that constitutes the effectiveness of an actor's performance. Zeami aligns Appeal with the complementary achievement of Magnitude.

Being (*u*) (有) and Non-Being (*mu*) (無). The terms are opposites that figure in a variety of ways in Buddhist thought. They are sometimes translated as Existence and Non-Existence.

Bending (*shiore*) (萎). Literally, "withering," as of a flower. The beauty to be seen when a touch of age falls upon a blossom at the height of its bloom.

Bone (*kotsu*) (骨). One of the three basic elements in *nō* performance. The term is said to have originated with the aesthetics of calligraphy, in which Bone represented the basic strength of the stroke. See also Skin, Flesh.

Changeless Flower (*shōka*) (性花), Changing Flower (*yōka*) (用花). Terms used by Zeami to illustrate the fundamental and ephemeral aspects of *nō* performance.

Delicacy within Strength (movement) (*saidō*) (砕動). Literally, a "pulverizing movement", a movement of the body so that it seems to "break" into many pieces. The movement appropriate to the performance of Demon roles in the Kanze school. Zeami contrasts this with the Rough Style of movement, not approved by his school.

Eternity (*jōjūfumetsu*) (常住不滅). Literally, "unchanging and indestructable," a term with Buddhist overtones borrowed by Zeami to illustrate the virtues of *nō* performance.

Externalization (*mushufū*) (無主風). Literally, a "manner without an owner," an art that shows no inner mastery. Zeami uses the term in contrast to Internalization.

Fascination (*omoshiroki*) (面白き). A term, usually translated as "pleasant" or "entertaining," that is given a wide range of meanings by Zeami when describing the *nō*. These range from "fascinating" through such allied meanings as "effective," "moving," "successful," "enjoyable," "memorable," and "interesting."

Feeling That Transcends Cognition (*mushinkan*) (無心感). A term sometimes used to explain the escape from discriminative thinking in *zen* enlightenment, used by Zeami to describe the pleasure of watching a superior *nō* performance.

Five Skills of Dancing (*gochi*) (五智). The five elements required for perfection in *nō* dancing. They are, in order: Self-Conscious Movement, Movement beyond Consciousness, Mutuality in Balance, Mutuality in Self-Conscious Movement, and Mutuality in Movement beyond Consciousness.

Flesh (*niku*) (肉). One of the three basic elements in *nō* performance. The term is said to have originated in the aesthetics of calligraphy, in which Flesh represents the love of the calligrapher for his art. See also Bone, Skin.

Flower (*hana*) (花). A central metaphor in Zeami's conceptions of the *nō*, used as a means to verbalize the development of true artistic accomplishment.

Fulfillment (*jōju*) (成就). Literally, "bringing to successful completion", a term used by Zeami to describe an emotionally complete performance.

Function (*yō*) (用). Derivative elements in a *nō* performance that arise from the Substance of the performance, but do not constitute that element itself. See also Substance.

Grace (*yūgen*) (幽玄). A word originally found in Chinese philosophical texts meaning "dim, deep, mysterious." When adapted into Japanese, the term began to shift from its religious and philosophical implications to artistic ones. Zeami generally used the word to represent the epitome of elegance and grace suggested by the behavior and dress of court ladies. In *waka* poetry, however, the term came to have significant overtones of transcendental mystery and depth.

Heart (*shin*) (心), see Sight.

Highest Fruition (*jōka*) (上果). An ideal level of performance corresponding to the upper three of Zeami's nine levels.

Internalization (*yushufū*) (有主風). Literally, a "manner with an owner," an art that shows true inner mastery. Zeami uses the term in contrast to Externalization.

Law of Cause and Effect (*inga*) (因果). A fundamental Buddhist concept that governs all situations. Every action that is a cause will have a result or effect; in the same way, every resultant action has its cause.

Level (*kurai*) (位). A word used frequently by Zeami to distinguish between various degrees of accomplishment in the *nō*. No actual rank or status is suggested.

Magnitude (*take*) (長). A term that literally suggests height, used in the sense of refinement. Zeami contrasts Magnitude with the complementary achievement of Appeal.

Melancholy Elegance (*aware*) (あわれ). A literary virtue with a long history in the canon of Japanese aesthetics. Originally the term derived from the sound of a cultivated person's emotional response to something seen or heard that is moving (as in the English "ah!"). By the time of Zeami, the term had come to mean as well the ability of art to conjure up in a cultivated person a sense of the evanescence of beauty.

Mood (*kakari*) (懸). Literally, an "appearance," an atmosphere created by the *nō* that Zeami sees as one of those beyond cognition or description.

Movement beyond Consciousness (*buchi*) (舞智). Literally, "understanding the dance," the second of Zeami's Five Skills of Dancing.

Mutuality in Balance (*sōkyokuchi*) (相曲智). Literally, "understanding mutual skills," the third of Zeami's Five Skills of Dancing.

Mutuality in Movement beyond Consciousness (*butaifūchi*) (舞体風智). Literally, "understanding the way of the arts of the dance," the fifth of Zeami's Five Skills of Dancing.

Mutuality in Self-Conscious Movement (*shutaifūchi*) (手体風智). Literally, "understanding the way of the art of the hands," the fourth of Zeami's Five Skills of Dancing.

Novelty (*mezurashiki*) (めづらしき). One of the terms used by Zeami to describe the nature of the Flower.

Peerless Charm (*myō*) (妙). Literally, "charming, exquisite, mysterious, wonderful," a term from Tendai Buddhism much favored by Zeami, who uses it in a number of contexts to express complementary meanings. In particular, the highest of Zeami's nine levels of artistic excellence, the Flower of Peerless Charm, employs the term.

Perfect Fluency (*yasuki kurai*) (安き位). A level of performance at which the artist can execute his artistic aims without hindrance.

Perfect Freedom (*taketaru kurai*) (闌けたる位). Literally, a "stage of high advancement," a term used by Zeami to describe the ease and freedom available to the performer who has truly mastered his craft. Some scholars see the term as closely related to Magnitude, but generally the sense of Perfect Freedom in context is somewhat different.

Placidity (*mukuyagi*) (むくやぎ). A term used by Zeami to suggest the qualities of pliability and latitude in a *nō* performance.

Role Playing (*monomane*) (物まね). The term used by Zeami to indicate the movements and sentiments appropriate to the performance of a particular role in the *nō*. Although the word literally means "imitation" or "mimicry," the kind of naturalistic acting style suggested by the English word was never Zeami's intention; rather, he stressed that the essential spirit of the role was to be the object of the actor's art.

Rough (movement) (*rikidō*) (力動). Literally, a "strong movement" used for demon roles. Zeami disapproved of this type of performance, and cautioned against the style. See also Delicacy within Strength.

Sequence (*dan*) (段). Originally a musical term, in *nō* the Sequence refers to a unit within the structure of a play in the *jo ha kyū* progression. Sequences can be further broken down into smaller musical and dramatic units. Each play normally contains five Sequences. The first constitutes the *jo*, the next three the *ha*, and the final Sequence the *kyū*.

Self-Conscious Movement (*shuchi*) (手智). Literally, "understanding the hands," the first of Zeami's Five Skills of Dancing.

Sight (*ken*) (見), Sound (*mon*) (聞), Heart (*shin*) (心). Three qualities necessary in a truly successful *nō* performance.

Skin (*hi*) (皮). One of the three basic elements in *nō* performance. The term is said to have originated in the aesthetics of calligraphy, in which Skin represents the gentleness of the stroke. See also Flesh, Bone.

Sound (*mon*) (音), see Sight.

Sphere of Accomplishment (*gaibun*) (我意分). (1) The term used by Zeami to suggest the realm claimed by an artist who can make full use of his own unique potential. (2) Various stages of achievement by the actor as he comes to realize his potential.

Subscription Performance (*kanjin nō*) (勧進能). Performances given for the public to raise money, often for the construction and repair of shrines and temples. The troupes were usually hired for such occasions, and, at Zeami's time at least, the funds did not normally go to the actors themselves.

Substance (*tai*) (体). Literally, "body" or "essence," a term originating in the Buddhist doctrine of the three universals: essence, form, and function. Eventually these conceptions, as used in the practice of *zen*, became influential in the aesthetics of *renga*, and, eventually, in the *nō*.

Three Role Types (*santai*) (三体). Literally, the "three bodies" or three fundamental categories of *nō* roles, the old person, the woman, and the warrior.

Transciency (*mujō*) (無常). Originally a Sanskrit Buddhist term meaning impermanence, the ceaseless change that is the only constant in the phenomenal world.

True Flower (*shōka*) (正花). Zeami uses this term to stand for the highest level of the middle three of his nine levels.

Two Basic Arts (*nikyoku*) (二曲). The two arts of the dance and the chant, fundamental to the *nō*.

2. JAPANESE-ENGLISH GLOSSARY

The Japanese-English glossary contains those terms left in Japanese in the text, words and phrases for which no suitable English equivalent or approximation could be found. Equivalents for musical terms, in particular, are exceedingly difficult to establish, as are terms for articles of clothing. A literal translation has sometimes been provided as a means to help explain the function of a particular term.

ageuta (high song) (上げ唄). A relatively high-pitched musical passage, with a fixed rhythm, that can run up to ten units of 5–7 syllables. The *ageuta* is often used for the entrance of the *shite* and for the opening choral passage.

banshiki (盤渉). The note B in ancient Japanese music theory. The mode built upon it is called *banshikichō*.

bugaku (dancing music (舞楽). Dances performed to classical court music developed in the Nara and Heian periods. In addition to Japanese dances, those modeled on Chinese and other Asian prototypes were included, as well. Some influences were felt from *bugaku* in the development of the *nō* theater.

dengaku (field music) (田楽). Originally the name given to the songs and dances performed by peasants while planting and harvesting. These were later performed as entertainment by professionals, who were collected into groups or guilds. *Dengaku* developed in a parallel fashion with *sarugaku* as a form of theatrical entertainment, but remained more miscellaneous and fragmentary in nature.

eboshi (烏帽子). The lacquered tall hat of a Japanese court official.

ennen (long life) (延年). The general name given to various types of performances held at Buddhist temples in connection with a variety of festivals and ceremonies. Eventually the professional *sarugaku* performers took over these functions from the clerics. Songs, dances, and skits were included.

ha (破). The middle section of a *nō* play in the *jo ha kyū* sequence. The term is sometimes translated as "development" or "exposition", but a literal translation, "breaking," suggests the increased dramatic and musical level of energy after the more composed and stately *jo*.

hakama (袴). Loose divided trousers worn by men.

hayabushi (rapid music) (早節). Zeami's term for a basic rhythmic structure in which one beat is linked to two syllables of the text. This pattern is particularly effective in the final highly charged moments in a battle scene or a similarly exciting moment.

hitatare (直垂). A man's outer garment, a lined over-robe worn over a *hakama*.

hito-utai (solo song) (一謡). A general term used by Zeami to refer to portions of the *shite*'s musical performance in the opening sequence, after the *issei*.

issei (solo voice) (一声). One type of entrance song for the *waki*, in a free rhythm, with a rich melodic style. Also, a similar type of entrance song for the *shite*. See also *shidai*.

jiutai (ground chant) (地謡). The chorus in the *nō*, which consists of from six to twelve performers, who sit in two rows at the side of the stage.

jo (序). The opening section of a *nō* play in the *jo ha kyū* sequence. The term is sometimes translated as "introduction" or "prelude," suggesting the slow and stately tempo at the beginning of the play.

kagura (god music) (神楽). The general term for Shintō music, in which various rites, dances, and pantomimes were included. Certain *kagura* pieces served as prototypes for the *nō*.

kakko (鞨鼓). A kind of drum, in use since Heian times, sometimes used in *nō* performances. The drum is placed on the stage and struck on both ends with special sticks.

kariginu (狩衣). A costume, literally a "hunting robe," worn for everyday activities by courtiers, usually made of heavy silk. The *ōkuchi* style of *hakama* was worn with it.

kinu (衣). A general term for one of the various kinds of upper robe worn over the *hakama*.

kiribyōshi (cutting rhythm) (切拍子). Zeami's term for a basic rhythmic structure in which one beat is linked to one syllable of the text. This pattern is often used at the end of a *nō* for a calm and majestic effect.

kirufushi (cutting music) (切曲). Evidently a section of music employed in a *kiribyōshi*. Zeami's use of the term is not altogether clear.

kosode (小袖). Literally, "small sleeves," the early prototype for the Japanese *kimono*.

kouta (short song) (小歌). Popular songs of the common people, often of irregular musical and poetic rhythm. Collections of these songs were made; the most famous of them is doubtless the *Kanginshū* (Collection of Leisure Songs) compiled in 1518. *Kouta* were sometimes incorporated into the *nō*.

kuri (く り). A musical term, the first of the three parts that make up a *kusemai* (*kuri*, *sashi*, *kuse*), performed in a free rhythm and rich melodic style.

kuse (曲). A musical term, the third section of a *kusemai* (*kuri*, *sashi*, *kuse*), usually in three sections, with a fixed rhythm. See also *kusemai*.

kusemai (曲舞). Literally, "unconventional dances." (1) A popular form of song and dance that began in the Kamakura period (1192–1336) and became particularly popular at the time of Kan'ami. (2) *Kusemai* as adapted into the *nō*. Usually the *kusemai* dance is placed in the climactic Sequence of the play. This *kusemai* (usually composed of three sections: *kuri*, *sashi*, and *kuse*) was given great artistic importance by Zeami.

kyōgen (狂言). Literally, "extraordinary words." The term refers both to comic actors and to the plays they present. (1) One or more *kyōgen* actors often appear during the course of a *nō* play, usually to tell the story of the play in monologue form and in simplified language between the two sections of the play proper. (2) Comic plays presented between *nō* plays as comic interludes by these actors.

kyū (急). The final section of a *nō* play in the *jo ha kyū* sequence. The term is sometimes translated as "climax" or "finale," but a literal translation, "rapid," conveys the quick tempo appropriate to the end of the *nō*.

mizugoromo (水衣). A robe with long, broad sleeves worn by either men or women, unlined, in the style of a tunic.

nō (能). Not a generic term in Zeami's time, but a word used to describe a specific play, or its text, as performed by a *sarugaku* troupe.

obi (帯). A man's or woman's sash, worn with a *kimono*.

ōkuchi (大口). Literally, "large mouth," a style of broad divided skirts worn by men. One kind of *hakama*.

ōshiki (黄鐘). The note A in ancient Japanese music theory. The mode built on it is called *ōshikichō*.

otoshibushi (descending music) (落し節). A type of melody that evidently descended rapidly in pitch. The exact usage of the term has not been determined.

renga (linked verse) (連歌). A poetic form, usually consisting of from two to a hundred parts alternating 5-7-5 and 7-7 syllable units. The form was popular in court and aristocratic circles at Zeami's time.

rongi (discussion) (論議). Usually a section of dialogue sung alternatively by the *shite* and the *waki*, or, on occasion, between the chorus and the *shite*. The rhythm is fixed.

sageuta (low song) (下げ唄). A relatively low-pitched musical passage, with a fixed rhythm, that usually follows a pattern of from two to four units of 7-5 syllables. It usually precedes the *ageuta*.

sarugaku (miscellaneous music) (猿楽 then 申楽). An entertainment, dating back to the Heian period, with roots in the performing traditions of China and Central Asia. Included were songs and dances, acrobatics, and conjuring tricks. Simple comic plays were also performed. By the Kamakura period (1192–1336), troupes of professional *sarugaku* performers were in existence. Narrative elements in their performances became more important as the form developed, and by the time of Kan'ami and Zeami, the troupes were highly skilled at presenting various kinds of entertainment, including *nō*.

sashigoe (naming voice) (指声). An older term for *sashi*, a lyrical passage sung either by the *waki* or the *shite* in a recitative fashion.

sashigoto (naming thing) (指事). Another term for *sashigoe*.

shakuhachi (尺八). The Japanese bamboo flute used in *nō* music.

shidai (次第). One type of entrance song for the *waki*, in a fixed rhythm in a simple style, which usually explains the background of the story. Also, a similar type of entrance song for the *shite*. See also *issei*.

Shiki samban (three rituals) (式三番). Dances of ancient origin that developed into the play *Okina*, the oldest surviving piece in the *nō* repertory. They were often presented at Shintō shrines and Buddhist temples for ceremonial purposes.

shirabyōshi (白拍子). Literally, "white beat," with two meanings: (1) A dance form, of humble origins, that evidently consisted of an introductory song plus other melodies to accompany a dance. By the thirteenth century, the nobility enjoyed watching these performances. (2) A person who performs those dances. These dancers were usually women and courtesans.

shite (the Person Who Does) (仕手). The chief actor in the *nō*. There is only one such role in each play. The performer is usually masked, and his costumes are the most elaborate.

shōmyō (声明). The traditional method of chanting the Buddhist sutras.

shura (修羅). Sometimes written as *ashura* (阿修羅). Originally in Indian mythology, a devil who fights with the gods. Introduced into Buddhism, the *shura* became a kind of devil by nature fond of fighting. In Buddhist theories of transmigration, the *shura* represented one of six worlds through which the souls of living beings must pass. In the *nō*, the term was applied to plays dealing with the spirits of dead warriors who relive their sufferings in the realm of the *shura*.

shushi (magician) (呪師). Originally performances by priests that involved rites and spells. Eventually those functions were taken over by professional players. *Shushi* performances were appreciated for the elaborate costumes employed and for the agility of the actors.

sōga (fast song) (早歌). Sometimes referred to as *enkyoku* (宴曲), the genre includes songs composed for banquets and other entertainments.

suikan (水干). A court official's robe, something like a *kariginu*, usually made of thin silk.

suō (素襖). A simplified form of *hitatare*, usually worn by the common people in Zeami's time.

tachiai (performing together) (立合). (1) A performance in which various actors, sometimes from competing troupes, danced together in an ensemble number. (2) A competitive performance, on the basis of which the best troupe or actor was chosen.

tadautai (只謡). A type of chant that uses the irregular rhythms of *kouta*.

taiko (大鼓). A barrel-shaped drum set on a stand so that it can resonate freely. The *taiko* is played with two sticks that have beveled ends.

tanka. See *waka*.

tate-eboshi (立烏帽子). One style of *eboshi* headdress, a standing cap.

tayū [or, in a suffix, *dayū*] (大夫) (a rank). In a *sarugaku* troupe, usually the chief actor, who performs the *shite* roles.

tsure (companion) (つれ). Subsidary actors in a *nō* play.

tsuzumi (鼓). There are two varieties of *nō* hand drums, the *kotsuzumi* (小鼓), small drum and the *ōtsuzumi* (大鼓), now often referred to as *ōkawa* (大革), (large drum). Both are struck with the fingers.

waka (Japanese poem) (和歌). (1) A poetic form is thirty-one syllables, arranged in a pattern of 5-7-5-7-7 syllables, which became the standard form of court poetry. Also called *tanka* (short poem) (短歌). (2) In a *nō* play, the section of the text, usually after the dance of the *shite* in the Fifth Sequence, in which a *waka* is recited. Often the play itself is based on the history of significance of the poem, which serves the author as a kind of kernel for his whole conception.

waki (side) (脇). The second most important category of *nō* performers, after the *shite*. The *waki* serves as a foil for the *shite* and often sets the scene. He is never masked.

waki nō (脇能). The opening piece in a sequence of *nō* dramas assembled for a day's performance. *Waki nō* usually concern a god and are of a ceremonial and congratulationary character.

3. IMPORTANT PERSONS MENTIONED IN THE TEXT

The listing that follows is a mixture of historical personages, historic persons serving as characters in the *nō*, and, on occasion, literary characters used as models for characters in the *nō*, where they are in fact treated as though they were historical characters. There are a few persons mentioned in the various treatises—minor actors and others—concerning whom no biographical information is available. No entry has been made for them.

Ama no Uzume (天鈿女). A heavenly goddess who was supposedly the ancestor of an ancient family ruled by women called the Sarume. The family is recorded as having performed ritual dances at the Yamato court.

Amaterasu (天照). The goddess of the sun, the ancestor of the imperial family.

Aoi no Ue (葵上) (Lady Aoi). The first wife of Genji in *The Tale of Genji*. In the novel she dies in giving birth to Yūgiri, their son. The jealousy felt for her by Lady Rokujō is the subject of the *nō* play *Aoi no Ue*.

Ariwara no Narihira (在原業平) (825–880). A renowned poet of the Heian period and the model for the courtly lover as portrayed in *The Tales of Ise*.

Ashikaga Yoshimitsu (足利義満) (1358–1408). Third Shōgun of the Ashikaga family, he was the most charismatic political figure of his period, a brilliant diplomat, and a crucial patron in the development of the *nō*. His interests in art and architecture were also profound.

Ashikaga Yoshimochi (足利義持) (1368–1428). The eldest son of Yoshimitsu and the fourth Ashikaga Shōgun.

Ashikaga Yoshinori (足利義教) (1394–1441). Sixth Ashikaga Shōgun and the fourth son of Yoshimitsu.

Atsumori (Taira no Atsumori) (平敦盛) (1169–1184). A gallant young warrior killed during the civil wars by Kumagai Naozane. The touching story of his death is recounted in the *nō* play *Atsumori*.

Bidatsu (敏達) (538–585). Traditionally, the thirtieth emperor of Japan. Buddhism became popular under his rule.

Dōami (道阿弥) (died 1413). A master performer in the Hie troupe of Ōmi *sarugaku*. He was much favored by Ashikaga Yoshimitsu, who gave him the name Dōami. Previously he had gone by the name of Inuō (犬王). Much of what is known about him appears in *Reflections on Art*.

Enami (榎並) (c. 1400?). The head of the Enami troupe of *sarugaku*. No details are known concerning his career.

Fujiju (藤寿). (fl. ca. 1436). A well-known teacher of *renga*; he was recorded as still active in 1436, when over seventy years of age.

He was also a gifted *shakuhachi* player, and was known for his skill in a variety of artistic pursuits.

Genji (源氏). The hero of *The Tale of Genji*, a handsome prince who embodies the literary virtue of Melancholy Elegance (*aware*).

Giō (祇王) and Gijō (祇女). Two *shirabyōshi* dancers who won the favor of Taira no Kiyomori (1118–1181), then at the height of his power. They later retired to become Buddhist nuns. An account of their lives forms an important incident in *The Tales of the Heike*, and the *nō* play *Giō* dramatizes their encounter with Kiyomori.

Hanayasha (花夜叉). Head of the Shinza troupe of *dengaku*. No details are known concerning his life.

Hata no Kōkatsu (秦河勝) (c. 600). An artist, probably a naturalized Chinese or Korean, traditionally given credit for having begun the theatrical entertainments that eventually became the *nō*. His name appears in various ancient records.

Hata no Motoyoshi. See Motoyoshi.

Hata no Ujiyasu (秦氏安) (c. 960). Ancient records indicate that Ujiyasu prepared entertainments for the Emperor Murakami. His name is mentioned in Book Three of the *Honchō monzui* (Literary Gems of the Japanese Nation), a compilation of poems and prose pieces in Chinese assembled around 1060.

Hyakuman (百万). A female *kusemai* performer popular in the latter part of the fourteenth century. Zeami made her the central character in his play *Hyakuman*.

Inuō. See Dōami.

Itchū (一忠) (c. 1330). A leading performer of the Honza troupe of *dengaku* and an important teacher of Zeami's father Kan'ami.

Iwatō (岩童) (c. 1400). Iwatō was the head of the Hie troupe of Ōmi *sarugaku*. After Inuō's death, he was a leading figure in all of *sarugaku*.

Jinen Koji (自然居士) (c. 1300). A lay priest of the Rinzai *zen* sect famous for his eccentric conduct. He is the central figure in the *nō* play *Jinen Koji*.

Kagetsu (花月) (dates uncertain). A famous male entertainer who became the model for the *shite* in the *nō* play *Kagetsu*.

Kan'ami (観阿弥) (1333–1384). The father of Zeami and head of the Yūzaki or Kanze school of Yamato *sarugaku*. He lifted the artistic and aesthetic standards of his art by combining the best elements of the Yamato and Ōmi styles. In 1374, when his troupe performed in the capital, Ashikaga Yoshimitsu saw the troupe and became patron of father and son. Kan'ami continued to act for the common people who had originally formed his audience, and died after performances at the Sengen shrine in Suruga (now within the city limits of the city of Shizuoka). Kan'ami is sometimes referred to by his full name Kanze Kan'ami Kiyotsugu.

Ki no Gon no Kami (紀の権の守) (dates uncertain). According to various records, he was associated with a temple in Nara, then went to Hie in Ōmi, and eventually became the founder of the *sarugaku* troupe associated with that place. It is probable that he is the Ki no Kami mentioned in Section 23 of *Reflections on Art*.

Kiami (喜阿弥) (c. 1350). Also known as Kameyasha (亀夜叉), of the Shinza troupe of *dengaku*. One of the leading actors of his time.

Kimmei (欽明) (539–571). Traditionally the twenty-ninth emperor of Japan. In 562, Buddhism was first introduced into court circles.

Kiyotsugu. See Kan'ami.

Kiyotsune (Taira no Kiyotsune) (平清経) (died 1183). An important warrior in the civil wars who drowned himself when he saw that his family would go down to defeat. His ghost is the *shite* of the play *Kiyotsune*.

Komparu Mitsutarō (金春光太郎) (c. 1350). Head of the Enami, later known as the Komparu, troupe of *sarugaku* and a contemporary of Kan'ami.

Komparu Zenchiku (金春禅竹) (1405–1468). Zeami's son-in-law and student; second only to Zeami as a playwright and theoretician of the *nō*. He was active in building the great traditions of the Komparu school of *nō*.

Kūkai (空海) (744–835). The Buddhist priest who traveled to

China and returned to Japan to found the Shingon sect of Buddhism. He began the great complex of temples at Mt. Kōya. Famous also as a poet in Chinese, a writer of texts on Buddhism, and a calligrapher.

Lady Ise (伊勢) (died 939). Lady-in-Waiting during the reigns of the Emperors Uda and Daigo. A noted *waka* poet.

Mitsutarō. See Komparu Mitsutarō.

Motomasa (元雅) (1394?–1432). Zeami's elder son and a talented performer in *sarugaku*. His death in Ise Province may have been brought about for political reasons, but the circumstances are obscure.

Motoyoshi (元能) (dates uncertain). Zeami's second son. He is thought to have performed as a musician in his father's troupe. He recorded his father's recollections in the *Sarugaku dangi*, translated here as *An Account of Zeami's Reflections on Art*. At one point in his life, he evidently became a Buddhist priest.

Murakami (村上) (926–967). Traditionally the sixty-second emperor of Japan. Supposedly a noted musician and a gifted administrator.

Nan'ami (南阿弥) (died 1381). A highly respected *sarugaku* performer who was an important influence on Kan'ami. Few details are known about his life.

On'ami (音阿弥) (1398–1467). The actor who succeeded his uncle Zeami as head of the Kanze troupe. The two went not friendly, however. On'ami eventually received Shōgunal patronage and Zeami himself was exiled.

Ono no Komachi (水野小町) (c. 860). An important *waka* poet and reputedly one of the great beauties of her age. There are a number of *nō* plays about her, including *Sōshi arai Komachi*, *Sotoba Komachi*, *Kayoi Komachi*, *Sekidera no Komachi*, and *Ōmu Komachi*.

Ōtomo no Kuronushi (大伴黒主) (c. 890). One of the celebrated poets of his period. Although he was from a noble background, few details about his life have been preserved.

Lady Rokujō (六条御息所). The noblewoman in *The Tale of Genji*, in love with Genji, whose angry spirit haunts Lady Aoi when she is giving birth to her child. The incident is recounted in the *nō* play *Aoi no Ue*.

Sasaki Dōyo (佐々木道誉) (1306–1373). An important retainer of Ashikaga Takauji (1305–1358), the founder of the Ashikaga Shōgunate. A powerful figure politically, Dōyo had a particular interest in the *nō*. He is mentioned in the *Taiheiki*. See Helen McCullough, tr., *The Taiheiki, A Chronicle of Medieval Japan*, pp. 94–95 and p. 105.

Seiami (井阿弥) (c. 1410). An actor and writer of *nō*, contemporary of Zeami. No significant details are known concerning his life.

Seigan Koji (西岸居士) (dates uncertain). A lay Buddhist entertainer cited for his fame in *Reflections on Art*.

Shizuka (静) (c. 1180). The mistress of the general Minamoto Yoshitsune, who protected him when his brother Yoritomo attempted to have him assassinated. A famous character in literature, she is the model for the *shite* in the *nō* play *Yoshino Shizuka*.

Prince Shōtoku (Shōtoku Taishi) (聖徳太子) (573–621). Prince regent under Suiko, statesman, and scholar, who promulgated the 604 constitution and did much to increase the spread of Buddhism. One of the great figures of early Japanese Buddhism, around whom many legends have collected.

Sugawara no Michizane (菅原道真) (845–903). A court scholar and gifted poet in both Chinese and Japanese. After rising high in the administration, he was slandered and forced into exile. One of the most significant cultural figures in early Japanese history.

Sushun (崇峻) (died 592). Traditionally the thirty-second emperor of Japan. He was active in the debates concerning the adoption of Buddhism.

Suiko (推古) (554–628). Empress, traditionally the thirty-third ruler of Japan. Her prince regent, Prince Shōtoku, was a great statesman and scholar.

Tamarin (玉林) (c. 1400). A famous *renga* teacher at the time of Zeami. Few details concerning his life have been preserved.

Tōgan Koji (東岸居士) (died 1283). A lay priest and disciple of

Jinen Koji, who used dance and music to attract laymen to his religious lectures. He is the model for the *shite* of the *nō* play *Tōgan koji*.

Tsuchidayū (露太夫) (c. 1400). The name given to two gifted *kyōgen* actors who performed with the Kanze troupe. No biographical details are available. In the translation they are referred to as Tsuchidayū the First and Tsuchidayū the Second on those occasions when a distinction can be made between them in the original text.

Ukifune (浮舟). A daughter of Prince Hachi and the chief heroine of the last part of *The Tale of Genji*. Loved by both Kaoru and Niou, she attempts to commit suicide, an incident that figures in the *nō* play *Ukifune*.

Yōmei (用明天皇) (540–587). Traditionally the thirty-first emperor of Japan, who succeeded Bidatsu.

Yūgao (夕顔). Genji's first great love, who appears in chapter IV of the first book of *The Tale of Genji*. She dies mysteriously when spending the night with him, and is the *shite* in the play *Yūgao*.

Zōami (増阿弥) (c. 1400). The most gifted actor in the Shinza troupe of *dengaku*, and an important contemporary of Zeami.

4. LIST OF PLAYS AND ENTERTAINMENTS MENTIONED IN THE TEXT

Following is brief information about the plays mentioned in the text. Multiple titles are provided as appropriate. If a translation has been located, a citation is provided from the sources listed below. When no translations have been located in English, additional citations in French are cited. Authorship of the plays is often difficult to determine. The authors cited below reflect the efforts of recent Japanese scholarship. Some of the texts of the plays have, of course, been altered since performances given in Zeami's time, but most are considered to be at least reasonably close to the originals.

Tentative English titles have been given for the plays when possible. In this regard, the handbook *A Guide to Nō* by P. G. O'Neill (Tokyo: Hinoki Shoten, 1953) has been invaluable. When plays are not available in translation, an attempt has been made when possible to suggest their subject matter.

Sources Cited

Keene	Keene, Donald, ed. *Twenty Plays of the Nō Theatre*. New York: Columbia University Press, 1970.
Matisoff	Matisoff, Susan. *The Legend of Semimaru*. New York: Columbia University Press, 1978.
NGS	Nippon Gakujitsu Shinkōkai, ed. *Japanese Noh Drama*. 3 vols. Tokyo: Kenkyusha, 1956–1960.
O'Neill	O'Neill, P. G. *Early Nō Drama*. London: Lund Humphries, 1958.
Renondeau	Renondeau, G. *Le Bouddhisme dans les nō*. Tokyo: Maison Franco-Japonaise, 1950.
Shimazaki	Shimazaki, Chifumi. *The Noh*, Vol. 1, *God Noh*, and Vol. 3, *Woman Noh*. Tokyo: Hinoki Shoten, 1976.
Sieffert	Sieffert, René. *Nō et Kyōgen*. Paris: Orientalistes de France, 1979.
Tyler 1	Tyler, Royall. *Pining Wind: A Cycle of Nō Plays*. Ithaca: Cornell University East Asia Papers, No. 17, 1978.
Tyler 2	Tyler, Royall. *Granny Mountains: A Second Cycle of Nō Plays*. Ithaca: Cornell East Asia Papers, No. 18, 1978.
Waley	Waley, Arthur. *The Nō Plays of Japan*. New York: Grove Press, 1957.

Plays

Aioi (*Twin Pines*) (相生). An alternate name for *Takasago*.

Akoya no Matsu (*The Pine of Akoya*) (阿古屋の松). A play by Zeami, no longer performed. The legend of the pine is found in Book 2, Chapter 9 of the *Heike Monogatari* (*The Tale of the Heike*).

Ama (*The Fisher Girl*) (海人). Author unknown, but earlier than Zeami. Translation in NGS, Vol. 3.

Aoi no Ue (*The Lady Aoi*) (葵の上). Based on an incident in *The Tale of Genji*, is probably a revision by Zeami of an earlier text. Translation in NGS, Vol. 2, and Waley.

Aridōshi (蟻通). Aridōshi is the name of a Shintō god around whom the play centers. The play is by Zeami. Translation by Sieffert.

Ashikari (*The Reed Cutter*) (芦刈). An adaption by Zeami of an earlier text. Translation in Keene.

Atsumori (敦盛). A play about the death of the Taira courtier Atsumori, killed by Kumagae Naozane. By Zeami. Translation in Waley.

Atsuta (熱田). An older name for the play *Gendayū*.

Aya no taiko (*The Large Drum of Damask*) (綾の大鼓). An older name for *Koi no omoni*.

Chikata (千方). A lost play. The play probably dealt with the legend of Fujiwara no Chikata, a rebel against the Emperor Tenchi (626–671). The story is described in the *Taiheiki*, Book 16, and elsewhere. See NGS, Vol. 1, p. 35.

Eguchi (江口). The setting of the play, the village of Eguchi, is the name of the place where the courtesan known as Eguchi no Kimi was buried. Kan'ami is the author. Translation in NGS, Vol. 1 and Tyler 1.

Fue monogurui (*The Madman with the Flute*) (笛物狂). The former title of the play *Tango monogurui*.

Fujisan (富士山). A play, probably by Zeami, about the god of Mt. Fuji.

Funabashi (*The Floating Bridge*) (船橋). A play by Zeami adapted from an earlier text. Funabashi concerns two lovers who died when the planks of a bridge were removed by their parents so that they could not meet. The play has an earlier title, *Sano no funabashi*.

Furu (布留). The play, a *waki nō*, is no longer performed. The play is named for Furu, the location of Isonokami shrine, near Kyoto. Zeami was the reputed author. Translation in Tyler 1.

Fushimi (伏見). A play, no longer performed, reputedly by Zeami. The title refers to a site near Kyoto.

Gendayū (源太夫). The play deals with Gendayū and other Shintō gods at the Atsuta shrine. The play is probably by Kiami and was formerly called *Atsuta*.

Hakozaki (箱崎). A *waki nō*, no longer performed. The title refers to the Hakozaki Hachiman shrine near Fukuoka in Kyushu.

Hanagatami (*The Flower Basket*) (花筐). A play by Zeami. Translation by Sieffert.

Hanjo (*Lady Han*) (班女). A play by Zeami, based on a Chinese legend of the Han Dynasty. Translation in Keene.

Hatsuse (初瀬). A play, possibly about the Hase temple, by Zeami, now lost.

Hatsusei Rokudai (*Rokudai at Hatsuse*) (初瀬六代). An independent *kusemai* by Zeami. The subject matter is taken from Book Twelve of *The Tale of the Heike* and deals with Rokudai, the young son of Taira no Koremori and the last of the Heike to be executed.

Hatsuwaka (初若). A *nō* for which the text is now missing.

Hibariyama (*Hibari Mountain*) (雲雀山). The play is attributed to Zeami and deals with the legend of the Minister of the Right, Toyonari, who abandons his daughter in the mountains. Related in theme to another play attributed to Zeami, *Taema*, which is not cited in the treatises.

Higaki (桧垣). A play by Zeami in which the ghost of the *shirabyō-shi* dancer Higaki appears.

Hōjōgawa (*The River for the Hōjōe Ceremony*) (放生川). A play by Zeami that deals with the festival called Hōjōe (The Release of Living Things) held at the Iwashimizu Hachiman Shrine on Otokoyama, near Kyoto. For a description of the festival, which includes ceremonies both Buddhist and Shintō elements, see William and Helen McCullough, trs., *A Tale of Flowering Fortunes*, pp. 403–404. The play had an earlier title, *Yawata Hōjōe*.

Hyakuman (百万). A play by Zeami concerning the *kusemai* performer Hyakuman. The play had an earlier title, *Saga no dainembutsu no onna monogurui*. Translation in Sieffert and Tyler 2.

Ishikawa no jorō (*The Courtesan of Ishikawa*) (石河の女郎). A play by Zeami, now lost.

Izutsu (*Well Curb*) (井筒). A play by Zeami, based on an incident in *The Tales of Ise*. Translation in NGS, Vol. 2 and Tyler 2.

Jigoku (*Hell*) (地獄). An early *kusemai* based on Buddhist themes. See also *Utaura*.

Jinen Koji (自然居士). A *nō* by Kan'ami in which an incident involving the eccentric lay priest Jinen Koji is recounted. Translation in Tyler 1.

Kasama (笠間). A play, no longer performed, concerning a rebellion against Ashikaga Ujimitsu (1357–1398), in which the traitor attacks his own father, Kasamajūrō.

Kashiwazaki (*The Promontory of Kashiwa*) (柏崎). A *nō* by Enami about a woman from Kashiwa whose husband dies while on a trip to Kamakura.

Kayoi Komachi (*Komachi and the Hundred Nights*) (通小町). This *nō*, by Kan'ami, was probably revised by Zeami. The play concerns the Heian poet Ono no Komachi and her lover Fukakusa no Shōshō. An older name for the play is *Shii no Shōshō*. Translation in Keene.

Kinuta (*The Cloth-Beating Block*) (砧). A *nō* by Zeami about the loneliness, madness, and death of a wife separated from her husband. Translation in NGS, Vol. 3 and Tyler 1.

Kiyotsune (清経). Zeami's play about the defeat and death of the warrior Taira no Kiyotsune. Translation in NGS, Vol. 1.

Koi no omoni (*The Burden of Love*) (恋の重荷). A play by Zeami about an old gardener who falls in love with a court lady.

Komachi (小町). Another title for *Sotoba Komachi*.

Kōya (高野). Another title for *Kōya monogurui*.

Kōya monogurui (*The Madman at Kōya*) (高野物狂). A play attributed to Zeami about a father searching for his son, who has become a priest on Mt. Kōya.

Kōya Shizuka (高野静). An alternate title for *Shizuka*.

Kōya Shōnin (空也上人). A play, no longer performed, about the Tendai Buddhist priest Kōya Shōnin (903–972). The name Kōya is also often given the pronunciation Kūya.

Kusakari (*Grass Cutting*) (草刈). The text of this play cannot be identified with certainty, but it seems to closely resemble that of *Yokoyama* (横山), a play that concerns the attempts by

Yokoyama Jurō Harunao to obtain legal restoration of his Musashi fief from the Kamakura Shōgunate. The play is no longer performed.

Matsugasaki (*The Pine Promontory*) (松崎). A *nō* by Zeami's son Motomasa. The title is a place name.

Matsukaze (松風). The play by Zeami concerning two fishergirls, Matsukaze and Murasame, and their lost love for the courtier Yukihira. An earlier version of the play possibly by Kiami, was called *Shiokumi*. Translations in NGS, Vol. 3, Keene, and Tyler 1.

Mekurauchi (*Beating the Blind*) (盲打). The play has been lost.

Michimori (道盛). A play by Iami, revised by Zeami, about the death of the Taira warrior Michimori. Translation in *Monumenta Nipponica* 24, No. 4 (1969).

Miidera (三井寺). Author uncertain. A play about a woman who finds her lost son at the Miidera temple. Translation in NGS, Vol. 3.

Morikata (もりかた). The play is lost and no details are known concerning the text.

Moriya (守屋). A play, no longer performed, about the rebellion of the courtier Mononobe no Moriya (died 587) against the Soga family. Moriya attempted to destroy the growing influence of Buddhism.

Motomezuka (*The Sought-for Grave*) (求塚). A play by Kan'ami that dramatizes a poem from the *Man'yōshū*. Translation in Keene and NGS, Vol. 3.

Nembutsu (*A Prayer to Buddha*) (念仏). A *sarugaku* play, now lost.

Nishikigi (*The Brocade Tree*) (錦木). A play by Zeami. Translation in Keene.

Obasute (*The Deserted Crone*) (姨捨). A play by Zeami about an old woman who is abandoned to die. Translation in Keene.

Oimatsu (*The Aged Pine*) (老松). A *waki nō* by Zeami in which the spirit of a celebrated pine tree appears. Translation in Shimazaki, Vol. 1.

Okina (翁). Literally, "The Old Man," a group of dances that go back to at least the tenth century and serves as a religious prototype for the *nō* drama. Performances of *Okina* are only given at times of special celebration.

Ominaeshi (女郎花). The play, now lost, was reputedly by Kiami. The title refers to a type of yellow flower that blooms abundantly in Japan and often figures as a subject for *waka* poetry.

Ōsaka (*Meeting Slope*) (逢坂). Probably an alternate title for the play now known as *Ōsaka monogurui* (*Osaka Madman*) (逢坂物狂) by Zeami. The title refers to a well-known slope on the road leading north from Kyoto that was often mentioned in *waka* poetry. Translation in Matisoff.

Raiden (*Thunder and Lightening*) (雷電). A play about the anger of the ghost of the Heian courtier Sugawara no Michizane over those who forced him into exile. The author has not been determined. The play has an older title, *Tenjin*.

Rokudai. see *Hatsuse Rokudai.*

Saga no dainembutsu no onna monogurui (*Prayers of the Madwoman at Saga*) (嵯峨の大念仏の女物狂). An earlier version of the play *Hyakuman.*

Saigyōzakura (*Saigyō and the Cherry Tree*) (西行桜). A play by Zeami about the great priest and post Saigyō (1118–1190).

Saikoku kudari (*Going down to the Western Provinces*) (西国下り). A *kusemai* with a text by Tamarin, with music added by Kan'ami.

Sakagami. An older title for *Semimaru.*

Sakuragawa (Sakura River) (櫻川). A play by Zeami concerning a woman searching for her lost son, who has sold himself into slavery for her sake.

Sanemori (実盛). A play by Zeami about the death of the aged warrior Taira no Sanemori, who dyed his white hair to hide his age before going into battle. Translation in NGS, Vol. 1.

Sano no funabashi (*The Floating Bridge at Sano*) (佐野の船橋). An alternate title for *Funabashi.*

Satsuma no kami (*The Governor of Satsuma*) (薩摩の守). An alternate title for *Tadanori.*

Seisuiji (清水寺). A *kusemai*, the text of which has been lost. The temple of the title, Seisuiji, is doubtless the famous Kiyomizu temple on the hills of Kyoto.

Semimaru (蟬丸). A play by Zeami concerning the blind and exiled prince Semimaru and his sister Sakagami, a wild creature who wanders aimlessly from place to place. The play has an older title, *Sakagami*. Translation in Keene.

Shakuhachi (尺八). A *dengaku nō*, now lost. The title refers to the bamboo flute used in traditional music.

Shibabune (Brushwood Boat) (柴船). The text of this *nō* play has been lost.

Shigehira (重衡). A *nō*, no longer performed, that concerns the warrior Taira no Shigehira who was executed during the 1185 civil wars.

Shii no Shōshō (*The General of the Fourth Rank*) (四位の少将). An older title for the play *Kayoi Komachi*.

Shiogama (*Salt Pan*) (塩釜). Another name for the play *Tōru*.

Shiokumi (*Scooping Salt Water*) (塩汲). An older name for the play *Matsukaze*.

Shirahige (白髭). Literally, "White Beard," a *kusemai* danced by Kan'ami and set to music by him. The text concerns a legend involving the Shirahige shrine in present day Shiga Prefecture.

Shizuka (静). A play about Shizuka, the mistress of the Minamoto general and hero Yoshitsune. The play is known in some versions as *Kōya Shizuka*. The play is thought to have been written by Kan'ami and revised by Seiami.

Shizuka ga mai (*Shizuka's Dance*) (静が舞). Evidently an earlier version of the play later known as *Yoshino Shizuka*.

Shōkun (昭君). An early play, author unknown, about the beautiful Chinese princess of the Han Dynasty, Wang Chao-chün (Ō Shōkun in a Japanese rendering), who was sent off to the desert to propitiate the barbarians. Translation in Keene.

Shōshō (*The Generals*) (少将). A play about the return of Naritsune and Yoshiyori from exile during the 1185 civil wars. The text is lost.

Sotoba Komachi (*Komachi on the Stupa*) (卒都婆小町). A play by Kan'ami concerning the famous Heian poet and beauty Ono no Komachi. Translations in NGS, Vol. 3, Waley, and Tyler 2.

Suma Genji (*Genji at Suma*) (須磨源氏). A *nō*, the text of which was adapted by Zeami, concerning the exile of Prince Genji at Suma Bay, an important incident in the novel.

Sumidagawa (*The River Sumida*) (隅田川). A *nō* by Motomasa about a woman looking for her dead son. The basis for the 1964 opera by Benjamin Britten, *Curlew River*. Translation in NGS, Vol. 1.

Sumiyaki (Charcoal Burning) (炭焼). A *nō* for which the text is lost.

Sumiyoshi no sengū (*The Moving of the Shrine at Sumiyoshi*) (住吉の遷宮). The play may be by Kan'ami, but the text is lost. The shrine was moved in 1374, and the play might have been composed at that time.

Susano-o (須佐之男). The text of this play has been lost. In Shintō mythology, Susano-o was the violent and unruly god, brother of Amaterasu, who was banished from heaven by his sister.

Tadanori (忠度). A play by Zeami about the Taira warrior and poet Tadanori. An alternate title is *Satsuma no kami*. Translation in NGS, Vol. 2.

Taisan Pukun (alternately *Taisanmoku*) (The Great Lord of Mount T'ai) (泰山府君). A play by Zeami concerning the Lord of Mt. T'ai, a sacred mountain in the western part of Shantung province in China, through whose power the cherry trees in Japan bloom three times longer than usual.

Takasago (高砂). A *waki nō* by Zeami about the famous old couple who live by the bay of Takasago and represent the "double pine" of peace and longevity. Translations in NGS, Vol. 1 Shimazaki, Vol. 1, and Tyler 1.

Tamamizu (*Jeweled Water*) (玉水). The play is no longer performed. The title refers to the pure water of the Tama river at Ide, to the south of Kyoto, a spot that figures in several well-known *waka* poems.

Tango monogurui (*The Madman at Tango*) (丹後物狂). A *nō* by Iami, revised by Zeami, no longer performed, about a father who has lost his child.

Tenjin (*The God of Heaven*) (天神). An older name for the play *Raiden*.

Tōei (藤栄). A *nō*, author unknown, concerning the generosity of the prime minister of the Kamakura shōgunate, Hōjō Tokiyori (1227–1263). Tōei, the *shite*, has confiscated his nephew's lands, which Tokiyori restores.

Tōgoku kudari (*Going down to the Eastern Provinces*) (東国下り). A *kusemai* by Tamarin that describes the feelings of Taira no Morihisa, who is on a journey to Kamakura during the 1185 civil wars. Translation in O'Neill.

Tōrō (たうらう). Nothing is known about this work, possibly by Kan'ami.

Torōkyō (都良香). A *dengaku tachiai*. The text is not known. This entertainment may have dealt with an early Heian poet Miyako no Yoshika (834–879), whose name when read in the Chinese fashion is pronounced like the title of the play.

Tōru (融). A play by Zeami about the palace and magnificent gardens of Minamoto no Tōru (822–895), a *waka* poet, nobleman, and son of the Emperor Saga. The Gardens contained a miniature replica of a bay in the province of Mutsu, where salt was collected; this explains an earlier title for the play, *Shiogama* (*Salt Pan*).

Tōru no otodo (*The Great Minister Tōru*) (隔の大臣). A play about Minamoto no Tōru (822–895). The text is lost. Not the same play as *Tōru*.

Tsuchiguruma (*The Barrow*) (土車). A *nō* play by Zeami in which son and retainer set out to find the boy's father, who has become a priest.

Tsunemori (常盛). A play about the Taira general Tsunemori. It is no longer performed.

Tsutsumi no taki (*Cascade of Drums*) (鼓の滝). A play, no longer performed, about which little is known.

Ukai (*The Cormorant Fisher*) (鵜飼). A *nō* play by Enami, revised by Zeami. Translation by Waley.

Ukifune (浮舟). A *nō* with revisions by Zeami. The play deals with Ukifune, the heroine of the final book of *The Tale of Genji*.

Ukon no baba (*The Riding Ground of Ukon*) (右近の馬場). A *nō* play by Zeami in which three priests quote poetry and watch a dance by the spirit of the famous cherry trees at Ukon.

Unoha (*The Cormorant's Wing*) (鵜羽). A *nō*, no longer performed, that concerns the Shintō goddess Toyotamahime.

Unrin-in (雲林院). A *nō*, author unknown, based on *The Tales of Ise* and the life of the courtier Ariwara no Narihira. The

Unrin-in, a famous temple in Kyoto during Zeami's time, served as the locale for the play and gave it its title.

Utaura (*The Soothsayer*) (歌占). A play by Motomasa that encorporates part of an early *kusemai* called *Jigoku*. The play concerns the happy reunion of father and son.

Yamamba (*The Mountain Hag*) (山姥). A *nō*, possibly by Zeami, about a famous mountain witch. Translation in NGS, Vol. 2 and Tyler 2.

Yashima (八島). A *nō*, possibly by Zeami, about Minamoto Yoshitsune's famous battle against the Taira at the bay of Yashima. Translation in Renondeau and Tyler 1.

Yasuinu (安犬). An alternate title for the play *Kasama*.

Yawata (*The God of War*) (八幡). An earlier title for the play *Yumiyawata*.

Yawata hōjōe (*The Hōjōe Ceremony at the Yawata Hachiman Shrine*) (八幡放生会). An earlier title for the play *Hōjōgawa*.

Yorimasa (頼政). A *nō* by Zeami about the warrior Minamoto no Yorimasa, killed early in the civil wars of 1185. Translation in Sieffert and Tyler 2.

Yōrō (*The Care of the Aged*) (養老). A *waki nō* by Zeami about the god of a magic waterfall, the water of which can cure illness. Translation in Shimazaki, Vol. 1.

Yoroboshi (*The Stumbling Boy*) (弱法師). A *nō* by Motomasa about a child who prays to the goddess Kannon and is eventually reunited with his father. Translation in NGS, Vol. 3.

Yoshino Shizuka (*Shizuka at Yoshino*) (吉野静). A play by Kan'ami in which Shizuka aids Yoshitsune's escape by dancing for his pursuers. An earlier version was known as *Shizuka ga mai*. Translation in Tyler 2.

Yukiyama (Snow Mountain) (雪山). Only fragments of the original text are preserved in the writings of Zeami. The actual subject of the play cannot be determined.

Yumiya (*Bow and Arrow*) (弓矢). A *tachiai* piece in which three old men carry out dances of felicitation. The title may refer to Yumiya Hachiman (alternately pronounced Yawata), the god of war.

Yumiyawata (*The Bow at Hachiman Shrine*) (弓八幡). A *waki nō* by

Zeami about the god of the Yawata Hachiman Shrine on Otokoyama near Kyoto. An earlier title for the play was *Yawata*. Translated by Ross Bender in *Monumenta Nipponica* 33 (Summer 1978).

Yura no minato (*The Harbor at Yura*) (由良の湊). A *kusemai*, presumably by Kan'ami. The full text is now lost. Yura is located on the Sea of Japan to the northwest of Kyoto.

Selected Bibliography in Western Languages

Some Other Translations of the Treatises of Zeami

Teachings on Style and the Flower (Fūshikaden)

Nobori, Asaji, ed. *Kadensho, A Secret Book of Noh Art.* Osaka:
Union Services Co., 1975.

Sakurai, Chūichi, and others. *Zeami's Kadensho.* Kyoto: Su-
miya-Shinobe Publishing Institute, 1968.

Sieffert, René, tr. "De la Transmission de la fleur de l'inter-
prétation," *La Tradition secrète du nō*, pp. 1-112.

Whitehouse, Wilfrid, and Sidehara Michitarō, trs. "Seami jūroku bushū. Seami's Sixteen Treatises," *Monumenta Nipponica* 4, (July 1941), 204-239; and 5 (December 1942),
466-500.

The True Path to the Flower (Shikadō)

Sieffert, René, tr. "Le Livre de la voie qui mène à la fleur,"
La Tradition secrète du nō, pp. 143-149.

Tsunoda, Ryusaku; Wm. Theodore de Bary; Donald Keene,
eds. *Sources of Japanese Tradition*, pp. 296-303.

A Mirror Held to the Flower (Kakyū)

Sieffert, René, tr. "La Miroir de la fleur," *La Tradition secrète
du nō*, pp. 115-140.

Disciplines for the Joy of Art (Yūgaku shūdō fūken)

Izutsu, T., tr. "Observations on the Disciplinary Way of Noh,"

The Theory of Beauty in the Classical Aesthetics of Japan, pp. 105-114.

Sieffert, René, tr. "Le Livre de l'étude et de l'effet visuel des divertissements musicaux," *La Tradition secrète du nō*, pp. 165-171.

Notes on the Nine Levels (Kyūi)

Izutsu, T., tr. "The Nine Stages," *The Theory of Beauty in the Classical Aesthetics of Japan*, pp. 97-104.

Nearman, Mark J. "Zeami's *Kyūi*: A Pedagogical Guide for Teachers of Acting," *Monumenta Nipponica* 33 (Autumn 1978), 299-332.

Sieffert, René, tr. "L'échelle des neuf degrés," *La Tradition secrète du nō*, pp. 175-178.

Tsunoda, Ryusaku; Wm. Theodore de Bary; Donald Keene, eds. *Sources of Japanese Tradition*, pp. 292-296.

Finding Gems and Gaining the Flower (Shūgyoku tokka)

Izutsu, T., tr. "Collecting Gems and Obtaining Flowers," *The Theory of Beauty in the Classical Aesthetics of Japan*, pp. 115-134.

FURTHER READINGS IN ENGLISH ON THE NŌ

What follows is a selection of particularly useful materials.

Bethe, Monica, and Karen Brazell. *Nō as Performance: An Analysis of the Kuse Scene of Yamamba*. Ithaca: Cornell University East Asia Papers, No. 16, 1978.

Hare, Thomas W. *Zeami's Style: A Study of the "Mugen" Noh Plays of Zeami Motokiyo*. Ph.D. dissertation, University of Michigan, 1981.

Hoff, Frank, and Willi Flint, eds. "The Life Structure of Noh." Adapted from the Japanese of Yokomichi Mario. *Concerned Theatre Japan* 2 (Spring 1973), 209-256.

Imoos, Thomas. "The Birth of the Japanese Theatre." *Monumenta Nipponica* 24, no. 4 (1969), 403-414.

Inoura Yoshinobu. *A History of Japanese Theatre I, Noh and Kyogen.* Tokyo: Kokusai Bunka Shinkokai, 1971.

Keene, Donald. *Nō, the Classical Theatre of Japan.* Palo Alto and Tokyo: Kodansha International, 1966.

Konishi Jun'ichi. "New Approaches to the Study of Nō Drama." *Bulletin of Tokyo Kyōiku University Literature Department*, March 1960, pp. 1-31.

Matisoff, Susan. *The Legend of Semimaru.* New York: Columbia University Press, 1978.

McKinnon, Richard N. "Zeami on the Art of Training." *Harvard Journal of Asiatic Studies* 16 (June 1953), 200-224.

Ortolani, Benito. *Zenchiku's Aesthetics of the Nō Theatre.* New York: Riverdale Center for Religious Research, Study no. 3, 1976.

Pilgrim, Richard. "Some Aspects of *kokoro* in Zeami." *Monumenta Nipponica* 24, no. 4 (1969), 136-148.

——. "Zeami and the Way of Nō." *History of Religions* 12 (November 1972), 136-148.

Raz, Jacob. "The Actor and His Audience: Zeami's Views on the Audience of the Noh." *Monumenta Nipponica* 31 (Autumn 1976), 251-274.

Tsubaki, Andrew T. "Zeami and the Transition of the Concept of Yūgen." *Journal of Aesthetics and Art Criticism* 30 (1971), 55-67.

Ueda Makoto. *Literary and Art Theories in Japan.* Cleveland: Press of Case Western Reserve University, 1967. Chapter 4, "Imitation, Yūgen, and Sublimity."

Watsuji Tetsurō. "Japanese Ethical Thought in the Noh Plays of the Muromachi Period." Translated by David Dilworth. *Monumenta Nipponica* 24, no. 4 (1969), 467-498.

Yamazaki, Masakazu. "The Aesthetics of Transformation: Zeami's Dramatic Theories." Translated by Susan Matisoff. *Journal of Japanese Studies* 7 (Summer 1981), 215-258.

Yasuda, Kenneth. "The Dramatic Structure of *Ataka*, a Nō Play." *Monumenta Nipponica* 27 (Winter 1972), 359-398.

————. "A Prototypical Nō Wig Play: *Izutsu*." *Harvard Journal of Asiatic Studies* 40 (1980), 399-464.

————. "The Structure of *Hagoromo*, a Nō Play." *Harvard Journal of Asiatic Studies* 33 (1973), 5-89.

WORKS CITED IN THE TRANSLATIONS

Brower, Robert, and Earl Miner. *Japanese Court Poetry*. Stanford: Stanford University Press, 1961.

Collcutt, Martin. *Five Mountains, the Rinzai Sect Monastic Institution in Medieval Japan*. Cambridge: Harvard University Press, 1981.

de Bary, Wm. Theodore, ed. *The Buddhist Tradition in India, China, and Japan*. New York: Modern Library, 1969.

De Visser, M. W. *Ancient Buddhism in Japan*. Leiden: E. J. Brill, 1935.

DeWoskin, Kenneth J. *A Song for One or Two: Music and the Concept of Art in Early China*. Ann Arbor: Center for Chinese Studies, University of Michigan, 1982.

Dubs, Homer H., tr. *The Works of Hsüntze*. London: Arthur Probsthain, 1928.

Dumoulin, Heinrich, S.J. *A History of Zen Buddhism*. New York: Pantheon Books, 1963.

Harich-Schneider, Eta. *A History of Japanese Music*. London: Oxford University Press, 1973.

Izutsu, Toshiko and Toyo Izutsu. *The Theory of Beauty in the Classical Aesthetics of Japan*. The Hague: Martinus Nijhoff, 1981.

Katō Genchi and Hoshino Hikushiro. *Kogoshūi or Gleanings from Ancient Stories*. London: Curzon Press, 1972.

Keene, Donald. *Twenty Plays of the Nō Theatre*. New York: Columbia University Press, 1970.

Kitagawa Hiroshi and Bruce T. Tsuchida. *The Tale of the Heike*. Tokyo: University of Tokyo Press, 1975.

Liao, W. K. *The Complete Works of Han Fei Tzu*. London: Arthur Probsthain, 1939.

Legge, James. *The Chinese Classics*. 5 volumes. Hong Kong: Hong Kong University Press, 1960. Various other editions also available.

Liu, James J. Y. *The Art of Chinese Poetry*. Chicago: University of Chicago Press, 1962.

Malm, William P. *Japanese Music*. Rutland, Vermont: Charles E. Tuttle, 1959.

McCullough, Helen G., tr. *The Taiheiki, A Chronicle of Medieval Japan*. New York: Columbia University Press, 1959.

———, tr. *Tales of Ise*. Stanford: Stanford University Press, 1968.

———, and William McCullough, trs. *A Tale of Flowering Fortunes, Annals of Japanese Aristocratic Life in the Heian Period*. Stanford: Stanford University Press, 1980.

Minagawa Tatsuo. "Japanese *Noh* Music." *Journal of the American Musiological Society* 10 (1957), 181-200.

Miner, Earl. *Japanese Linked Poetry*. Princeton: Princeton University Press, 1979.

Needham, Joseph. *Science and Civilization in China*. Vol. 4, *Physics and Physical Technology*, Part I, Physics. Cambridge: Cambridge University Press, 1962.

Noma Seiroku. *Japanese Costume and Textile Arts*. New York: Weatherhill, and Tokyo: Heibonsha, 1974.

O'Neill, P. G. *Early Nō Drama, Its Background, Character, and Development*. London: Lund Humphries, 1958.

Phillipi, Donald, tr. *Kojiki*. Princeton: Princeton University Press, 1969.

Shaver, Ruth M. *Kabuki Costume*. Rutland, Vermont: Charles E. Tuttle, 1966.

Shaw, R.D.M., tr. *The Blue Cliff Records*. London: Michael Joseph, 1961.

Sieffert, René. *La Tradition secrète du nō*. Paris: Gallimard, 1960.

Suzuki, D. T. *Essays in Zen Buddhism*, 1st series. London: Luzac and Co., 1927.

Suzuki, D. T. *Essays in Zen Buddhism*, 3rd series. London: Luzac and Co., 1934.

———. *Manual of Zen Buddhism*. Kyoto: Eastern Buddhist Society, 1935.

Tsunoda, Ryusaku, Wm. Theodore de Bary, and Donald Keene, comps. *Sources of Japanese Tradition*. New York: Columbia University Press, 1958.

Waley, Arthur, tr. *The Analects of Confucius*. New York: Vintage Books, n.d.

———, tr. *The Book of Songs*. New York: Grove Press, 1960.

———, tr. *The Way and Its Power*. London: George Allen & Unwin, 1934.

Watson, Burton. *The Complete Works of Chuang Tzu*. New York: Columbia University Press, 1968.

———. *Early Chinese Literature*. New York: Columbia University Press, 1962.

———. *Hsun Tzu, Basic Writings*. New York: Columbia University Press, 1963.

———. *Japanese Literature in Chinese*. 2 volumes. New York: Columbia University Press, 1975.

———. *Records of the Grand Historian of China, translated from the Shih Chi of Ssu-ma Ch'ien*. New York: Columbia University Press, 1961.

Wilhelm, Richard, tr. *The I Ching*. Princeton: Princeton University Press, Bollingen Series XIX, 1967.

Yampolsky, Philip, tr. *The Platform Sutra of the Sixth Patriarch*. New York: Columbia University Press, 1967.

Index

We have attempted to include as many names and terms as possible. Some key words, such as Flower, *shite*, *waki*, *sarugaku*, *nō*, and references to Zeami himself are so numerous that no separate entries have been prepared. Terms are entered as they appear in the text and in the main entries of the glossaries, where details and translations as appropriate can be found.